Routledge Revivals

Gambling, Work and Leisure

Since the legalisation of off-course cash betting in 1960, and the rise of varying forms of gambling, the British have come to be known as a nation of gamblers. Until this study was published in 1976, barely any evidence existed against which to assess the claim that gambling had become a major social problem. The authors present data drawn from area surveys carried out in Swansea, Sheffield, Wanstead and Wood-ford, and explore how well previous sociological theories of gambling agree with their findings, particular in connection with certain aspects of work and leisure. Examining different forms of gambling, including betting, bingo and gaming machines, the chapters consider how gambling choices vary between different social groups, and how much time and money is spent on them. With the internet making it easier than ever before to place bets, this title is especially relevant, and provides a systematic basis for an explanation of gambling in relation to social structure.

T0361934

Gambling, Work and Leisure

A Study Across Three Areas

D. M. Downes, B. P. Davies,
M. E. David and P. Stone

Routledge
Taylor & Francis Group

First published in 1976
by Routledge & Kegan Paul Ltd

This edition first published in 2013 by Routledge
2 Park Square, Milton Park, Abingdon, Oxon, OX14 4RN

Simultaneously published in the USA and Canada
by Routledge
711 Third Avenue, New York, NY 10017

Routledge is an imprint of the Taylor & Francis Group, an informa business

Publisher's Note
The publisher has gone to great lengths to ensure the quality of this reprint but
points out that some imperfections in the original copies may be apparent.

Disclaimer
The publisher has made every effort to trace copyright holders and welcomes
correspondence from those they have been unable to contact.

A Library of Congress record exists under LC control number: 76378739

ISBN 13: 978-0-415-72086-1 (hbk)
ISBN 13: 978-1-315-86669-7 (ebk)
ISBN 13: 978-0-415-72087-8 (pbk)

Gambling, work and leisure:
a study across three areas

D. M. Downes
B. P. Davies
M. E. David
P. Stone

Routledge & Kegan Paul

London, Henley and Boston

First published in 1976
by Routledge & Kegan Paul Ltd
39 Store Street,
London WC1E 2DD,
Broadway House,
Newtown Road,
Henley-on-Thames,
Oxon RG9 1EN and
9 Park Street,
Boston, Mass. 02108, USA
Set in 10 on 11 point Times Roman
and printed in Great Britain by
Willmer Brothers Limited, Birkenhead

ISBN 0 7100 7708 4

Contents

Preface

If our experience is any guide, research into gambling is an advanced form of risk-taking. The project on which this study is based began as long ago as 1964, and should certainly have been completed by 1970. Of the five or six 'lost' years, at least four can be attributed to delays in what are technically the most straightforward processes of research production: computer analysis and actual publication. In fact, two years elapsed before the processing of the results from the 1968 surveys could begin; and whilst a much fuller version of this book had been prepared for publication by early 1973, the rapid build-up of publishing costs led the publishers in 1974 to request a scaled-down version instead. Readers may well be grateful for this last decision, since the present version is far less data-intensive than the first.

Miriam David was a research assistant on the project from 1968–9; and she has edited much of Chapters 3 and 5–11 of the original study to produce this book. Her collaboration at this latter stage has proved invaluable. Peter Stone was first a research assistant and second, Research Officer, on the project until 1970. His main contribution was to lay the groundwork for the empirical side of the study, by converting the raw data into a form amenable to analysis, no easy task against a background of computer delays and financial stringencies. Bleddyn Davies was joint director of the project throughout, though after 1970 commitments elsewhere unfortunately limited his contribution to writing the chapter on methodology and advice on the statistical aspects of the analysis. David Downes was also joint director of the project, and – thanks to the opportunity afforded by a Senior Research Fellowship at Nuffield College, Oxford – carried out the rest of the analysis and wrote all but Chapter 3 of the book. He also collaborated in the production of this version of the text.

Along the way, we have become indebted to many people for various forms of aid, advice and encouragement. Our thanks in particular go to Sheila Hillier; John Keohane; Gene Eriksen; David Little; Dorothy Rapoport; Robert Herman; Anne Sedley; Clive Payne; Roy Carr-Hill; and Bridget Atkinson. For the later stages of data processing, we are especially grateful to Mrs Margaret Hall, of the Computer Unit at the London School of Economics. The surveys would have been far more difficult to carry out without the kind co-operation of the Departments of Sociology at the Universities of Sheffield and Swansea.

The project could not have been undertaken without substantial financial and institutional support. The Social Science Research Council contributed a grant towards the cost of the analysis. The London School of Economics, both through a grant from its Social Research Division and the facilities of its Library and Computer Unit, have also aided the project. Most of the cost of the research was borne by the Churches' Council on Gambling, whose Secretary, the Rev. Gordon Moody, gave the project its initial impetus, and encouragement and advice throughout. We should stress, however, that from its inception, the project was conducted quite independently of the Churches' Council.

Finally, we would like to thank all those involved in the interviewing; first, those who carried out the interviewing so well on our behalf; and second, those who co-operated in giving us valuable information about their work and leisure.

Part one

Issues in the study of gambling

1 Gambling as a sociological problem

There have been remarkably few sociological attempts to account for gambling – and this applies whether 'accounting' is taken in the sense of explanation, in the sense of understanding, or as covering both simultaneously. Whatever the reasons for this strange gap in sociological accounting – and the sheer absence of reasonably comprehensive empirical evidence may be among them – it should soon be filled by the re-emergence in fashion of carefully conducted small-scale ethnographic inquiries, and the growing availability of officially designed statistics and opinion polls. As things stand, the theoretical perspectives against which such data can be weighed may turn out to have been false starts, or of severely limited use. Nevertheless, they are all we have, and for their authors to have constructed them at all is a high contribution in a field otherwise bereft of all but polemic.

Gambling as play

In the most consummate attempt yet to give play its due in the creation of culture, Huizinga's *Homo Ludens*,[1] gambling is given short shrift as a parasitic, materialistic and entirely negative activity: the dark side of play. Huizinga was concerned to define play as exhaustively as possible and to link the 'play instinct' with institutions and activities hitherto conceived as embodying the antithesis of play: law, war and philosophy (as well as those conveniently viewed as closer to play: literature, art and music). By sheer force of protean example Huizinga seeks to convince us that 'civilization does not come *from* play like a babe detaching itself from the womb: it arises *in* and *as* play and never leaves it.' The less scope for play to flourish, the more its spirit is suppressed or eliminated in institutional life, the less scope also for civilization to survive. Huizinga could see regimented leisure as far more inimical to civilization than overwork in which the spirit of play was nevertheless alive.

It is on this basis that Caillois[2] seeks to build a sociology not merely *of* games but derived *from* games. He repudiates the view that games can be reduced to mere residues of former tradition, or childish imitations or substitutes for 'real' life. He defines play as (a) *free*, not compulsory or forced; (b) *separate*, circumscribed within limits of time and space, carved out from 'ordinary life'; (c) *uncertain*, as to its outcome; (d) *unproductive*; (e) *governed by rules*; and (f) *'make-believe'* – 'accompanied by a special awareness of a second reality, or of a free unreality, as against real life' (p. 10). He then distinguishes four characteristics as underlying the myriad forms assumed by play: *competition* (agon); *chance* (alea); *simulation* (mimicry); and *vertigo* (ilinx) – the names in brackets are the closest terms in classical or modern language to the ideal types Caillois wishes to distinguish.

The main contrast in which we are interested is that between agon and alea. Agon stresses the ability of contestants to surmount obstacles and opponents to achieve victory. Alea renders the outcome quite independent of the players. Both stress the equality of the contestants under the rules, but seek to bring this about in different ways: agon by handicapping or equalizing *skills* as far as possible: alea by compensating with profit as closely as possible to the risk involved. In agon the contestants rely upon their own abilities and seek to minimize the role played by chance; in alea 'it is the very capriciousness of chance that constitutes the unique appeal.' The player is active in the one, passive in the other.

> In agon, his only reliance is upon himself; in alea ... he depends upon everything *except* himself. Agon is a vindication of personal responsibility; alea is a negation of the will, a surrender to destiny ... Both, however, obey the same law – the creation for the players of conditions of pure equality denied them in real life (pp. 17–19).

Hence their natures are both oppositional yet complementary, a compatibility heightened by the battening of alea onto the uncertainty of outcome contrived in agon by the equalization of chances. In simulation, the escape from oneself to play the role of another, and in vertigo, 'the attempt to momentarily destroy stability of perception and inflict a kind of voluptuous panic upon an otherwise lucid mind' (p. 23), as in the whirling games of children and ecstatic dances, no such implication of equality occurs. The germ of Caillois's evolutionism emerges.

Each type contains the seeds of its own corruption: *agon* through professionalization, cheating, the ritualization of the means of victory over and above the point of the game; *alea* through the degeneration of the appreciation of impersonal chance into the belief in luck, destiny, superstitions, etc.; *simulation* through the *loss* of self in role-play, or (in modern societies) over-identification with fantasized hero-figures, as in fan-worship; and *vertigo* through the synthesizing or alteration of consciousness by resort to drugs.

Of the possible combinations of competition, chance, mimicry and vertigo, only two are truly compatible: competition–chance, and mimicry–vertigo. The latter are seen as typical of 'Dionysian' societies, ruled by masks, possession, shamanism and magic – Amerindian, Australasian, and African tribal societies exemplify this combination. The former are seen as typical of comparatively 'rational' societies – Chinese, Assyrian, Roman and Inca – in which order and merit are the basis for social cohesion. The latter are rooted in primeval fears of the unknown which they palliate by recourse to pantheism and ecstasy; the former have at least *some* notion of a *cosmos*, of a universe which can be ordered and perceived as stable in crucial respects. To Caillois, civilization can exist only in so far as the former displaces the latter as a principle of social organization.

Whatever one makes of Caillois's evolutionism, especially in the wake of Lévi-Strauss and the destruction of tribal cultures in large parts of both the American continent and Africa by civilizations which then consign their victims to the shanty town and the pursuit of alea, his central distinction seems valid, and leads him to pose the issue of the consequences for agonistically oriented societies of the stubborn persistence of the aleatory principle. Wealth/poverty, glory/obscurity, power/servitude are relatively constant polarities even in the most egalitarian societies. Despite reforms and even revolutions, most people are 'unable radically to change their station in life. From this arises the nostalgia for crossroads, for immediate solutions offering the possibility of unexpected success, even if only relative. Chance is courted because hard work and personal qualifications are powerless to bring such success about' (p. 114). Alea therefore seems, under these conditions, a necessary complement to and compensation for agon. Hence, while modern democratic societies may deplore alea and seek to eliminate it along with mimicry and vertigo, it remains tenacious and paradoxically compensates (as indeed do mimicry and vertigo) for the cruelties of merit.

Caillois cites one powerful instance of the importance of games of chance in the modern world, choosing – ironically in view of his evolutionary ideas – the Jogo de Bicho in Brazil. This lottery is played[3] by 60–70 per cent of the population, each spending *on average* 1 per cent of his monthly income *daily* on the game. All manner of corruptions are involved in its machinery and disposal of winnings, but for Caillois its main drawback is *economic*. 'The game practically immobilizes an appreciable part of disposable income by causing it to circulate too quickly. It is thus unavailable for the nation's economic development or for improving the standard of living of the inhabitants.' Once committed to gambling, capital is virtually immobilized, since winnings are usually reinvested. The Jogo de Bicho symbolizes the waste and unproductiveness of gambling.

In criticism of Caillois, two further points should be made:

1 His assessment of the aleatory factor in egalitarian societies does not cover the well-documented link between aristocratic life and gambling. If alea survives and even flourishes chiefly for compensatory reasons, why should the class most beneficently endowed with wealth and status be so clearly committed to upholding the 'Sport of Kings' and the green baize? Happily, the answer can easily be given from within Caillois's own model: those whose status is based on the aleatory principle of heredity will cultivate it at play.

2 A more serious criticism is that Caillois does not really convey the *meanings*, as distinct from the formal *essences* of different forms of games, and especially of gambling. He generally treats games as self-evidently attractive since victory or profit accrue from them, or as attractive in terms of distinctive attributes, e.g. they are free, spontaneous, etc., unlike the workaday world of everyday life. But this comes close to the very reductionism he sought to avoid at the outset. He analyses games in terms of their formal properties with great assurance; but we are left wondering why people really play them.

For illumination on that score, we turn to the work of Erving Goffman.

Gambling as action

Goffman's essay on games and gambling[4] is so beautifully structured that the argument is best put by condensation rather than by rearrangement of its parts. Analysing outwards from the archetype of two boys tossing a coin *for* the coin, he ends by rendering gambling intelligible in the context of a total culture. The culture in question is naturally that of the USA: but the range of application is universal.

In all games of chance or skill, the outcome is problematical, the odds ideally equal. The span of play covers four quite separate phases: 'squaring off' – in which the boys decide to toss for the coin; determination – in which it describes its parabola and lands; disclosure – in which the outcome is revealed; and settlement – the winner takes the coin, or the play is renewed. These phases inhere in any game, and also in most events in everyday life, But in marriage, for example, while the span can cover anything from a few weeks to a lifetime, it usually approximates to the latter rather than the former. 'The distinctive property of games and contests is that once the bet has been made, the outcome is determined and payoff awarded *all in the same breath of experience*' (p. 156). Everyday life is usually quite otherwise; it is the *uninterrupted* nature of the sequence which gives most forms of gambling their intensity, though the lengths of each phase and the pause between them are variables which differ from game to game.

It is in his discussion of the *consequentiality* of gambling that Goffman lays the foundations for an understanding of its career structures, the termini of which are occupied by the hardened or 'compulsive' gambler on the one hand, and by the professional gambler on the other. In general, the consequentiality of gambling – 'What winning allows and losing disallows the player later on to do' – is far more manageable than that of real life chance-taking. But what makes gambling consequential *at all* is the staking of money on the outcome of the bet, a practice conventionally held to originate in the human desire for gain. In a related essay,[5] however, Goffman allows a different view: that the purpose of the stake is to induce a correct seriousness in the attitude of players towards the game.[6] In common with Huizinga and Caillois, Goffman stresses that play and seriousness, far from being antithetical, eventually contrive to promote the most appropriate attitude-set towards games, which can only be enjoyed *to the full* if the players not only abide by the rules but do so with conviction. If players drift off the field halfway through a game, or play inattentively or absent-mindedly, the game is to a large extent spoilt for the rest of the players. As Huizinga first observed, it is the spoilsport, not the cheat, who is most inimical to the spirit of play. Moreover, play is not simply different from everyday life: the occasion, and often the setting for it, have to be *set apart from* everyday life, and this circumscription is not simply to facilitate the action – it is to maintain the boundaries between play and everyday life, boundaries which are fragile and have to be carefully contrived and sustained.

The stake is the player's commitment to *serious* play: it is also

15

the prime determinant of its consequentiality. For play can become *too* serious and, as a result, increasingly consequential for the player. The greater the consequentiality, the more *fateful* the enterprise becomes. Over time, he may plunge too deeply, and what began as serious play becomes fateful action – as to why he might be drawn into such a spiral at all, we can only follow the path set out by Goffman.

The human condition is primordially fateful. The life of even the best actuarial risk is fraught with danger, both physical and psychic. Men have accordingly arranged their lives to minimize risk, and to reassure themselves. Even so, certain occupations persist which amount to 'practical gambles', shot through with problematic consequentiality and abnormally vulnerable to contingency: financially risky commercial roles; physically dangerous jobs; jobs whose holders operate against a tight margin of success and failure; performing jobs subject to switches of fashion; roles whose occupants man the boundaries of civil order – the police; the armed forces; criminal roles and professional sportsmen. Yet even in these roles, procedures and norms are developed which minimize risk and contingency as far as possible. By 'copings' (taking physical care, being provident) and by 'defences' (taking psychic care to anticipate eventfulness), men seek to ward off uncertainty and contingency.

Fatefulness cannot be entirely eliminated. But even if it could, ambivalence would persist about such 'safe and momentless living'. For, in Western society at any rate, and American society in particular, we still believe that the truest record of an individual's make-up is revealed in his reaction to fateful activities sought out *without obligation*. It is these activities which constitute *action*, a term which had its slang beginning in the gambling world, for 'gambling is the prototype of action'. The term has been diffused and commercialized far beyond these boundaries, perhaps because 'we have become alive to action at a time when – compared to other societies – we have sharply curtailed in civilian life the occurrence of fatefulness of the serious, heroic and dutiful kind' (p. 193).

Action of the former kind is now to be found in commercialized sports; non-spectator risky sports; commercialized settings for action – casinos, race-tracks, fairs, amusement centres, etc.; and arenas for 'fancy milling', resort to large, tightly packed gatherings which offer the promise of excitement, contingency and proximity to 'real action' performers. Brief penetrations into high living are increasingly commercially provided by casinos, restaurants, airlines, even pubs and filling stations with an overlay of glamorous service. Action is routinely available – at a price – for those who need it only transiently, irrespective of their social and psychological state (though it is much more appealing to men than to women). Action celebrates self-determination via the revelation of *character* under stress. Certain properties of character (as distinct from those of skill, training and technical accomplishment) can emerge only during fateful events. The performer is judged, 'essentialized', against the showing he makes at such times, is accorded a 'strong' or a 'weak' character in terms of moral extremes. The principal attributes of character to which his performance can attain are courage; gameness; integrity; gallantry; composure; and presence of mind. 'Character' can be dramatically acquired or lost – hence the particular appeal of action. '*Character is gambled* ... The self can be voluntarily subjected to re-creation' (p. 238). Even if material loss ensues, a real gain of character can occur.

Action, then, is not mere impulsiveness or irrationality, nor is the chief motivation to gamble the desire for gain. 'The possibility of effecting reputation is the spur.' Those who never risk never avail themselves of the opportunity to gain or lose 'character' in this way: they thereby lose direct connection with some of the values of society, though they may vicariously experience them via the mass media. Soap operas, thrillers, Westerns, what the French term 'histoires héroiques', re-establish and confirm our connection with values concerning character. Yet it is via gambling that men commonly struggle to achieve character in a society which has all but arranged action out of everyday life.

The force of Goffman's essay on gambling is that he lifts gambling out of the moral abyss into which successive generations of commentators and reformers have consigned it and renders possible a consideration of its meaning which is freed from *a priori* associations of a negative kind. It may well be that there is a hint of bathos in his insistence on seeing the rather drab routines of, say, fruit-machine players as even an attenuated pursuit of the heroic. But, without his analysis, we are reduced to a behaviourist model of a mindless automaton seeking profit from a machine which has been skilfully designed to minimize that eventuality. His analysis also makes sense of features of 'this sporting life' which would otherwise be inexplicable. In his social mapping of the world of the race-track, Marvin Scott[7] echoes Goffman in his characterizations of the jockey as the 'last in the line of "men of honour" ', displaying attributes of coolness, gallantry and integrity most crucially when *under pressure*: 'risk-taking is an essential prerequisite for a jockey to "emerge" '.

Such doubts as arise from his essay relate not to his analysis of gambling, action and character but to the relations he draws between these phenomena and the encircling culture and social structure. Goffman depicts a culture composed of two diverse value patterns:

prudential and incremental coping (the Calvinist way) and action (what in another context have been termed the 'subterranean' values of toughness, excitement and disdain for routine work).[8] These systems can, as far as individuals are concerned, be treated in everyday life as straight preferences or as uneasy choices, which co-exist as alternative guidelines for behaviour.

Goffman does not allow himself to be drawn as to the likely distribution of such choices throughout the social system. 'Certain segments of each community seem more responsive than others to the attraction of this kind of action' (p. 200). 'Fatefulness, which many persons avoid, others for some reason approve, and there are those who even construct an environment in which they can indulge it' (p. 214). These are statements which give little help in assessing *for whom* action as he describes it is likely to be most attractive. He does suggest that lower-class street gangs – 'well organized for disorganization' – are most open to fateful activities of a physical danger kind because – in a circular vein – such action is relatively 'least disruptive' and 'most tolerable' for their members. The cult of 'masculinity' ascribed by Miller[9] to lower-class culture in general is also seen by Goffman as fatefully inclined, though he prefers to subsume 'masculinity' under the rubric of 'character', rather than the reverse.

Do we then ascribe the probability of choosing prudence or action to a straight class-based matrix of cause and effect? This is exactly the kind of prediction which Goffman wishes to avoid. How do we account for the co-existence of such apparently incompatible value systems? The answer is that society needs both. 'The individual allows others to build him into their own plans in an orderly and effective way. The less uncertain his life, *the more society can make use of him*' (p. 174). However, 'although societies differ widely in the kinds of character they approve, no society *could long persist* if its members did not approve and foster this quality [i.e. integrity]' (p. 219, italics supplied). Society can afford to license integrity-generating action because 'the price of putting on these shows is likely to provide an automatic check against those who might be over-inclined to stage them' (p. 238). Finally, Goffman slides away into an ambiguous quasi-functionalism:

> Social organization everywhere has the problem of morale and continuity. Individuals must come to all these little situations with some enthusiasm and concern, for it is largely through such moments that social life occurs, and if a fresh effort were not put into each of them, society would surely suffer. The possibility of effecting reputation is the spur. We are allowed to think there

is something to be won in the moments that we face so that society can face moments and defeats them (pp. 238–9).

The chief issues that remain to be explored within Goffman's own terms of reference might be set out as follows:

1 How do the puritanical manage to survive psychologically in an action-packed culture? While Goffman's analysis was of the exact opposite question, it inevitably raises its mirror image.

2 How did it come about that the spheres in which action is now centred, gambling and mass spectator sports etc., have displaced spheres in which fatefulness of the 'serious, heroic and dutiful' kind gained fuller expression? There is precious little reference to what has happened to political and religious definitions of character in Goffman's work.

3 Do those who undertake the 'practical gamble' of everyday life – men in physically dangerous jobs, etc. – find themselves more, or less, drawn to the pursuit of action in the sphere of sport and gambling, or is there no necessary connection between the two? This remains a central ambiguity of Goffman's analysis. Some of these issues are, however, clarified further by the third perspective, to which we now turn.

Gambling as strain

In a monumental, but unfortunately unpublished, work completed in 1949 Devereux[10] provides what is still the most rounded and comprehensive attempt to account for the nature of gambling in relation to the social structure of the USA, or indeed of any society, urban-industrial or otherwise. To an astonishing extent, he anticipated the themes later developed rather differently by Caillois and Goffman. A then graduate student of Talcott Parsons, he approached his theme within a rigorous structural-functional framework, and rarely has the strength of that method been better exemplified. Indeed, the charges commonly made against structural-functionalism as a doctrine seem rather irrelevant when, as here, its utility as an organizing conceptual framework paid such rich dividends. There is, of course, the customary due paid to equilibrium-maintenance – but the doctrinal trappings are fortunately detachable from the substantive argument, a separability pointed to elsewhere by Homans[11] and Gellner.[12]

It would be futile in the space available to attempt an adequate summary of the full range and complexity of Devereux's argument. Rather, we shall focus initially on his characterization of gambling as predominantly characterized by *strain*, and then on his attempts to answer the following questions:

1   What are the bases for the social disapproval of gambling; and why, in the face of that disapproval, does it persist?

2   What are the social determinants of gambling?

To Devereux, while gamblers *affect* the cognitive detachment of rational, economic man, as in the attention paid to odds and probabilities, and in the cold-blooded reaction to success or failure, the façade hides the fact that each stake placed at hazard subjects the gambler to a

> veritable emotional shower bath . . . to the flesh and blood gambler, the situation is full of promise, but it is also full of mystery, and danger, and meaning . . . it is also fraught with strain: the conflicting valences and ambivalences of hope versus fear, risk versus security, power versus helplessness, and faith versus doubt are playing complicated melodies within his consciousness. The result is an intolerable, but not necessarily wholly unpleasant, state of tension (p. 695).

Paradoxically, this tension is often deliberately heightened by gamblers, who clearly find it pleasurable as *strain*. But it remains intolerable, and the gambler seeks ways to resolve it. Real pleasure may also lie in tension-*resolution*, which is all the more heightened the greater the strain involved. Gambling is an ordeal which produces tensions which *ought* to be intolerable but are effectively managed by self-discipline:

> it seems obvious that whereas the gambler may 'enjoy' these tensions, he is still fundamentally ambivalent about them. Having once exposed himself to the situation, he takes extraordinary pains to make himself comfortable within it. . . . Although most of the mechanisms function as accommodation devices, permitting gamblers to make the most of a bad situation . . . many of them also figure positively among the basic motivational elements in gambling (p. 743).

Clearly Devereux is here near to formulating the view of gambling as the prototype of action, and what to him are techniques of accommodation are to Goffman 'copings' and 'defences' – the belief in luck, the resort to animism, the investiture of luck as an attribute of people and of particular objects; the mental 'writing-off' of a stake to reduce eventual disappointment; the equation of stakes with business investments or with recreational expenditures; the focus on *odds* (the stake: jackpot ratio) rather than *probabilities* (the number of prizes: number of players ratio) in lotteries; and the belief in 'systems' as distinct from rational calculation of probabilities. Devereux's insistence on the strain and ambivalence inherent in gambling, whilst very close in meaning to Goffman's emphasis on the revelation of character *under pressure*, matches his analysis of strains and ambivalences inherent in the dominant culture. To Devereux, the answer to the conundrum of why gambling elicits such powerful disapproval (to the point of remaining almost wholly illegal in the USA, except in the State of Nevada) and yet persists and even flourishes despite such disapproval, is best sought by analysis of 'fundamental cleavages and ambivalences' within a common culture rather than as the product of friction between conflicting groups and codes. Any adequate theory of gambling should provide *homologous* accounts of the dynamics of gambling as a phenomenon, the dynamic of the social reaction to gambling, both as expressed by different groups and as institutionally based, and of the relationship between the two phenomena. The account which Devereux provides takes him back to Weber's theory of the spirit of capitalism and its relationship to the Protestant ethic.

The structural features of capitalism: an 'open' market; a generalized money system; political order; some *'laissez-faire'*; the institution of contract; and the system of private property, cannot be sustained and operated without certain kinds of motivation on the part of the individual. A capitalist society will seek to standardize as far as possible certain ideal-typical characteristics in its citizens:

1 *Economic self-interest of a 'rational' kind* 'Money', 'profits' etc. are the clear goals of the economic system and should govern economic behaviour. But since men need 'non-logical rules to live by', the economic world must be institutionally separated from the larger social framework, and outside it, its values should not apply, e.g. wives are not to be treated as means to economic ends, judged impersonally, etc.

2 *Competition* For maximal efficiency, the economic system needs high levels of aspirations, effective channels for vertical mobility, ideological stress on equality of opportunity, and a visible correlation between effort and reward. At different stages of capitalistic growth, however, different motivations assume functional priority and are stressed accordingly:

in the early stages of capitalistic growth, the stress on *thrift* ensures *accumulation*, and the build-up of wealth needed for capital formation;
in later stages, the stress on *consumption* ensures expansion;

21

in all stages, the stress on work-discipline ensures stability of interaction.

3 *Institutional mechanisms* to bolster the economic system but *at the same time* to protect the broader systems from its potentially disruptive consequences. Devereux is here presumably referring to such institutions as the banking and credit systems, which service both producers and consumers with capital for expansion and consumption yet which operate on the basis of certain criteria whereby capital flow is processed in more rather than less 'functional' directions.

4 *Cultural definitions* to create and maintain appropriate motivations. These motivations find their origins in, and help regenerate, the Protestant ethic:

(a) as it derived from Calvin, it signalled the decline of the retreat from the world of monasticism, and the apotheosis of the Kingdom of God on earth;

(b) it promoted the study of science (cf. Merton's analysis of the seventeenth-century will to know God by his works);

(c) it stressed reason as God's gift to man;

(d) and of the individual conscience as productive of economic freedom;

(e) its stress on predestination incurred distrust of fellow men not visibly blessed by membership of the Elect;

(f) it promoted religious sanctification of work: the 'calling';

(g) it led to the sanctification of private property, as held in trust and 'stewardship' for God.

Not all of these elements were new: but Protestantism gave them coherence and divine sanction. (d), (f) and (g) in particular have become *residual values* central to American (to some extent, Western) culture. Sources of strain, however, are not difficult to pinpoint in this holistic system. It is not simply that strain originates from sources of conflict *extrinsic* to the system, as, for example, in the stubborn refusal of merit and reward to correlate, and in the ironical consequence that virtue has too often to be its own reward since few others are forthcoming, a state of affairs which would be more acceptable if the un-virtuous were not so visibly and numerously blessed instead; or in the strain exercised by the puritan ethic on the foundations of personality, where rationality vies with illogicality, and asceticism with hedonism. These strains could *ideally* be accommodated were the Protestant value system sufficiently institutionalized and intensively absorbed, though the cost in guilt, shame and anxiety over a wide area of human behaviour would probably be increased. It is, rather, in the sources of strain *intrinsic* to the role of the Protestant ethic in the rise of capitalism that conflicts more difficult to accommodate arise:

1 The system is inherently frustrating: it generates dissatisfaction in order to expand.

2 Some value-conflict is endemic in capitalism: thrift *v*. consumption; prudence *v*. risk-taking. This value-conflict is particularly acute as the transition is made from early capital-formation to full-blown consumer capitalism, in which the protestant 'vocabulary of motives' loses some of its functionality with regard to the economic system. Wealth as an end-in-itself is stressed far more, and the loss of the 'stewardship' motif leaves conspicuous consumption and status competition as *the* suitable criteria against which 'success' is to be judged. However, the core values of puritanism, whose decline has been prophesied since the 1660s, retain great power: even the irreligious or amoral feel impelled to 'get ahead' as a worth-while goal, irrespective of straight cash rewards; the fruits of success are increasingly suspect as the rise in GNP fails to provide any automatic 'pay-off' in terms of spiritual fulfilment – the hollowness of a purely materialistic success remains one of the great themes of our culture.

3 Some value-conflict is endemic between *capitalism and parent Christianity*: the affective neutrality of the economic order, with its stress on impersonality, self-interest, ambition and competitiveness, clashes with Christianity's central injunctions as to love, humility and self-sacrifice. This conflict is acted out in the dualism between work and the family, as for example in the conflict which arises when the values of the work-place are carried into the home, and vice versa.[13]

4 The development of capitalism towards 'rationality' – via machine technology, systematic economic analysis, scientific market information, bureaucratic business organization, etc. – and away from chance, bold, risk-taking entrepreneurship narrows the scope for initiative to activities defined as disruptive of established business norms and conventions. '*Risk has become a disutility, to be avoided, minimized, or insured against.*' Speculators, when successful, tend to be regarded as immoral, unworthy and *lucky*. However, ambivalence towards speculation rarely becomes hostility, since to attack it is very close to attacking the entire rationale of the economic system.

'Society' handles these conflicts by structural and symbolic differentiation and segregation. It is broken up into several differentiated sub-systems, each governed by norms appropriate to its own functional requirements. Segregation is comprised of the spatial and temporal separation of these sub-systems, and the symbolic definition of appropriate contexts. Barriers to communication and role segmentation keep these contexts separate. Finally, the over-riding ethical conflict is resolved by ranking different sets of values in terms of some major scheme of allocation. Under this scheme, the major organizing imperatives of capitalism are officially defined as work, routine, thrift, prudence, conservatism, rationality and discipline. Such values as boldness, initiative, risk-taking and the pursuit of chance (shrewd or otherwise) are rated much more dubiously as necessary evils, which cannot be repudiated, but should only fleetingly be identified with, and are generally assigned to 'deviants', or specialists. Competing or threatening values are segregated contextually, 'ideal' values are confined to 'sacred' contexts. Dubious values may generate *sub rosa* contexts – in Devereux's view, this is most appropriate where the structural needs to be met are derived from and created in functional in-adequacies and strain *within* the dominant system.

The disapproval of gambling centres around a basic theme: gambling rests on *chance*, and chance is a non-ethical (even *anti-ethical*) basis for the distribution of reward. Hence, its existence is a threat to the rationale in which work, merit and reward are supposed to go hand in hand, and even helps emphasize the extent to which they do not do so. Gambling is thus a threat to a properly ethical orientation, helps break down 'rationality', and fosters super-stition and fatalism. In sum, gambling appears to be an *in principle* violation of capitalism. The nub of Devereux's thesis is that, in fact, the values deplored in gambling are by no means peculiar to it or foreign to the broader culture. They may in fact functionally relate to the legitimate economic system. Since these values cannot be attacked in their relation to the latter, it is only with regard to gambling, where the same values crop up in segregated contexts, where they *can* safely be attacked, thus safely 'grounding' the tensions and ambivalences they produce, and simultaneously rein-forcing and bolstering the dominant system.

That gambling survives and even flourishes testifies to its meeting of needs, both social and personal, which are not, perhaps cannot be, fulfilled in other ways, at least in capitalist societies.

1 *The protest against budgetary constraints* Few gamblers realistically suppose that gambling will truly be for them a short-cut to wealth, though it is a convenient pretext for fantasy along these lines. Their gambles are on the whole far too petty and far too limited to be more than a minor break with their budgetary discipline. Yet this break is all-important – for what irks in everyday life are the constant reminders of the needs for budgetary control, of income limitations and the gap between even modest aspirations and reality. In this closed-circuit world, where no dramatic increases

in wealth are possible, the gambler can at least protest against the tyranny of the 'budget'. Winnings are usually 'blown' or perhaps rebet, though large prizes may be consumed via more solid purchases generally out of reach except to high income groups. Even if loss ensues, the pleasures of *anticipating* a win can be seen as worth the effort. A chance element is brought into the serious and orderly realm of earned income. But the break is usually carefully controlled, and the stakes kept small *relative* to income.

2 *The protest against rationality* Many gamblers ignore or choose to suppress even that element of rationality which does obtain in gambling. In such cases, a blow is struck against a rationality which is viewed with resentment as governing too many of life's pleasures, while leaving its central mysteries unsolved.

3 *The protest against ethics* Chance is non-ethical: its pursuit therefore entails *some* protest and escape from ethical constraints, especially puritanical ones. The guilt thus engendered, however, frequently involves the gambler in a great deal of self-mystification as to his motives, which he sustains by resort to symbolic refutation and disguise: 'All in fun', etc.

4 *Thrill-seeking* Gambling involves a cycle of tension accumulation and resolution. The respectable can experience the 'safe deviance' involved in acting out the counter *mores* of daring and risk-taking in a segregated setting, which renders its insecurities 'less real' than those of everyday life. It can thus alleviate anxiety and boredom.

5 *Competitiveness and aggression* In many forms of gambling, these motivations can be stepped up and indulged behind a 'playful' façade. In such games, rules and settings are provided in which what Goffman terms 'character contests' can be acted without any overlap into 'real life'.

6 *Problem-solving* Gambling, like crossword puzzles and chess (though with the additional contingency of the stake), provides artificial, short-term, miniature 'capsule' problems – and their resolution – for those who enjoy them, and who are either starved of them or who perhaps cannot face or solve them in real life. This particular motivation was amplified by Herman[14] in his analysis of horse-track betters as exemplars of displaced decision-making, compensating in gambling for work situations in which they lacked the scope for creative decision-making.

7 *Teleological motivations* Man imposes moral order on causal order, and generates legitimate expectations thereby. Chance events often run counter to legitimate expectations, dramatizing man's ultimate ignorance and helplessness, and raising anew the problem of meaning. Men are more imbued with legitimate expectations than women due to their far more intensive involvement in the rationalistic rhetoric of the work sphere. Women are thus more 'philosophical', 'intuitive', etc., *not* because inherently so, but because they are more cut off from the moral order of the economic sphere. Chance events, which can only be incorporated in science as symptoms of inadequate knowledge, nevertheless pose problems of meaning which men resolve by resort to transcendental schemes, as in religion, magic and superstition. In our heavily rationalistic culture, gambling is the *only* area in which permissive attitudes towards such notions as luck and superstition prevail. Gambling thus encapsulates the area of mystery diffused throughout life in general but culturally 'silenced' in most institutional areas. It becomes, therefore, a laboratory for probing the meaning and grounds of the self's relationship to things and nature. Since religion imposes a different teleology, based upon an inscrutable deity, gambling is not simply non-religious but *counter-religious*.[15] Gambling signifies a break in the moral closure of the dominant system. 'Am I lucky?' has a *cosmic* significance, but no final answer is possible: hence the gambler is forever 'testing' his luck.

8 *Extrinsic or contextual motivations*
(a) The wager always concerns an *event* with its own event – specific interests, e.g. football, horse-racing, etc. Intrinsic interest in the event may precede the desire to stake a bet on its outcome, and may be drawn upon to assuage any guilt feelings that would otherwise stem from gambling.

(b) All gambling takes place in some concrete *social setting*, which may attract in other betters for social reasons, a desire to be 'one of the boys', 'not spoil the fun', etc.; 'social gambling' may thus be compared with 'social drinking'. 'Charity' bets are also structured to drag in motivationally neutral players.

(c) *Associations* of a symbolic kind, e.g. racing as the 'sport of kings', and the link between cards and gaming and spas and 'high society' may appeal to players who would otherwise be neutral towards gambling. As Goffman has stressed, commercial entrepreneurs are well aware of the status passage thus provided.

In sum, 'most motivational themes woven into gambling do *not* stem from ... "human nature", but are (mainly) derived in a process of interaction with a particular social and cultural environment' (p. 986). To Devereux, the prime sociological determinant of gambling resides in where people stand in relation to this environment. In his view, the 'core culture' of American society remains the economic/religious/ethical synthesis of puritanism. And it is the challenge presented to that culture by secularization, the acquisitive materialism of the full-blown consumer capitalism to which it has given birth and the counter-mores it has thrown up, which accounts for the tremendous inconsistencies and conflicts of American culture.

The old puritan hegemony remains strongest in rural and small-town areas; among the lower middle class; and among protestants. It weakens the more one moves away, in *any* direction, from this centre of gravity. It has tremendous *staying-power*: it has been 'breaking down' since the mid-seventeenth century yet still constitutes the 'official' and approved set of values for modern America (and, for that matter, modern Britain). Its persistence can be attributed to its functional relationship to crucial imperatives of the social and economic structure. It will be most intensively 'carried' by those playing roles most salient for the *transmission* of that culture: not only churchmen, but magistrates, headmasters, and local government officials.

The clear implication is that gambling varies *inversely* with the sway exerted by this culture. Among the Protestant middle class, it is likely to be predictable, of very small scope, and within the permissible limits of recreational expenditure. It operates principally as a 'safety valve' which frees the individual temporarily from budgetary constraints. This pattern of occasional and petty gambling is also the norm for the majority, whose dominant patterns of life organization lie outside gambling, though its incidence will grow the more one moves away from the small-town middle-class Protestant matrix.

By contrast, 'heavy' gamblers – those who play with sufficient frequency and for sufficient stakes so that gambling becomes a major focal centre of individual life organization – have no sense of a 'budget'. The role is incompatible with middle-class norms and membership – it is hence a safe target for moralists to condemn 'excessive' rather than 'petty' gambling as 'demoralizing'. Gambling is more habitual the greater the absence of the traditional constraints of middle-class life: i.e. ties to job, family, neighbourhood, church, regular work and incremental income, satisfactory career lines, and *some* visible relationship between effort and reward. Since many of these constraints apply also to the 'respectable' working class, habitual gambling is a *slum* rather than *stable* working-class activity. Gambling of a habitual kind is also more likely in the criminal 'demi-monde', the upper class and the 'beau monde': in the first, 'windfall' spending has status-conferring power; in the second, it represents a ritualized affirmation of superiority; and in the third, where it often *is* excessive, it stems partly from the insecurities about the stability of one's *nouveau riche* status, and partly from the reassurance provided by reassertions of 'character' in fashionable contexts. In all except perhaps the upper-class case, it remains, however, fraught with strain and ambivalence, for 'the problem is not a simple matter of opposing groups and philosophies, and their relative positions of dominance within the community. Much more fundamentally, it is a problem of basic inconsistencies and ambivalences within a common culture, and of basic cleavages within the individual conscience' (p. 769).

Conclusion

There is a certain logical continuity in the three perspectives dealt with above. Caillois provides us with the notion that modern urban industrial societies, among others, have opted for the cultural matrix based on a combination of agonistic and aleatory principles and have largely shed or suppressed the principles of mimicry and vertigo. Goffman suggests that forms of action archetypically embodied in gambling have attained a salience they formerly lacked. And Devereux suggests a socio-historical model within which Goffman's analysis can to some extent be placed: a cultural dynamic in which puritanism vies with alternative world views in a society whose central imperatives are increasingly threatened by the force of their inner contradictions.

The work of Goffman and Devereux is explicitly based upon the relationship between gambling and the American social structure. However, British society shares perhaps the most crucial characteristic germane to Devereux's theorization: a rough similarity in the relationship between the Protestant ethic and the rise, and subsequent development, of capitalism. That immense dissimilarities also obtain between the two societies, and that these make comparative theorization very difficult indeed, should never be forgotten in the application of American-based theories to British society. But that should not serve as a blind to their relevance.

2 Gambling as a social problem

In his analysis of the history of the laws on vagrancy in England, Chambliss[1] showed the sensitivity of the relationship between the definitions accorded vagrancy, and the nature of its differentiation from other 'social problems', and changes in the social structure at different times from the early Middle Ages to the present day. In examining the history of gambling as a 'social problem' in England, it is helpful to adopt much the same perspective: that is, to attempt to relate changes in the legal definition of, and social response to, gambling to changes in the encompassing social structure, as well as the changes in gambling practices which were only partially independent of the socio-legal context which framed this operation. It should be stressed that any similarity between Chambliss's endeavour and our own is of approach rather than substance. Vagrancy, as Chambliss demonstrated, was never a unitary phenomenon, but a portmanteau term whose elasticity was very useful to law-makers and social controllers, a label which could be attached to measures against beggary or brigandry as the need arose. Gambling, collectively considered, does not – in contrast – appear on the statute book at all. Measures against gambling (with one exception) were aimed at specific forms of betting and/or gaming practice; and it is the *variation* in our piecemeal attempts at the control of specific forms of gambling that provides the substance for inferring structural implications.

The exception is a crucial one: the 1845 Gaming Act which rendered all gambling debts unenforceable by law. Rubner[2] asserts that this Act was the first in which the *moral* issue was paramount, in which the Puritan opposition to gambling on ethical grounds finally overcame the remnant of eighteenth-century licence, and whose main purpose was to dissociate the Victorian establishment completely from the adjudicatory role of the law in settling gambling disputes. There is certainly some force to his argument that before 1845 the character of anti-gambling legislation was *ad hoc* and instrumental, designed to combat extreme abuse, cheating or games (such as hazard) which gave flagrantly unfair odds to some players rather than others; or to seek to limit gaming, along with other forms of recreation, when these seemed injurious to the state – as in the famous 1541 Act banning the playing of a host of amusements whose pursuit was held to be detrimental to the practice of archery. The 1845 Act also strengthened the measures already in existence against gaming houses, and it is certainly the case that in the second reading of the Bill, the Home Secretary, Sir J. Graham, stated the purpose of the Bill as to 'put down gambling, which had lately very much increased in this country, and produced such pernicious and fatal effects'.[3]

It is more doubtful, however, whether the passing of the Act either constituted the *first* in which the moral issue was paramount, or indeed whether the moral issue *was* paramount in this particular case. The 1823 and 1826 Acts illegalizing lotteries, and bringing an end to the long run of state lotteries, begun under Elizabeth I and held at least annually throughout the eighteenth century, could be held to contain as strong a moral purpose as the 1845 Act – though no debates are reported in Hansard for these Acts, they stemmed originally from the 1808 Select Committee on Lotteries, which reported unequivocally against their being held, and uncovered a mass of corruption in their operation, and in the surveyance of the illegal insurances which had grown up around them.

> It has been represented to your Committee that the Lottery and the illegal insurances are inseparable; that the former cannot exist without the latter for its support; ... In truth, the foundation of the lottery is so radically vicious that ... under no system of regulations which can be devised ... [can parliament] ... adopt it as an an efficient source of revenue.

Efficiency and the amount of revenue collected were not their sole concern, however:[4]

> Idleness, poverty, and dissipation are increased [by the effect of the lottery] ... truth betrayed, domestic comfort destroyed, madness often created, crimes are committed, and even suicide itself is produced. ... And this unseemly state of things is to continue, in order that the state may derive a certain annual sum from the partial encouragement of a Vice, which it is the object of the law, in all other cases, and at all other times, most diligently to repress.

The language of the 1844 Select Committee is classically restrained by comparison.

This may simply serve as another example of Victorianism preceding Victoria, the high moral tone of the turn-of-the-century reformers paving the way for the massive restructuring of institutions of her reign. But in character, as well as in tone, the 1808 Select Committee Report appears far more moralistically concerned with the 'vicious' aspects of gambling than that of 1844. The 1808 Committee lambasted corrupt officialdom and recommended the outright abolition of the lottery (foreign lotteries and private lotteries were already illegal); the 1844 Committee expressly *denied* any intention of interfering with betting and sought only to suppress gaming houses, not gaming as such. They saw betting as on the decline from the excesses of the eighteenth century, and sought to rid the courts of the burden of settling gambling disputes, rather than seeking to suppress gambling by the removal of the legal context. Indeed, the main purpose of the 1845 Act seems to have been a clean-sweep systematization of the law on gambling along classical *laissez-faire* principles, rather than an onslaught on gambling *per se*: [5]

> At present, wagers are chiefly confined to sporting events, but the practice of Wagering is still deeply rooted ... and the practical imposition of pecuniary penalties for wagers would be so repugnant to the general feelings of the people, that such penalties would scarcely be enforced, or, if enforced, would be looked upon as an arbitrary interference with the freedom of private life.

> In the earlier periods of European civilization it was thought to be the duty of Governments to exercise a minute superintendence and control over all those private actions of the members of the community ... and thence arose the laws on our Statute Book which prescribed to the different classes of the people what apparel they should wear, what Games they should play at, what amount of money they might win or lose, how their tables should be served ... Such Regulations are out of date.

The Committee went on to recommend that wagering should be freed of such penalties as had become attached to it in the previous century (such as the Statute of Anne banning bets of more than a certain amount on games – the issue as to whether or not this should apply to horse-racing had never been settled in the courts) as well as rendered unenforceable by law. This brought English gaming law into line with that in Scotland and on the continent, and was justified by the Committee in terms of saving the courts' time from disputes which called for 'private settlement' rather than legal adjudication.[6]

The minutes of evidence of the 1844 Select Committee refer to examples of disputes which certainly verged on the ludicrous – one instance was of the court being asked to settle the outcome of a wager as to whether or not a man had jumped over a table backwards – but the witnesses called, and the questions put to them, revealed as much concern over the enforcement of the existing law on gaming houses as on the nature and extent of gambling in general, or on the consequences of involving the law in settling gaming disputes. It was clearly a matter of great concern to the Committee that gaming houses were flourishing in the West End much as illegal lottery and insurance transactions had flourished in the City before the abolition of the lotteries in the 1820s. (The City was relatively free from gaming houses, according to the evidence of Harvey, the Commissioner of the City Police Force.) The evidence of both Mayne (a Metropolitan Police Commissioner) and Baker (a Westminster Police Superintendent) stressed the disparity between the task the police were expected to carry out (the suppression of gaming houses) and the powers given them to do so – a familiar sounding complaint in modern terms, with a long ancestry. The police knew of at least fifteen gaming houses in Westminster alone, but could not proceed against them for lack of evidence: the police feared action for trespass; they could obtain warrants for entry only by a procedure – the sworn testimony of two householders that an establishment was used for gaming – which gave warning to the gamesters; they were not authorized to search the pockets of those found on premises that *were* raided, so that their only real chance of ensuring convictions was to catch the game in full spate. These restrictions, coupled with the neighbourly reluctance to inform, led not only to police fears of exceeding their powers, which might damage both their careers and the 'moral character' of the force; but also provoked suspicions that the gamesters were out to trap them into making false arrests, by setting up a fund for the purpose of bringing an action against the police once they had been lured into making a false raid on rigged premises (Mayne claimed that an action for trespass against a policeman could, if successful, 'effect his ruin').[7] Baker claimed to have been 'almost worn out' by the gamesters' ruses, who threatened revenge for police actions taken against gaming houses, followed him round, and so on. On balance, it needed only the sketchiest organization to avert the possibility of successful police action, and while the Committee appeared both surprised and alarmed by the lack of police success in closing the 'copper hells' under existing powers, they concluded by recommending stronger police powers, for instance, their authorization to search the persons of those found on premises suspected of gaming.

Two points emerge from the police evidence to the 1844 Committee: one, the police were already very skilful at presenting their case for greater powers (or more manpower, or both); two, the seeds of police ambivalence towards their role in regulating gambling were well and truly sown in their perception of the difficulties of prosecution where public collusion, either in the positive sense of active collusion, or the negative one of 'not informing', occurred with the deviants. Future Committees and Commissions were to express similar surprise and alarm at the reluctance and failure of the police to secure convictions against illegal gambling on anything other than a token scale. The 1923 Select Committee on Betting Duty could not understand why so few convictions had been obtained in Sheffield. Police reluctance to take the burden of upholding anti-gambling laws against street betting were an important factor in the legalization of (properly regulated) off-course cash betting in 1960. And Lord Kilbracken in 1968 expressed his criticism of police inactivity in prosecuting casinos which were contravening the 1960 Act by gaming for unequal chances. (The *ex parte* Blackburn case against the police actually forced them to prosecute clubs as the 1968 Act amending (and securing) their status was being debated.) Police–gambler collusion does not officially emerge as a factor of any significance; rather, it was the damage to the 'moral character' and standing of the force brought about by gambler–public collusion which, over a century, built up police reluctance to enforce the unenforceable, and lobby for the legalization of virtually all forms of gambling. But it is generally accepted that many policemen were bookies' runners: though how extensively and systematically so, and how far senior officers were involved, is a matter for further research.[8]

Other themes ran through the 1844 minutes of evidence which echo earlier concerns as well as presage later developments. One of these relates to what sociologists have come to term 'boundary maintenance', or that set of social processes to do with differentiating phenomena from one another in terms of acceptability and respectability.[9] In the eighteenth and early nineteenth centuries, Stock Exchange transactions were seen as far closer to gambling than is the case today. Perennial as the speculative element is in any stock market dealing, in the sense that certain variables cannot be allowed for,[10] in the period up to the mid-nineteenth century, a great many stock market transactions were illegal, stock dealings were poorly, if at all, regulated, and the overlap between stock

33

market speculation and sheer gambling was openly admitted. Several exchanges in the 1844 Select Committee reflect this overlap. For example, the Commissioner of the City Police Forces is asked:

> Would not that [the question of the higher classes setting an injurious example to the lower] apply equally to those illegal [i.e. time bargain][11] speculations on the part of the large tenders [in the City] as it would to betting on the Derby on the part of gentlemen interested in the Turf?

> Precisely . . . but I think it is a matter of little importance to hear and to know that men of large fortune have transferred from one to the other £100,000; but I think it is a very undesirable thing that mechanics and persons engaged in industrous pursuits should be crowding around thimble-tables, and going into gamble-booths, and losing their money. *I think the moral and social inconveniences would be much greater from the latter.* At the same time, I admit that the evidence of the one palliates, and perhaps justifies the conduct of the other – and hence the undesirableness of both (para. 859, pp. 74–5).

This passage raises the other themes connected with the complex reaction to gambling in the nineteenth century and today: one, the concern over the 'example' set the poor by the profligacy of the rich; two, the perception, then tentatively expressed, that the latter mattered less, morally and socially, than the indulgences of the poor. The first attitude, that 'example' should be a major consideration in rich–poor relations, was put to several witnesses. For instance, Adams, the Chairman of the Middlesex Quarter Sessions, was asked:

> 'Is gaming encouraged by the example of "leading personnages" who game?'
> 'I do not think that one apprentice more or less would go to the copper hells because the first gentleman in the land did or did not gamble' (para. 616).

That the replies in general discounted the ill-effects of ill example (as did Lamb in his attack on this 'popular fallacy')[12] does not alter the extent to which the issue evidently preoccupied the Committee. The background of the gaming excesses of the eighteenth-century aristocracy and of the Regency period clearly mark these questions, a reminder that the anti-gambling legislation of the eighteenth century was chiefly aimed at the threat posed to large fortunes by excessive as well as crooked play. The reaction against the aristocratic style in gaming, as in dress, leisure and morality, heralded by Wilberforce, the Clapham Sect and ultimately by Utilitarianism and moral evangelism, was accompanied in the 1830s and 1840s by the political threat to the aristocracy by the new middle class 'The Middle Classes in the 1840s attacked the aristocracy through campaigns against the game laws, as well as against the Corn Laws.'[13] Less directly, much the same might be said of the new gaming law. The very raising of the issue drove home the extent to which the upper classes and royalty had not only put their fortunes at risk and set a bad 'example' – their excesses also gave radicalism its nearest equivalent to the pre-revolutionary *ancien régime*.

The related theme, that however reprehensible the gambling of the rich, that of the poor proved the greater threat, loomed larger as the century progressed. Clause 2 of the 1845 Act was levelled expressly against the gambling of the higher classes – namely, against hazard, roulette, and other games, where the bank was kept by the person to whom the house belonged, and where there was a dead pull against the player.[14] The object of the Bill was to 'protect the public, high and low, against *improper* Gambling' (italics supplied).[15] For some, detestation of gaming went with near veneration of betting. One Captain Rous who in the debate hoped that 'the first Conviction under it would be the Crockford Club House', stated before the Committee that 'betting is not offensive: quite the reverse. England would not be fit for a gentleman to live in if it were prohibited.'[16] (This did not prevent the banning of betting houses eight years later.)

To sum up, the first expression of predominantly *moral* opposition to a form of gambling to find legal expression was the banning of the State lottery in the 1820s, following the recommendation of the 1808 Select Committee, rather than the 1845 Gaming Act. Before the early-nineteenth century legislation had primarily been designed to check the excesses of upper-class gaming, as in the post-Restoration period, or to check gambling, along with other recreations, as injurious to the State. Preceding legal enactments, gambling was opposed and presumably held in check by the formal opposition of the Church. In a predominantly rural society, however, communities would exercise their own controls over excessive gaming, and it would only be in the eighteenth century, with its combination of stability and prosperity for the upper class, that the excessive gaming of a leisure class could develop into a style. Urbanization and industrialization were to alter the context of leisure for the working classes, and present the authorities for the first time with a formidable task: suppression, rather than reform, of emergent uses of leisure increasingly defined as *peculiar* to the working class. The withdrawal of the upper classes from popular forms of gambling in preference for the Stock Exchange strengthened this trend.

The Betting Houses Act of 1853 was passed without debate after a brief statement in the Commons by the Attorney General to the effect that 'the evils which had arisen from the introduction of these establishments were perfectly notorious and acknowledged upon all hands.'[17] The only need was to differentiate these houses, 'in which the owner holds himself forth to bet with all comers', from 'that description of betting ... which had prevailed at such places as Tattersall's, where individuals betted with each other, but no one ... held a bag against all comers.' The fine liberal sentiments prefacing the 1844 Report were absent from the Attorney General's speech, and the rather tentative opposition to both 'high and low' gambling of that Committee gave way to outright condemnation of the 'mischief arising from the existence of these betting shops ...' The problem was clearcut:

> Servants, apprentices and workmen ... took their few shillings to these places, and the first effect of their losing was to tempt them to go on spending their money, in the hope of retrieving their losses, and for this purpose it not infrequently happened that they were driven into robbing their masters and employers. There was not a prison or a house of correction in London which did not every day furnish abundant and conclusive testimony of the vast number of youths who were led into crime by the temptation of these establishments, of which there were from 100 to 150 in the Metropolis alone, while there was a considerable number in the large towns of the provinces.

Licensing would discredit the Government, and increase the problem rather than prevent it.

What had provoked such a stiffening in the tone as well as the character of anti-gambling legislation? In part, the situation in 1853 had been created by the Act of 1845. With wagering contracts unenforceable at law, and gaming houses facing stronger police powers, cash betting became the most economic form of wager for both punters and entrepreneurs. But this does not account satisfactorily for what was evidently a mushroom growth of betting houses: and since the 1853 Act set the pattern for gambling legislation for the following hundred years, it is worth looking for trends which the 1844 Committee had missed in their definition of the situation in largely eighteenth-century terms.

In the early-nineteenth century, the complex chain reaction set off by industrialization and urbanization involved recreational changes which in their turn were subject to the changing relations between the social classes. Brian Harrison[18] has cited W. Howitt's claim in 1838 that the decline in brutal sports represented a 'mighty revolution' in popular pastimes, and summarizes the processes underlying this decline: urbanization deprived working people of space, mechanization deprived them of physical exercise during working hours; both processes imposed economy in *time*, which came to be husbanded by codifying sporting rules and the abandonment or tighter regulation of games of uncertain duration, hunting and soccer for example. At the same time, middle-class notions of 'rational' and 'fulfilling' leisure as a *preparation* for work, instead of as an end in itself, gained over the old rural and aristocratic co-operation between the classes in unhealthy or dangerous blood sports. Arguably, gambling quickly became subject to the same degree of regularity and routinization. It was opportune that the sport of horse-racing and the growth in sophistication of horse-breeding had, by mid-century, progressed to the point where meetings and facilities were sufficiently developed to provide a calendar for racing which gave a routine to betting, and a structure for handicapping and the provision of odds.[19] But the chief developments in horse-racing had taken place in the eighteenth century. What gave it such impetus as a form for betting in the mid-nineteenth century on was chiefly the convenience it provided for those 'masses' of working people brought together, for the first time in history, and faced with a problem of leisure.

The 'problem' was self-created. As Burns[20] had stressed:

the swamping of everyday life by industrialization has not been succeeded by a mere ebbing, or forcing back, of the flood. Social life outside the work situation has not re-emerged, it has been created afresh, in forms which are themselves the creature of industrialism, which derive from it and which contribute to its development, growth and further articulation.

Taking his cue from Chapman's thesis that 'the 10 Hours Act was by far the most important landmark in 19th century social history',[21] Burns argues that the working-class movement can be said to have 'created' leisure by successfully challenging the immersion of everyday life in industrial work in face of the power of industrial capital. But the leisure thus gained was won in terms of 'freedom from' labour, not 'freedom to' pursue other ends. The 10 Hours Act was fuelled by the hostility aroused by punitive working conditions and rules, excessive health risks and fatalities and the shackling of women and children to factory labour: the leisure that resulted was a vacuum 'which was largely filled, even to begin with, by the amusement industry.'[22]

In pre-industrial society, work and leisure were far less clearly demarcated. Equally important, most men were content with subsistence economy;[23] when that was achieved, work slackened or stopped altogether. The rhythm of work was set by the seasons and ritualized by the festivals and holidays of church and community. Time hung. Industrialization was as much a matter of breaking down the resistance to *routine* and *incessant* labour innate in such a psychology as it was about new techniques. The demand for leisure came only as the last vestiges of pre-industrial life were fast disappearing.

The upsurge of betting among the new urban working class, and the strong reaction against it, are fully intelligible only in the context of the newly created dualism between work and leisure. Thomas has argued that the triumph of industrialism came not by the force of economic or legal compulsion, but by 'the force of habit and even a sense of duty'. It is more likely that the latter took hold only when the former presented little alternative to working people than adaptation to the new regimes of work, or a revolutionary displacement of the economic and social arrangements which supported them. The early industrialists imposed a rigorous, even savage, labour discipline, with elaborate systems of fines, with campaigns against holidays and wages, and with sabbatarianism and allied attempts to check the violent forms of recreation to which the workers of the time were habituated. The old incentives to labour – subsistence, communal responsibility, craftsmanship – were wrenched aside to make way for the regimentation of the wage and the factory. While wage labour had become more predominant since the seventeenth century, Hill has conveyed the deep resistance to it in his remark that 'factory discipline must have seemed as irrational, as irrelevant to one's own interests, as unfree, as army discipline today.'[24] Both masters and men now regarded work as an imposition which only a strong constitution could bear. Idleness was the natural state: the habit of work had to be rigorously imposed upon recalcitrant material, and must not be allowed to break.

One of the classic, and mainly neglected, conflicts of capitalism (in England at least) is that between the attempt made on the one hand to control working-class leisure, largely by the suppression, or stringent regulation, of drink, gambling and a host of other amusements; and, on the other hand, the rush to cater for their tastes at a nice commercial profit. The situation was nicely summarized in the Wildean quip about newspapers fulminating against gambling on the front page whilst relying for their sales on the racing information given at the back. From the 1850s on, betting and horse-racing became increasingly interdependent and increasingly big business.[25]

It is not a freak of language that the words 'bookmaker' and 'welsher' creep into popular speech in the early sixties. The old punting had been done inside the trade. Gully, prize-fighter, punter, race horse owner and member of parliament, and his like, had betted with their fellows. But now a public with leisure to enjoy desired to come in. . . . To assist it, a whole range of new publications came into existence. In 1859, *Sporting Life*, appeared as a weekly; in 1881, it increased to four days a week; in 1883 it became a daily . . .

In 1877 Henry James felt impelled to attend the Derby, so Festive had the occasion become, whose atmosphere he described majestically as one of 'gross plebeian jollity', in which 'the people that of all peoples is habitually the most governed by decencies, proprieties, rigidities of conduct, was for one happy day unbuttoning its respectable straight-jacket . . .'[26]

The double standard, whereby the rich gambled legally while the poor did so illegally, was by now thoroughly entrenched as an aspect of class warfare. For while, for the last several decades, thousands had flocked to the major races at Epsom, Ascot, Doncaster, etc. – Richard Baxter, who opposed all betting, had once been 'pelted' down the streets of the Yorkshire racing town[27] – millions cooped up in the cities and towns could bet only through the street bookmaker (since the 1853 Act), and local Watch Committees had made it their duty to outlaw such practices. So immense were the variations in local provisions, however, that parliament was repeatedly called upon to illegalize street betting nationally, which it duly did in 1906. The Bill was attacked by several members as 'class legislation of the worst type',[28] but these objections were brushed aside. To the Government spokesman, street betting was gambling 'in the most acute and urgent form'.[29]

It should not be forgotten that in the midst of the generally repressive and intolerant views taken of working-class gambling by the authorities and spokesmen for public morality, there was a vein of real humanitarian concern for the misery undoubtedly caused by excessive gambling, as by extensive drink and brutality. Mayhew had observed the costermongers' addiction to Sunday gambling, when at one fell swoop takings for the week, stock, cart and all would be lost.[30] Fifty years later Lady Bell wrote:[31]

I would give a great deal to be furnished with some brief, plain, convincing argument against staking money on chance, which

39

would seem to the man of small means a cogent reason for giving it up. To tell him that if he loses he will be ruined is not final, since he will reply that if he wins he will be enriched. And every now and again a working-man does win, and thereby acquires in one moment a lump sum of capital that would be accessible to him in no other way.

(She thought that the most feasible compromise was for public lotteries to be organized by the State, a solution favoured by Colquhoun in 1808[32] and Keynes in 1933;[33] on the premise that some gambling is ineradicable, both argued that a state lottery with a mass of small prizes would both provide revenue *and* keep gambling in check. Other forms of gambling could then be safely abolished. Keynes argued that the less 'pretence of skill' the better, and that 'gambling should be cheap, fair, frivolous and on a small scale. . . . I think it would add to the cheerfulness of life if punctually everyone in the country was to wake up each Sunday morning stretching out for the Sunday papers with just a possibility that they had won a small fortune. It is agreeable to be habitually in the state of imagining all sorts of things as possible.'[34] Premium bonds come nearest to meeting these suggestions, but without meeting the other assumption – that other forms of gambling would diminish.)

Victorian legislation survived in the main until 1960. Despite the rise in the twentieth century of new forms and strategies of gambling – principally pools betting and greyhound racing – the illegality of off-course cash betting was retained. By 1960 the law was a mare's nest of anomaly and contradiction. Governments had by then tried to tap betting for revenue – in the 1926–9 experiment which failed to produce anything like the returns expected. The 1932–3 Royal Commission had, in general, upheld the legislative *status quo*, whilst that of 1950–1 guardedly recommended the legalization, under strict control, of off-course cash betting facilities. It is nevertheless difficult to account adequately for why this position was eventually enacted in 1960. The establishment of premium bonds in 1957 may have been a precedent for the Government finally to accede to sporadic demands for the ending of the disparity between cash and credit betting off-course. But it could equally have been used as a reason for deferring such a move, arguing along the Keynesian line above. Certainly the Exchequer had an interest in the revenue that might eventually accrue from taxing off-course cash betting turnover: and the police had reiterated their reluctance to enforce the unenforceable. But these factors had been present for the past century – what tipped the balance? The answer probably lies in that peculiar openness to commercial suggestion which characterized the 'never had it so good' period of Macmillan's administration. The government which had introduced premium bonds and sponsored the creation of commercial television could with equanimity and an appeal to democratic principle end the proscription of what was, after all, the major form of gambling in Britain. The post-war experience of full employment, and the lack of any increase in gambling throughout the relatively prosperous 1950s, took the edge away from the opposition to the measure.

The immediate aftermath of the 1960 Act was of a sharp upsurge in the extent and variety of the forms of gambling legally available, and of moral unease at the scale of gambling apparently thus unleashed. Since the intention of the 1960 Act had simply been to legalize the existing volume of off-course cash betting, and to constrain inducements for the expansion of betting or facilities to encourage betting – betting shops were not to advertise, were to provide no services *other than* those for the placing of bets, etc. – the reaction was to be expected. The phrase 'a nation of gamblers' became a journalistic cliché. By the mid-1960s, however, most anxiety attached to the unanticipated side-effects of the 1960 Act – the loophole allowed by the so-called 'Vicar's Charter' (which allowed 'clubs' – the phrase was not defined, but was intended to cover mainly charitable organizations – to recoup their expenses by charging an entrance fee for the playing of games of equal chances) was exploited by the financial interests which had been waiting in the wings to develop the potential market for club gaming of a commercial type. A feature of the clubs and casinos which sprang up by the mid-sixties was their complete freedom from legal regulation as the result of poor parliamentary draftsmanship. Even so, the law was technically against the playing of games of unequal chance for profit, and a concerted campaign against them would undoubtedly have succeeded in closing them, or forcing them to conform to the law. As Kilbracken pointed out in the debate on the 1968 Bill intended to remedy this and other anomalies, thirteen out of the fourteen cases brought against casinos had upheld the law, and only police reluctance to prosecute a club for a second time (with far stiffer penalties) and to prosecute the large clubs, enabled them to survive. (It was left to a private citizen, Raymond Blackburn, to put legal pressure on the police to enforce the law – which was changed by the 1968 Act just in time to prevent acute police embarrassment.)

Police and governmental strategy appeared, however, to be evolving in response to innovations in the relationship between organized crime and the new gaming 'empires'. Fear that the easy and massive profits accruing from unregulated commercial gaming would capitalize the transformation of what had been small-scale and localized protection rackets into large-scale criminal syndicates along American lines were dramatized by the careers of the Krays and the Richardsons and their networks in the mid and late sixties. In retrospect, their strategies and organizations were still too 'under-developed' to benefit from the advice that Cressey maintains they were offered by American criminal organizations,[35] but their example certainly eased the passage of those clauses in the 1968 Bill which provided for the setting up of the Gaming Board, independent of the police and with its own inspectors, but with very considerable powers to uphold or rescind licences for gaming on grounds which amounted to suspicion of criminal involvement. It was assumed by 1968 that tight regulation and control was preferable to the attempt at renewed suppression, that to 'drive gambling underground', either by illegalization or over-taxation, would be to abandon its control to criminal entrepreneurs. The focal concern of legislation was no longer the formal suppression of gambling *per se*, but the calibration of social control mechanisms to prevent the unwanted side-effects of poorly regulated gambling, and to forestall the commercial promotion of inducements to gamble.

In conclusion, there are perhaps five periods in which the emergence and definition of gambling as a social problem can be related to changes in social structure. First, in the period up to the end of the seventeenth century, a basically agrarian society regulated gambling principally in terms of its nuisance value and occasionally in terms of its purely recreational threat to State interests. Second, in the eighteenth century, with the hegemony over social life exercised by the aristocracy and gentry, its regulation – in a flood of Acts between the late-seventeenth and mid-eighteenth century – was designed to protect the landed interest by enactments specifically against frauds, gaming with minors, and the legal enforceability of wagers over £10. Third, in the late-eighteenth to mid-nineteenth century, the differentiation of gambling transactions from capitalist transactions and the integrity of contract was ensured in the 1845 Act, whilst the City was freed from the burden of the contaminating side-effects of the State lottery in 1823. Fourth, from the mid-nineteenth to the mid-twentieth century, as Pizzorno has suggested,[36] the middle-class values of 'thrift, austerity and production were either adopted by, or "wished on to" the working class, but became obviously incompatible with their situation in industrial society', or rather, with their adumbration of a culture which was in many respects counter to that of the middle class. Fifth, 'in a society devoted increasingly to the values of leisure and consumption rather than to those of production, leisure presents itself as an alternative source of ethical values to those founded in production and work.'[37]

In a society whose economic structure and relative prosperity still depend very much on the latter, the rise of the former presents formidable problems of ethical strain and value conflict, both within individuals and between different groups.

3 The research strategy

The only official statistics on gambling available in 1965 (the year the study began) were revenue from the duty levied on certain types of gambling, chiefly football pools; statistics relating to the grant and renewal of bookmakers' permits and betting office licences; figures of totalizer receipts, and rather unreliable estimates of bookmakers' profits, based upon returns made by the bookmakers to the Horserace Betting Levy Board.

Almost the only data available from social and economic research in this country was contained in the *Report of the Royal Commission on Betting, Lotteries and Gaming, 1949–1951,* and in the report of the small national sample survey carried out for the Commission by the Government Social Survey.[1] There were also data on gambling contained in the Family Expenditure surveys carried out by the Government, though the data on gambling were presented in, judging from other data, a single global average which appeared grossly to under-estimate the expenditure on gambling.

As a basis for theorizing we chose to describe through survey methods how much time, attention and money were devoted to forms of gambling. As a background, however, we chose to investigate the reasons for a development of gambling since 1960, and analyse data on betting shop licences, permits and profits. These are briefly discussed before we explain the general methodology.

Variations in betting shop profits between county boroughs in 1962–3

The analysis of variation in betting shops relied on data on profits for one year, 1962–3. We attempted to examine the correlation between these profits and the occupational structures and sexual

44

division of labour of the areas, to develop a theory of gambling. The results show a correlation between volume of betting and employment in basic industries in the predicted direction, but it is not significant. The explanation for this weak relationship may lie in choice of indicators of employment. A supplementary indicator was involuntary unemployment in 1931 and this had an impact on betting shop profits partly because of its collinearity with the key indicator of traditional heavy industry: male employment. A second interpretation is that in 1961 male employment rates reflected the countervailing effects of low wages, and the culture of communities dependent on traditional heavy industries. It was predicted that low wages would have a negative, and the culture of communities a positive, effect on betting. This interpretation is not compatible with another finding – the substantial negative impact of women's activity rates. This indicator was used as a proxy for material prosperity and presumed to have a positive impact on betting. The result could also mean that past circumstances have more effect on supply and demand, and therefore the volume of betting, than current circumstances.

Basically, the analysis of betting shop profits was not capable of adequately testing elaborate hypotheses. For instance, it was not possible with the data to assess the relative importance of cultures based on occupational structures with a high risk of unemployment, disablement or death with marital role segregation. The effects of these demand factors could not be separated from those of supply (determined in part by past demand and associated with the same industrial structures that accompanies present demand). The dependent variable itself, betting shop profits, was certainly subject to large measurement errors whose correlation with the values of independent variables were unknown. Moreover, even true profits are an inexact indicator of the volume of betting. More important perhaps, indicators used were crude variables whose separate effects it was essential to distinguish in order to predict betting. This study was not able to do that.

Participant observation in a betting shop and the analysis of betting slips

It was hoped that participant observation in betting shops would also give us insights on which to base a theory. Otto Newman's work[2] has since yielded suggestions about the motivations of betters that are compatible with those of Devereux.[3] Our own attempt was not so successful, since it coincided with the recession in the British economy which led eventually to devaluation, and the betting industry was hit by a reduction in consumption. Betting shops were not at that point taking on any staff without previous experience and after considerable trial-and-error, the idea of conducting 'behind-the-counter' field research was abandoned.

For rather different reasons, support was not forthcoming for a proposed analysis of betting slips. It was hoped an analysis of slips would tell us, at the very least, the pattern of expenditure by type of bet; at best, given a knowledge of the area and clientèle, the pattern of betting by social class, sex, and intensity. The National Association of Bookmakers rejected the idea and so closed a promising possibility. One major bookmaking group did offer to allow us to analyse their used slips, but we felt it necessary to have a representative sample. Not knowing the extent of that group's activities, we could not usefully proceed with the analysis.

The structure of the betting shop industry in Glamorganshire

An investigation of the structure of the betting shop industry also seemed a useful source of theory. In Appendix 3 on the industry in Glamorgan, it is shown how, when betting shops were legalized, large firms dominated the market by such means as procuring most of the profitable sites. Some of the small bookmakers lacked capital, and others who had no taste for organized business became managers and settlers for the larger concerns. The concentration of ownership subsequently increased. Between 1961 and the end of 1966, the period of decelerating growth that preceded apparent saturation, the number of betting offices increased by 22 per cent, two thirds of which were offices of larger firms. Most of the shops were transferred from small owners to large concerns. Apart from the lack of profitable sites there were such barriers to the growth of the small firm as difficulties of managing more than one office and the lower rate of profit in a branch where it would be necessary to employ a manager. The large firm does not face comparable barriers to growth, because 'laying off' all but the largest bets becomes unimportant, and a central staff in indivisible units can encourage growth by the spreading of costs.

Both this concentration of ownership, and the Bookmakers' Federation, contributed to a substantially monopolistic market situation, but the introduction of the betting tax caused a breakdown in the Federation's system for preventing price competition. Firms adopted methods of attempting to recoup the tax from the punter according to the structure of their own bets placed. Nevertheless, the effects of the period of rigid price-fixing continued.

In Cardiff, the location of betting offices was influenced by the market, planning permission, and proximity to the public houses and clubs from which bookmakers and their owners had operated prior to legalization. Apparently, licensing magistrates have not employed any policy to reduce the extent of drinking before gambling.

These investigations were not complete when our main surveys were conducted, and so could not influence many of our most strategic decisions. Nevertheless, these preliminary findings did have some influence in that they reinforced our belief in the importance of supply generated by historical causes as a determinant of demand; and the importance of variations in supply between areas, large and small: and suggested how variations in the structure of bets might reflect the varying motivations of punters.

The surveys

Our approach to the survey reflects the conclusion drawn from these preliminary searches and the analysis of relevant literature that there is no body of theory to explain gambling behaviour. We could only hypothesize about a few types of gambling. One early strategic decision therefore was to define outcomes to be studied. Even if there were some characteristics that would predispose people to gamble in any form, it was unlikely that the relative importance of the factors would be the same for all forms of gambling. There would be some factors that would influence some forms of gambling but not others. Forms of gambling themselves offered varying combinations of characteristics – such as size of stake; the probability of winning; the time lag between decision, outcome, and benefit; the frequency of decisions. It seemed essential to allow for the separate analysis of as many types of gambling as proved identifiable and to experiment with alternative classifications.

A second decision was the type of factor likely to affect gambling outcomes. Both individual and group characteristics were expected to be important. Some individual characteristics might be related to personality traits. The distinguishable group factors were expected to include characteristics at very different levels of aggregation, such as affiliation to class, religions and community, family and work-place groups. Geographical factors were also considered. It could be expected that there would be marked differences in value systems between regions, depending upon rates of migration, and therefore affecting both attitudes and gambling behaviour. Other levels of geographical aggregation might be significant. For instance, activity might reflect different opportunities available for participation, as shown by the above study for one form of gambling. The level of geographical aggregation relevant is likely to vary between types of gambling. People probably travel further to use a provincial casino than to use a betting shop. Moreover, facilities that allow the activities which predispose persons to gamble in a particular way may vary between areas, such as being near enough to a football league club to attend matches which then might stimulate interest in football pools or fixed odds betting.

The design of the study, therefore, should at least allow for both levels of variable. Class and characteristics of groups associated with particular industrial structures required consideration when making the more basic strategic choices in the design of the study. Membership of work-place, religious and other community groups could be taken into account in questionnaire design. We would design a study to test the null hypothesis that broader geographical differences have no effect, even if it could not permit us to disentangle the relative importance of each influence. It was therefore decided to conduct area surveys drawn from different regions in England and Wales, and to analyse data for geographical sub-divisions within areas.

Another main objective of our sample design was to ensure an adequate representation of persons at the extremes of the distribution of social class. Some forms of gambling are reputed to be predominantly working-class activities. Some, indeed, were expected to be most important among members of the 'lower' working class. It was therefore important to have an adequate number of working class, and particularly lower working class people in the sample. There are other forms of gambling activity which were expected to be pursued mainly at the upper end of the class distribution. A pilot survey to demonstrate whether these preliminary ideas were adequate and necessary for the research design itself was next conducted.

The pilot survey: its lessons for the main survey

The aims of the pilot survey were:
(i) to extend the testing of the questionnaire as an instrument and of individual questions that composed it;
(ii) to gain experience of the method of sampling and the assumptions on which the stratification factors were based;
(iii) to throw light on the minimum sample size that should be aimed at in the main surveys;
(iv) to test the feasibility of interviewing whole households; partly to include the age group 18–20 (who were eligible to gamble but not at that time listed on the Electoral Register),

TABLE 3.1   *Sampling fractions and response rates by pilot survey zone*

Zone	Class and income	Fraction	Response rate %
1	high	1/7.76	71
2	low	1/27.70	53
3	mixed	1/54.60	67

but mainly to examine the association between gambling characteristics of household members.

Although over twenty versions of the questionnaire had been pre-tested prior to the pilot survey, the experience of conducting and analysing the pilot made it clear that further radical revisions were necessary.

The sampling frame for the pilot was a conventional one, the valuation lists, and few unexpected technical problems of incompleteness and inaccuracy arose, even in an area of London in which hereditaments may change their nature and use more frequently than in most. However, the low response rates to the pilot survey caused anxiety. Moreover, the response rates were lowest among households of low social class. This is illustrated in Table 3.1. In order to obtain a high percentage of the highest and lowest class and income groups, the area was divided into three zones, each with a different sampling fraction intended to yield fifty households. The gradient of response rates by class of zone is clear; but the big gap in rates was between zones 2 and 3.

Three main conclusions were drawn from the pilot survey response rates. First, that the training and management of interviewers should be our own responsibility in the main survey. The poor response in zone 2 apparently was due to poor interviewers, and reliance on a market research agency. Second, we should conduct individual rather than household interviews. The low response rate was also the result of interviewing all members of households. Where one respondent in a household objected to being interviewed, for whatever reason, the likelihood of conducting interviews with other members of the same household was drastically reduced: also, further intrusion into privacy is lessened when only one household member is approached for an interview. The price paid for the change was that the main survey could not analyse data on the extent to which families shared their patterns of gambling and use of leisure.

The third conclusion about responses was our mode of introducing the survey to prospective respondents. We should introduce the survey as being concerned with uses of leisure time. The pilot survey included questions on respondents' definitions of gambling which revealed that, irrespective of their own involvement, gambling was viewed with disapproval. Introducing the survey on the doorstep as one about gambling thus created a risk of non-response, some potential respondents wishing not to be associated with the activity, others who defined themselves as non-gamblers in advance assuming that they were of little relevance to the survey. Approximately one half of the questions on the main questionnaire were focused on leisure activities other than gambling, and also the term 'gambling' was not used in the questionnaire at all; questions related to specific betting or gambling activities. We therefore concluded that in the main survey, we should introduce the survey as being concerned with uses of leisure time, and that we would not press people into replying to questions on gambling which they did not wish to answer.

The results of the pilot survey justified the use of social class as a stratification factor, and the need for a large sample to cover frequent participation in gambling. The analysis also yielded some evidence about the extent and variation in participation between groups of respondents which contributed to our decision about sample sizes for the main survey, although the estimates yielded by the pilot survey were for an area whose composition is untypical and which were based on a sample with low response rates and therefore a high probability of bias.

The main surveys

The strategy determined that we conduct the survey in areas chosen from different regions. We discuss their choice, sampling procedures, questionnaire design, the strategy for data analysis and choice of statistical techniques.

(i) *The areas surveyed*

It was expected that regions, particularly those with little inflow of population, might have distinctive value systems, yet there would probably be substantial variations between districts sharing the facilities of major market areas. For these reasons we preferred to conduct surveys in three urban areas from different regions than a single national sample. Moreover, a national sample of the size needed for adequate analysis of gambling activities – some of which must be counted as rare traits – would have been more expensive than area samples. Area samples would also permit a more interesting analysis of the relationship between employment in different types of industry than a national sample. If we sampled from areas which had already been studied by sociologists, their prior insights might add new dimensions to the analysis. Of course, the analysis had to be restricted to three areas and so could not permit a proper experimental design, to compare and contrast ostensibly similar towns. The choice of areas was made so as to explore the consequences of a wide variety of factors rather than to attempt to test any explicit hypotheses.

The areas chosen were the county boroughs of Sheffield and Swansea and the former Municipal Borough of Wanstead and Woodford, from regions that are geographically and culturally distinct. Although both Swansea and Sheffield have substantial numbers of steelworkers, all three areas have large enough numbers of professional workers for them to be adequately represented in a sample, and for the populations to differ considerably. Swansea is a market and administrative centre; Wanstead and Woodford is a commuter area for non-manual workers in Central London: and both have been extensively researched. Sheffield relies on traditional industry and was being studied at the time.[4]

(ii) *The sample design*

The most accessible and reliable sampling frame for individuals is the electoral register, and this was used as a basis for the three samples. But it then included only those who are 21, or just under, and who have taken the trouble to register themselves as voters. Since the legal age of gambling is eighteen we had to devise a method of including those aged between eighteen and twenty-one. This problem has often been encountered. Commonly it has been solved either by the expensive, time-consuming and potentially biasing procedure of interviewing households and constructing a complete supplementary frame for the age-group, or by finding the number of that age-group in households containing a member of the same sample, and taking a supplementary and unrelated sample of the age-group. Both methods are liable to bias. The design chosen was a two-stage sample. The first stage was an equal-probability systematic sample of households, and the second stage was carried out by the interviewer in the systematic selection of one member of the household.[5]

(1) *The household sample* There are two possible sampling frames for households: the electoral register and the valuation list of the

51

rating authority. In principle the valuation list should be the more accurate and recent list of household spaces. In practice, as the pilot survey proved, it is difficult to use and is often less accurate than the electoral register. We, therefore, used the electoral registers.

Two methods of systematic sampling of households from the register exist. Moser and Kalton suggest the application of a fixed interval from a random start to give a sample with probability proportional to household size, from which elements would have to be rejected by random methods to give an equal-probability sample.[5] Yates[6] advises accepting a household only if the sampling interval indicated the first person listed in the household. Apart from inaccuracy in drawing the sample, there is a possibility of error in such a method. For instance, the addresses or dwellings listed are not always single household spaces; that is, some of the elements in the frame are clusters. Bias due to this is negligible where the clusters are rare and small. This appeared to be the case since no address sampled contained more than three households. Institutional households were in any case excluded from the sampling frame. The advantages of this sampling method were that the approximate household size – discounting those aged between 18 and 20 – and the number of households, given surnames at an address, were known before interviewing.

We attempted to secure a number of completed interviews that would support detailed description and analysis. We stratified with varying sampling fractions to increase the numbers of the extreme occupational groups, and their related income, family size groups. The problems for inference presented by such stratification are discussed by Blalock.[7] Generally, they are not severe where the sample is stratified by an independent variable, and where the explanatory variables are not independent of each other.

A total of 660 completed interviews were planned for with about 150 in each of the managerial/professional and unskilled manual occupations (using the Registrar General's classification). For Swansea and Wanstead and Woodford the estimates of yields for each polling district were made from enumeration districts to the 1966 Census-tract data. Since this Census-tract data was not available for Sheffield, estimates were made for constituencies by a regression analysis. Sheffield and Swansea were oversampled for the managerial/professional group, and Wanstead and Woodford for the semi- and unskilled manual group.[8] An assumed response rate also entered the calculations. The rates of 80 per cent for Swansea and 75 per cent for Wanstead and Woodford were based on previous surveys. The rate of 80 per cent for Sheffield was not based on such evidence. The methods and calculations for the primary sample of households, and expected results are shown in the appended tables (see pp. 62–4).

The method used to derive a sample of individuals from a sample of households was that invented by Kish. The Kish method was designed to ensure that a person has equal chance of selection for every person in a household for any size of household, the distributions of households by size for which this was true being American.[9] It provides simple rigorous rules by which an interviewer can select a respondent from a household; the interviewers first listing all persons aged 18 and over in the household, males first, and then referring to a pre-defined selection table.

(2) *Bias arising from non-response and interviewer effects* Of all sources of bias, the most serious are likely to be due to non-response and to non-random errors arising in the interview situation. Errors due to other sources are unlikely to be negligible. Various steps were taken to minimize interviewer bias (see pp. 64–7).

The potential for error due to non-response is more easily assessable. The response rates are shown in Table 3.2. Table 3.3 shows the analysis of types of non-response.

Dislike of London University was a more important cause of refusal in Wanstead and Woodford than elsewhere. The analysis of the proportions of the respondents who refused by word, successful contact having first been made with someone else in the household, suggested that there was no class bias in the incidence (see p. 66). Few respondents refused because of the nature and sequence of the questions in the interview situation, most refusals occurring before the commencement of the interview. To reduce the number of refusals, interviewers were sent back to addresses on at least two occasions, and a letter was also sent, which was most effective in Swansea, and least effective in Wanstead and Woodford.

Although the procedures adopted were similar in all three areas, they worked with less success in Wanstead and Woodford than elsewhere. Despite more intensive advertising the number of applicants was smaller, and less satisfactory interviewers were appointed. It is also likely that high activity rates for women, the importance of commuting, and other characteristics of the area, made it more difficult to obtain satisfactory interviewers. As the field period progressed, it became clear that the field-work in that area was unlikely to be successful without assistance. A research agency was commissioned to undertake 100 (of the 849) interviews. The non-comparabilities thus risked appeared likely to create only a small bias in a sample of 2000. It was judged that its most important effect on the study would be financial.

53

TABLE 3.2   *Non-response by area*

	Swansea	Sheffield	Wanstead and Woodford
Total no. of addresses (incl. potentially double/treble households assessed by the number of surnames) on the Electoral Register	1,015	921	953
Destroyed or vacant buildings	33	29	8
Duplicate case numbers for one household	126	65	96
Actual sample of dwellings	856	827	849
Number of completed interviews*	723	653	581
Number of unobtained interviews	133	174	268
Response rate (%)	85	79	68

*A check was made to ensure that obtained interviews had been conducted.

TABLE 3.3   *Sources of non-response by area*

Source of non-response	Swansea	Sheffield	Wanstead and Woodford
Respondent or contact refused*	87	130	191
Respondent unreachable or incommunicable†	41	35	67
Questionnaire not returned by interviewers	—	—	7
Wrong person selected and interviewed‡	5	9	3
Total non-response	133	174	268
Total eligible	856	827	849

* After letter sent out and two visits paid.
† Including the temporarily unavailable (e.g. being absent on a long holiday), the incommunicable (because, for instance, of senility or deafness), and the ill.
‡ Due to misapplication of Kish method by interviewer.

(iii) *The questionnaire design*

Since we had no theory on which to base the survey we chose to study a very broad range of characteristics of individuals in relation to gambling. Moreover, we assumed that gambling itself was embedded in a complex range of leisure activities. The final questionnaire developed from the pilot survey, therefore, sought a mass of detail on each individual in terms of his socio-economic status, his behaviour over a range of issues and his attitudes towards that behaviour.

First, the dependent variable – gambling – was defined widely. We chose nine separate types of gambling: football pools, betting on horses and/or dogs in a shop, on track or by credit, bingo, fruit machines, playing cards or games either in a pub or at home, or at a casino. We supplemented this list with brief questions about betting on the three big national races – Grand National, Derby, Ascot Gold Cup – fixed odds betting, newspaper competitions, raffles, lotteries and non-club bingo. For all types of gambling we asked each individual about how frequently he participated defined first in weekly terms and second in hours and minutes. For the nine key forms of gambling chosen we also asked for details on expenditure, outcomes and attitudes towards that specific activity as well as the social relations entailed.

Second, we asked all the questions about gambling in the context of general spare-time and specific leisure pursuits. We defined six areas of such pursuits – home-making and housework, hobbies, political and/or community activity, sports, study, entertainment – and detailed specific issues for each area. For these issues we also asked for frequency of involvement in terms of time spent.

Third, we tried to locate each individual's activities in its social and familial context. We therefore questioned about parental gambling, conjugal role and social relations. We also asked the respondent to evaluate why he or she did or did not participate in any gambling activities, and to express their attitudes to modes of living. In particular we tried to tap psychological states such as authoritarianism, belief in luck or chance and risk-taking by presenting a list of questions which apparently were indicators of such constellations of attitudes.

Fourth, to establish the social and economic characteristics of gambling, defined individually, we sought information on the respondent's background – age, sex, marital status, education and qualifications, religion, occupation present and previous, that of his or her parents and spouse, and household income. In this context we also asked the respondent to assess his present job, on a series of criteria such as autonomy, monotony and effort.

The questionnaire was quite lengthy and especially long for those who habitually participated in several forms of gambling. First, we expected each respondent to answer detailed questions for each form of gambling to enable us to analyse each one separately. Second, we had no way of anticipating which of the range of independent variables – socio-economic characteristics, psychological attitudes or social activities and relations – would yield the best explanations for the varieties of gambling that we had specified.

(iv) *The statistical analysis of the survey data*

Data were collected from each respondent to derive 3,000 raw variables. It was not difficult to select some of the more important dependent variables – forms of gambling – for the mapping of potentially important relationships, but the definition of composite variables and social indicators for analysis raised both theoretical and technical problems.[10] The requirements of exploratory 'fishing' activity, as Selvin and Stuart described the process of discovering relationships between a large number of variables, dominated decisions about the techniques of data analysis.[11] We discuss first the techniques used to derive the composite variables and social indicators and second the techniques used in this fishing operation for cause and effect relationships.

(a) *Composite variables and social indicators*

(1) *Gambling as the dependent variable*   The more we move from considering *one* form of gambling (to the exclusion of the rest) to *all* gambling, the more the activity becomes a 'more-or-less' rather than a 'yes-or-no' phenomenon. For theoretical purposes, it is desirable to take as the dependent variable gambling in the round rather than any one form, however popular that form might be. To this end we devised indicators of 'multiple gambling' which means a measure of the extent and intensity of gambling. First, we took only the nine basic forms and selected a frequency threshold at which regular seemed to be demarcated from more occasional gambling. For most forms, weekly or more often, seemed to be the dividing line. For on-track betting and casinos, a more realistic divide was between yearly or more and the rest. We then counted as 'multiple gamblers' those who gambled *above* the line chosen on *two or more* forms. The emphasis was on the *extent* rather than intensity of such. To rate highly, a respondent had only to do the

pools and play a fruit machine once a week. It proved a poor discriminator.

Next we allowed for unusually intensive and unusually extensive participation in one or several forms. We categorized as 'high' those who gambled *twice a week* or more on any one; once a week on any three; and/or once a fortnight on any four, and/or once a month on any five of the nine forms. The typology called Gambling Type I is as follows:

'High'   = Those gambling twice weekly or more often on any 1 form
          + Those gambling weekly or more often on any 3 forms
          + Those gambling fortnightly or more often on any 4 forms
          + Those gambling monthly or more often on any 5 forms

'Medium' = Those gambling weekly or more often on any 1 form
          + Those gambling fortnightly or more often on any 2 forms
          + Those gambling monthly or more often on any 3 forms
          + Those gambling yearly or more often on any 4 forms

'Low'   = Those gambling yearly or more often on any 1 form

'None'   = Those not gambling yearly or more often on even 1 form

This typology does seem to work quite well in providing a comprehensive and socially recognizable set of categories which differentiate the more intensive gamblers. Whether intensity is made up of the pursuit of one form of gambling very frequently, or of five forms of gambling more infrequently, they involve much the same frequency of gambling *events*. Type II extends this coverage.[12]

For AID (see below, pp. 61–2), a third measure of gambling was derived. This indicator is mean 'total' gambling frequency over a twelve-month period; the term total comprising participation in the nine basic forms of gambling. The unit whose frequency is measured is the gambling *session*, not the individual games in question. Clearly there are problems of equivalence involved: and the indicator excludes forms which arguably should have been included, e.g. raffles and premium bonds. On balance, we excluded them because their inclusion tended to dilute the variance achieved and they represent forms of gambling whose status as such is more problematic.

Both these measures are used to explain and test theories. Other measures are used to derive relationships within types of gambling such as expenditure, stake, outcome and form of gambling frequency.

(2) *Independent variables*   Composite indicators to use as independent variables were derived from the raw variables. For the main exploratory analysis thirty-eight basic indicators were developed. Some were modifications of socio-economic characteristics such as age, marital status, religion, religiosity, net household income and education. Others were more complicated derivations. The social

class variable was developed from the Registrar General's seventeen category socio-economic scale and collapsed into five groups. The same method was used for social mobility, basing the variable on father's occupation. The leisure activities' indicators relied on a similar method as that for gambling. The total frequency was derived by summing the frequencies of each item within a type of activity, e.g. political and/or community activity. For parental gambling and conjugal role-sharing the highest frequency from the check list of items was chosen.

The most complicated method used for deriving variables was factor analysis. This was used for attitudes towards job and to living. It was expected that gambling would be particularly sensitive to broad ideological perceptions. Devereux clearly links these broad attitude sets to gamblers' motivations.[13] He argued that in a society whose values emphasize material goals and their attainment through the economically rational (and risky) means of work and effort, gambling derives its 'meaning' by providing an economically irrational (and risky) means of attaining the material ends which norms dictate should be attained by work and effort. As such, attitudes towards gambling are ambivalent.

Adorno's model of the 'authoritarian personality' has features which are closely linked with the characteristics outlined by Devereux and has other features that may well affect gambling behaviour.[14] His F-scale therefore seemed to provide a basis for constructing indicators of such characteristics.[15] A set of statements was chosen, each being interrelated to reflect one of the principal dimensions of variation in attitudes.[16] The statements relating to each of the three dimensions are shown in Table 3.4. Respondents were asked to express the relative strength of their agreement with the propositions on a five-point scale.

The statistical technique used to derive indicators from the responses to the inventory was a three-factor maximum likelihood method (MLM) factor analysis. The literature concluded that the domains were statistically independent of one another. Therefore an orthogonal rotation was chosen. The three factors yielded by the analysis corresponded to conventionalism, a belief in luck, and a positive attitude to taking risks. The factor analysis was performed for each area separately and for the pooled sample. The loadings of each factor on the variables are shown in Table 3.5.

The significant loadings on this factor, although covering the items used for theoretical construction of 'rigid adherence to conventional values' or 'conventionality', also include two items that were not expected to be highly loaded on the factor.[17] The results agreed well as between samples.

TABLE 3.4 *The propositions relating to fate, risk-taking and conventionalism*

Domain A: Belief in fate and superstition
 1* Although many people may laugh I think that astrology can explain a lot of things
 4 Even if they don't always come true people should not ignore their horoscopes
 7 Luck is something you are born with
10 People who don't believe in fate are fooling themselves
13 Some things, like black cats and the number 13, really tell you a lot about your luck

Domain B: Attitudes to risk-taking and excitement
 2 The main thing in life is to guard yourself against any disturbances
 5 I never take risks if I can avoid them
 8 When I get bored I like to stir up some excitement
11 There's no fun in life if you always have to be careful
14 I really enjoy being in dangerous situations

Domain C: Authoritarianism or conventionalism
12 One should avoid doing things in public that appear wrong to others, even though one knows that those things are really right
15 Too many people today are living in a soft unnatural way; we should return to a more active, full-blooded way of life
 6 Respect for authority is the most important virtue a child should learn
 9 It is essential for learning and for effective work that our bosses tell us in detail what is to be done and exactly how to go about it
 3 Books and films and so on ought not to deal so much with the sordid or seamy side of life; they ought to concentrate on more pleasant and entertaining stories

* The numbers signify the order in which the propositions appeared in the inventory.

TABLE 3.5 *Factor I: The conventionalism or rigidity factor: loading on the variables**

Wanstead & Woodford		Swansea		Sheffield		All sample	
2	0·675	2	0·735	2	0·733	2	0·721
5	0·672	6	0·692	5	0·713	6	0·678
3	0·634	3	0·644	6	0·708	5	0·674
6	0·599	5	0·627	3	0·665	3	0·649
9	0·545	9	0·530	9	0·503	9	0·531
12	0·476	12	0·524	12	0·500	12	0·503

* Loadings of a variable on a factor show the correlation of the variable with that factor.

TABLE 3.6   *Factor II: Belief in fate or luck*

Wanstead & Woodford		*Swansea*		*Sheffield*		*All sample*	
4	0·685	1	0·695	1	0·706	1	0·700
1	0·680	4	0·647	4	0·640	4	0·625
10	0·537	13	0·458	13	0·448	13	0·460
7	0·520	10	0·388	10	0·411	10	0·437
13	0·496	7	0·336	7	0·325	7	0·384

All the loadings on Factor II in each of the areas and in the overall analysis which are significant are the items postulated as a 'belief in fate or superstition'. The rank order of the loading is, however, slightly different in the areas. No other items can be shown to be significantly loaded on this factor. The high loadings on Factor III are for items on the risk-taking domains other than 2 and 5. They are all significantly loaded on the factor and all other loadings are virtually zero. It is therefore clear that the pattern of correlation was what was expected, and that it differed little between the three areas.[18]

(b) *Relationships between variables*

In this most thoroughly inductive 'fishing' phase of model development, it is inefficient and unwise not to search for relationships of the dependent variable with as large a number of variables as might influence the pattern of predication, particularly where some of the causal factors are associated. Moreover, the form of prediction between the variables cannot be assumed: it must be discovered

TABLE 3.7   *Factor III: Attitude to risk*

Wanstead & Woodford		*Swansea*		*Sheffield*		*All Sample*	
8	0·624	8	0·587	8	0·572	8	0·591
14	0·517	11	0·483	11	0·561	11	0·513
11	0·501	14	0·459	14	0·430	14	0·470
15	0·373			7	0·416		

if important relationships are to be found for a theory. The traditional technique is multivariate tabulations. By trial and error the tabulations which best predict variations in the dependent variable are found. It was not practicable to attempt this. Stepwise regression analysis is more widely used where models must be based on relatively few observations. However, the use of this technique is based on rigid assumptions. It is a more valuable tool at later stages of analysis when the form of the relationships is clear and there is little doubt of the key variables.

Fortunately a new computerized technique came to our attention before the survey was undertaken – *Automatic Interaction Detector* (AID). It simulates the behaviour of a highly efficient, conscientious and insightful social survey analyst in finding the theoretically significant predictors of the dependent variable. The technique operates in a stepwise manner.[19] The result is a number of groups each of which is as homogeneous as the predictor variables allow with respect to the score of the individuals on the dependent variable. The variables defining the groups need not be the same for all; for example, some causal factors may influence gambling among men that do not influence gambling among women. The impact of the same variables can be shown to be of different magnitude – and indeed, in a different direction – for certain groups. Possible interaction effects are displayed. Although AID makes use of the language of hypothesis-testing, it would be inappropriate to test the significance of the differences. This is so because the associations are not pre-determined by the theory, as in a hypothesis-testing context, but have been created by a procedure that 'fishes' for differences, and whose results therefore reflect to some degree the effects of chance.[20] It is therefore legitimate to tabulate data using this 'fishing' procedure, but to test the significance of the models implicit in the form of the tabulations or the individual relationships within them, it would be necessary to collect new data. How important is an interaction effect – how great the departure from the additivity that Occam's Razor makes preferable – must remain a matter of judgment.[21]

AID is a valuable analytic tool. It can draw attention not only to the existence of interaction effects, but also to their nature. It can distinguish a situation in which the possession of a number of attributes, rather than merely one, is necessary for there to be high commitment to gambling. It suggests the most appropriate interaction term to describe this effect. For instance, gambling may not take place unless a respondent has three characteristics: an internal driving mechanism, a perceived probability of success, and some material incentive. The absence of any one of these may lead to a low level of commitment.[22] In this case the appropriate interaction term (incorporated in an additive model) would be the Booleian expression 'high internal driving mechanism *and* high perceived probability of success, *and* high material incentive'. Alternatively, gambling may take place with any one of these three factors present, making little difference whether more than one such factor was in operation. In this case, the Booleian expression which would define an appropriate term for an additive model would be 'high internal driving mechanism *or* high perceived probability of success *or* high material incentive.'[23] AID is also a valuable technique because it makes no assumptions about linearity or additivity and so can explain a higher proportion of the dependent variable than other techniques.[24] It is intelligible to the reader of a research report, and provides the analyst with a wealth of information on which to base his judgments.

However, AID yields only incomplete sketches for models. The model-building process requires that AID be used in conjunction with such other techniques as multiple regression analysis and multiple classification analysis (MCA). The latter has the advantage that it is easy to examine the overall effect of variables as classified predictors, as well as the effect of the actual classes of a particular predictor variable. It does not assume linearity although it does assume additivity.[25] Therefore, given limited resources, the intention of the project was to base the exploration on an extensive exploratory AID analysis to further develop each model by performing a series of MCA analyses, with different combinations of variables assumed to predict gambling, as finally estimating the model using multiple regression techniques. It was, however, realized that resources would not permit a thorough application of this strategy, if the analysis using AID was to be accomplished for an adequate number of dependent variables.

Note 1: The sample design

TABLE 3.8   *Basic data for fixing sampling intervals*

Area	No. of electors	No. of dwellings	No. of house-holds	Electors per h'hold	House-holds p. dwelling	Expected resp. rate
Sheffield	344,799	165,940	169,530	2·08	1·02	0·80
Swansea	114,385	52,150	53,950	2·19	1·03	0·80
Wanstead & Woodford	45,316	20,160	20,590	2·25	1·02	0·75

TABLE 3.9 *Sample sizes in all three areas*

Area	Completed inter- views	House- holds p. dwelling	Expected resp. rate	Sample size required	Sample size drawn
Sheffield	685	1·02	0·8	840	827
Swansea	685	1·03	0·8	832	856
Wanstead & Woodford	630	1·02	0·75	826	849
Total	2000			2498	2532

The sample size for a given number of completed interviews is calculated by dividing the number of completed interviews by the number of households per dwelling and the expected response rate, as shown in Table 3.9. Since at the time of sampling we knew that we were short of interviewers in Wanstead and Woodford, we reduced the expected number of completed interviews in that area, and increased the number for Sheffield and Swansea to keep the pooled sample size at 2,000.

The sampling interval for each stratum was obtained by dividing the stratum population by the product of the desired sample and the number of electors per household (to allow for the rejection of households in which the first listed name was not selected).

The results of stratification are shown in Tables 3.10–3.12. It

TABLE 3.10 *Estimated effects of stratification in Sheffield*

Sampling fraction	Estimated nos in sample in groups			
	A	B	C	Total
1/300	50	134	280	464
1/70*	85	71	220	376
Total	135	205	500	840
Expected Interviews†	108	164	400	672

Notes: A Socio-economic groups 1–4 (professional and managerial)
      B Socio-economic groups 10 and 11 (semi and unskilled manual)
      C Remainder
      Expected Interviews   Sample size x expected response rate
* Hallam Constituency
Expected response rate, 0·80

TABLE 3.11   *Estimated effects of stratification in Swansea*

| Sampling fraction | Estimated nos in sample in groups | | | |
	A	B	C	Total
1/100	40	141	237	418
1/25*	136	63	215	414
Total	176	204	452	832
Expected Interviews†	142	163	362	665

* Mumbles and Sketty wards
† Expected response rate, 0·80

TABLE 3.12   *Estimated effects of stratification in Wanstead and Woodford*

| Sampling fraction | Estimated nos in sample in groups | | | |
	A	B	C	Total
1/30	168	48	265	481
1/20*	38	17	62	117
1/15†	42	45	141	228
Total	248	110	468	826
Estimated Interviews‡	186	82	351	620

* Polling districts B2, B3, and S3
† Polling districts Wa3 and Wo4
‡ Expected response rate, 0·75

was impossible to obtain the desired number of interviews in group C by stratification by polling district without denuding most of the area of interviews. Even polling districts are sometimes too high a level of aggregation for efficient sampling, but smaller areas (e.g. enumeration districts) cannot easily be identified in the electoral register.

Note 2: Interviewer error and bias

The survey was timed so as to minimize the gap between it and the collection of the data on which the sampling frame was based. The Electoral Register, was published one month before work commenced. The best estimates of errors due to non-coverage – because no household corresponding to an address in the frame or due to printing errors in the Register – were 33 (out of 1,015 addresses) in Swansea, 29 (out of 921 addresses) in Sheffield, and 8 (out of 953 addresses) in Wanstead and Woodford. The errors of the interviewers in selecting their respondents using the Kish method are also quantifiable in so far as the relevant feature of their descriptions of household composition were correct. Five such mistakes were made in Swansea, nine in Sheffield, and three in Wanstead and Woodford. Coding and punching errors were minimized by the careful checking of questionnaires by senior personnel of the project; the careful preparation of coding frames based on a sample for each area of the completed answers to each open-ended question; the production of a coding manual; the employment of experienced coders; and their careful supervision. Errors in card punching and data analysis were minimized by punching from the precoded questionnaire; by having the cards verified; and for checking card images for order, case number and range limits.

High grade interviewers were recruited and prepared for the specific project task. They were selected by advertisement; of those making their written application in Swansea and Sheffield, a quarter were selected. The principal criteria used were availability at times of likely respondent accessibility; interest of conversation and an apparent absence of rigidly held views or a desire to impress or 'convert' the listener; presentability of appearance; an apparent interest in the aim of the project to explore reasons for the differing uses of leisure; an occupational background which included working, and in some circumstances managing people; and an educational background such as to suggest a sufficient degree of literacy and clarity of mind to perceive and record statements and situations fully and accurately. An attempt was also made to secure a mix of age, sex and class so that some matching of interviewer to respondent might be undertaken. Most of those selected at this stage had already had experience as interviewers. Selected candidates were exposed to a briefing, covering the aims of the project and the main questions in the schedule; a mock interview and three practice interviews.

In Swansea and Sheffield, at least, there was no reason to suppose that the fieldwork was likely to yield biases other than those arising from the nature of the questions and the dynamics of the interviewing situation in which competent interviewers faced samples weighted with persons of high and low social class. One feature of the situation is the large number of questions asked about gambling activities. This might be a subject about participation in which some respondents might feel embarrassment. Not only might this result in some under-reporting, and the under-reporting might be particularly prevalent in some groups whose activity relatively to that of other groups was theoretically important, but the probability of under-reporting might be related to interviewer characteristics. One possibility hypothesized in the literature is that under-reporting may vary with social distance: the higher the apparent class of the interviewer and the lower the class of the respondent, the greater the under-reporting is likely to be, since the interview situation tends to develop a dimension related to social control. In at least one experiment in a related area, drinking practices, under-reporting was negatively correlated with social distance; the authors hypothesizing that the interviewer was viewed as a professional to whom it would be safe to tell all.[26] It would, however, be dangerous to argue that such a result could be applied to a different set of activities in different local cultures on the other side of the Atlantic. However, the more general conclusion was that the interview takes the form of a developing of short-lived relationships in which respondents' answers come to reflect the norms that emerge in the course of it, and that may well have some validity.

It is the most immediately apparent characteristics of the interviewers – their sex, age and what is inferred from their clothing and speech – that affect the interview norms most. We hope that these were the characteristics that had most effect in the selection interview, and the supervisors' selection of interviewers. We tried to exercise some control over the factors affecting interview success, especially in matching interviewers to respondents towards the end of the field work period. In general, interviewers were expected to

TABLE 3.13   *Distribution of response rates by ward*

Response rates (%)	*Swansea*	*Sheffield*	*Wanstead & Woodford*
95 and over	1	–	–
90 and less than 95	2	2	1
85 and less than 90	5	1	–
80 and less than 85	4	4	2
75 and less than 80	1	2	3
70 and less than 75	1	2	2
65 and less than 70	1	2	6
60 and less than 65	–	–	1
55 and less than 60	–	–	1
50 and less than 55	–	–	1

carry loads in several areas, so that the interviewer effects would be spread across groups.

Although the procedures adopted were similar in all three areas, they worked with less success in Wanstead and Woodford than elsewhere.

Note 3: Response rates

Table 3.13 shows frequency distributions of response rates by ward. They closely reflect the overall means. The response rates for individual wards were most successfully held in Swansea, all but three rates exceeding 80 per cent. In Wanstead and Woodford, in contrast, only three rates exceeded 80 per cent, and five rates were less than 65 per cent.

4 Tests of hypotheses about patterns of gambling

Conventional wisdom in sociology dictates one sequence above all others: first theory, then data to test and/or elaborate that theory. In the task of survey design we were only too aware of this axiom. It was overshadowed, however, by the absence of any hypotheses, let alone a set of interrelated hypotheses amounting to a master theory, of overriding significance on gambling.[1] What did exist were a number of interesting theoretical leads and propositions which called out for further testing and elaboration, but none of which – taken alone – were of sufficient weight to form a pivot for the inquiry. The nearest to a full theoretical statement is that of Devereux,[2] but his structural-functional frame of reference predicted, for example, the persistence of gambling in a *sub rosa* status of illegality. The legalization of virtually all forms of gambling in this country in 1960 seemed *prima facie* evidence for rejecting his theory, whilst recognizing its suggestive powers and singling out from its theoretical *corpus* those propositions which seemed of continuing relevance. The situation of gambling theory, then, was one of the existence of interesting *pointers* rather than of any major theoretical statement around which to organize a full-blown study of gambling. We therefore determined to test these propositions as far as possible in a survey framework designed to reach other goals as well: namely, the gathering of primary information about a variety of forms of gambling, and the exploration of the relevance of differing commitments in leisure, socio-economic and attitudinal factors to gambling. In this way, we hoped to maximize the yield of the surveys: for to test one theory which falls flat is to waste the opportunity to test others and gather information which may enable us to generate yet more.[3] The former is worth-while only where a formidable theory has evolved which promises a greater

68

explanatory yield than the sum of other theories and propositions available at the time which relates to the same phenomenon.

Eight theories

With the above in mind, we proceed to an exploration and testing of eight theories of gambling. Some were specifically geared to the explanation of gambling; others were general theories of social deviance and were included because gambling, both historically and in certain current perspectives, connotes deviation from socially prescribed norms – though the emphasis now is only on the more intensive and costly forms of gambling. The theories differ, also, in their scope, covering in some cases *all* gambling, in others certain aspects or components of gambling only. They are, in their order of treatment below, theories based upon the notions of: (1) anomie; (2) alienation; (3) working-class culture; (4) structural-functional imperatives; (5) decision-making; (6) risk-taking; (7) 'home-centredness' and (8) 'work-centred' leisure.

The test population

All tests were carried out using a base population of *all men in the sample aged twenty-six to sixty-five*, the young and middle-aged. By controlling for sex, and eliminating the youngest and the elderly, we have tried to avoid any confounding that may unnecessarily interfere with the freedom of the hypothesized relationships to emerge. Further controls were impossible because we could not reduce our base population further without seriously impairing the reliability of the results. Unless otherwise specified, all tables are based on weighted data.

Tests

(i) *Anomie*

Propositions Anomie theory, as it has been Americanized by Merton out of Durkheim,[4] is basically a theory of the consequences for social deviance of a non-alignment between culturally prescribed goals and socially structured means to their attainment. In societies where the universe of discourse is that of individualistic democracy, structured inequality coexists with culturally induced expectations of uniform life-chances. It amounts to an assertion that no society can, at one and the same time, exhort its members to succeed materially whilst denying access to that goal to a majority of the population without consequences of strain which crystallize as 'deviant adaptations'. Heavy gambling is feasibly accounted for in this matrix.

The simplest test of anomie theory as it relates to gambling is to assume *uniform* adherence to the goal of material success. As access to this goal is restricted progressively the lower one's position in the social scale, we would hypothesize that the propensity to gamble should *increase* the lower one's position (and thus one's life-chances) in the social scale. Propensity to gamble should, therefore, be inversely related to social class as measured by current socio-economic grouping. *Within* class, however, some are better off than others: and their propensity to gamble should therefore be decreased.

A further deduction is that the *nature* of gambling would differ in the same directions: the worse the life-chances, the greater the risk component in gambling. Those with least hope of attaining the success goal through orthodox channels take the riskiest route to it through other channels.

One methodological point: Hirschi and Selvin[5] state that, in the case of delinquency, the correct test for anomie theory is the extent to which delinquency is inversely related to class, holding adherence to the success goal constant. While an objection to this view in the case of gambling is that gamblers can be viewed not only as 'innovators' and 'conformists' but also as 'ritualists' (the latter differ in that 'ritualists' over-adapt to the means, and lose sight of the goal), Hirschi and Selvin's point is still valid in relating anomie theory to gambling. (We did not have data on the degree of adherence to the success goal.)

We should stress that few sociologists would now accept anomie theory in its simplest form. They would expect 'intervening variables' to modulate and mediate the nature of commitment to the success goal. The chief 'intervening variables' would include sex and age, for which we have in part controlled. They would also include the nature of an actor's membership and reference groups (as in Runciman[6]); they would extend analysis to success goals other than that of material success (as in Downes[7]). But gambling as an activity is a classic example of the pursuit of material gain (a surrogate for success) by unorthodox means (a surrogate for adequate life-chances). It seems in order to make the simplest and most direct deductions from the theory. The absence of data on adherence to the success goal is, however, a serious drawback to the validity of the tests.

Tests
(a) Multiple gambling by socio-economic group by income.
(b) 'High-risk' element in gambling by socio-economic group by income.

Results   The most important results are shown in Tables 4.1 and 2.

TABLE 4.1   *% Gambling by class by income – Multiple Gambling Type I*

| | High | | High/medium | |
| | Low | High | Low | High |
Class	Income		Income	
Upper middle	8	8	25	57
Lower middle	32	23	70	71
Upper working	24	27	59	81
Lower working	31	37	80	57

TABLE 4.2   *% Gambling by class by income – Multiple Gambling Type II*

| | High | | High/medium | |
| | Low | High | Low | High |
Class	Income		Income	
Upper middle	15	13	38	66
Lower middle	32	26	70	77
Upper working	24	38	63	86
Lower working	33	42	81	79

According to our deductions, propensity to 'high' or certainly to 'high' or 'medium' gambling should increase as class and incomes lower. This deduction is partly borne out for 'high' gamblers only, in that the middle-class gradient is in line with the postulated trend: but the gradient breaks down for low-income working-class gamblers. If we ignore the income difference and concentrate on class, the gradient is as postulated for those earning *over* £1,000 p.a., but not for those earning *under* £1,000. The other results are even more out of line with deductions than the above. The tests for 'high-risk' betting were carried out for all betting on horses and dogs (off- and on-track) who bet at least sporadically. The upper middle-class group proved far too small in number for analysis (n=5). The differences between the remaining groups, whether analysed by class or income or both, were negligible.

71

Summary The deductions derived from anomie theory were not borne out by the data. In the case of 'high-risk' bets, the numbers available for the test were perhaps far too small for it to mean very much. But in the case of the tests involving the income-cum-class groups, the case most out of line with predictions was *not* those with small numbers. The most out-of-step group in this respect were the upper working class, earning under £1,000 p.a., a group which – if anomie theory means anything at all – should be particularly sensitive to the strains induced by the ends-means discrepancy, and particularly prone to gambling as a result. However, it may well be that this group is most oriented to goals other than those of material success, e.g. craftsmanship, and are therefore insulated to some extent against the pressures making for emulative materialism.

(ii) *Alienation*

Propositions Theories of alienation stem from Marx's global use of the concept to describe the condition of man-under-capitalism, estranged by the relations of production and commodity fetishism from the product of his labour and thereby from himself.[8] Modern theories of alienation at their weakest have equated the term with job satisfaction, but the best of these have stressed the multidimensional nature of alienation as an ideal-typical state (see Blauner[9]). As an indicator of alienation from work, we have tried to avoid the stress of job satisfaction – which too easily picks up mere surface discontents – and, following Blauner, have tried to place it on powerlessness in the work context. We selected from Blauner's questionnaire eight items for inclusion in our own, and factor analysis brought out two factors in particular. The first stemmed from items dealing principally with *autonomy* in the work role: freedom to work as preferred; an element of say in the way the job is done; and a chance to try out ideas of one's own. The second stemmed from items concerned mainly with excessive *effort*: having to work too fast most of the time; being too tired at the end of the day; and no freedom to work as preferred.

One proposition is that lack of autonomy in the work role will be associated with gambling, since the worker who is stifled in his work role will seek avenues of self-assertion in which he *is* free to do as he prefers, and *can* try out his ideas. Hypothetically, gambling provides him with such an avenue, functioning as more than a pastime for those who lack autonomy in work. Job effort is a less useful indicator of much the same principle, and here we would predict an inverse relationship between excessive job effort and gambling, since *prima facie* an indicator of lack of autonomy is the worker's powerlessness in the face of what he perceives as an unduly tiring and demanding work role.

A further indicator of alienation was thought to be the extent to which people participate in political and/or community activities. Whether canvassing or working in other ways for a political party or local pressure group, or a union, or simply taking part in local community affairs at any level, there is a certain implicit belief in one's ability to intervene in events, irrespective of whether the explicit aim is to promote social change or social welfare, or the reverse. But we cannot assume that non-participation in these activities amounts to alienation. Rather, we would argue that the degree of involvement in these activities indicates the degree of non-alienation. That is, participation in political and/or community activities is a sufficient but not a necessary indicator of non-aliena-tion. We would predict that such participation is inversely correlated with involvement in gambling, whose attractiveness as a demand on time, energy and money dwindles as alternative avenues of self-assertion are chosen.

Tests
   (a) Job autonomy by class by multiple gambling.
   (b) Job effort by class by multiple gambling.
   (c) Political/community activity by multiple gambling (middle class only).

Results For the hypothesis to be sustained, the trend should be for a *drop* in the percentages as one reads from left to right in Table 4.3. In only two of the eight lines does this broadly occur:

TABLE 4.3

		High	n	Middle	n	Low	n	None	n
		Multiple Gambling (Type I)							
% Low job	Upper middle	100	(8)	88	(45)	96	(32)	98	(49)
autonomy	Lower middle	42	(9)	66	(41)	70	(16)	52	(29)
	Upper working	31	(40)	36	(89)	28	(15)	33	(40)
	Lower working	39	(25)	24	(44)	62	(20)	0	(9)
% High job	Upper middle	44		52		29		61	
effort	Lower middle	87		52		57		40	
	Upper working	63		64		43		45	
	Lower working	58		63		71		51	

Key Each figure = per cent in each category rating low scores for job autonomy.
   Brackets = base population for each category.

for the lower middle and upper working-class groups on job effort. This is not enough to rescue the hypothesis, especially as the trend in these two cases is not repeated on the unweighted data. The results using the Type II indicator of gambling are much the same as for Type I. A point of interest revealed by this test is the very high proportion of the upper middle class who perceive their jobs as lacking scope for autonomy (see note at end of chapter).

The second test predicted an inverse relationship between involvement in gambling and involvement in political and/or community activities, and this prediction *was* borne out by the data (see Tables 4.4 and 4.5).

These tests are corroborated by the Type II gambling indicator and by the unweighted data. The test was carried out on the middle-class group only, since the relationship between this status and political/community involvement was marked. But extending the test to include working-class men did not affect this trend.

TABLE 4.4

| | | Gambling (Type I) | | | |
		High	Medium	Low	None
Political/community	Weekly	0	3	9	23
Involvement (%)	Monthly	1	10	10	25
	Yearly	27	28	32	25
	None	72	59	50	26
		100	100	100	100
		(n = 17)	(n = 86)	(n = 49)	(n = 79)

TABLE 4.5

| | | Political and/or community involvement | | | |
		High	Medium	Low	None
Gambling Type II	Weekly	0	1	16	22
	Monthly	14	36	46	52
	Yearly	12	9	14	12
	None	74	53	25	14
		100	100	100	100
		(n = 17)	(n = 29)	(n = 84)	(n = 101)

Summary The theory linking alienation to gambling must be rejected, since the most direct test showed no relationship between job autonomy and involvement in gambling. It should be stressed, however, that the main indicator of job autonomy was subjective perception rather than objective assessment. A second proposition *compatible with* the theory of alienation and gambling was sustained. It should be stressed, however, that the relationship between involvement in political/community activities and a decreasing involvement in gambling can be explained equally plausibly by theories which have little to do with alienation. One example would be that the value-system supporting political and/or community involvement is at odds with that supporting gambling *irrespective* of class or alienation at work. The first would stress the importance of self-realization through work-oriented collaborative social and political processes; the second would stress self-realization through the ideal of fun and play in leisure.

(iii) *Working-class culture*

Propositions A central theme in the sociology of contemporary Western societies is the cleavage between the two major social classes, middle and working. Without going into the history and ramifications of this theme, it is enough to note here the assumption that the two classes differ culturally, as well as economically; and a host of 'social problems' – or at least what constitute social problems from a middle-class standpoint – are often viewed as outgrowths of working-class *culture* (examples include delinquency, poverty and educational under-achievement). We thought it worthwhile to test the view (suggested by a variety of studies[10]) that gambling is primarily rooted in working-class culture, or at least that working-class culture is particularly fertile ground for the transmission of imperatives concerning gambling.

For the theory to work, we would not only have to show that the higher propensity to gamble exists in the working class (which is, in fact, the case, at least relative to the middle class – we have no data on the upper class), but also that those adhering most strongly to working-class culture *within* the working class display the highest propensity to gamble. To do this we must extract an indicator of working-class culture and demonstrate its colinearity with gambling.

Observers differ in their characterizations of working-class culture, but it is generally endowed with a higher valuation of physical toughness than occurs within the middle class; a preference for immediate pleasures as distinct from the middle-class pattern of deferred gratification; and a more powerful belief in luck, fate, destiny or chance – in short, fatalism – than the middle class, who incline rather more to a secular rationality. We included items on the last of these in the questionnaire (along with items on risk-taking and conventionalism). Factor analysis of these items (see Chapter 3) extracted a 'belief in luck' factor which we expect to be:

(a) more associated with working- than with middle-class men;
(b) more associated with high than with low propensities to gamble; and
(c) *most* associated with working-class men rated 'high' gamblers.

A second test related to parental gambling. While 'culture' is not a portmanteau passed on from generation to generation, the very notion of culture implies *some* continuity intergenerationally. If gambling is indeed an intrinsic part of working-class life, we should predict a strong relationship between present and parental gambling; we should also expect to see a greater rate of parental gambling in the working class than in the middle class. Parental gambling is defined as parents gambling regularly on any of the nine types of gambling under detailed scrutiny (see p. 215).

Tests
(a) 'Belief in luck' by social class.
(b) 'Belief in luck' by gambling.
(c) 'Belief in luck' by social class by gambling.
(d) Father gambled by social class by gambling.
(e) Mother gambled by social class by gambling.
(f) Either gambled by social class by gambling.
(g) Both gambled by social class by gambling.

Results (a) The data supported the prediction that 'belief in luck' was more characteristic of the working than the middle class; the strongest 'belief in luck' occurred among the lower working class (see Table 4.6). (b) The data refuted the prediction that a belief in luck would be positively related to the propensity to gamble (see Table 4.7). (c) The data refuted the prediction that working-class men with a 'high' gambling propensity would display the stronger 'belief in luck' (see Table 4.8). The same trend occurred when lower working- and upper working-class men were analysed independently.

(d–g) The data refuted the prediction that parental gambling would be more characteristic of working-class than middle-class men. They did show a marked positive relationship between parental gambling and the propensity to gamble *irrespective* of class. The

(a) TABLE 4.6

'Belief in luck'		Upper middle	Lower middle	Upper working	Lower working
Low	1	47	46	21	20
	2	23	30	30	20
	3	14 } 30	14 } 24	24 } 49	29 } 60
High	4	16	10	25	31
		100 (n = 133)	100 (n = 94)	100 (n = 178)	100 (n = 97)

(b) TABLE 4.7

'Belief in luck'		Multiple Gambling – Type I			
		High	Medium	Low	None
Low	1	25	24	30	44
	2	41	20	16	27
	3	14 } 35	28 } 56	36 } 54	10 } 29
High	4	21	28	18	19
		101 (n = 81)	100 (n = 215)	100 (n = 83)	100 (n = 123)

(c) TABLE 4.8

'Belief in luck'		Multiple Gambling – Type I (Working-class Men)			
		High	Medium	Low	None
Low	1	23	14	25	32
	2	38	20	16	30
	3	17 } 39	32 } 66	45 } 59	10 } 38
High	4	22	34	14	28
		100 (n = 64)	100 (n = 130)	100 (n = 34)	100 (n = 47)

highest concordance between generations was among middle-class men with a 'high' gambling propensity and father's gambling. These results should not be seen as tantamount to proving an intergenerational 'cause' of gambling, since the procedures that gave rise to them (subjects' replies to questions about parents' gambling) may have reflected a tendency for the more gambling prone to have a sharper perception of parental gambling, and vice versa (see Tables 4.9 to 4.12).

(d) TABLE 4.9

| | Current class | | | | Mobility (intergenerational) | | | |
	UM	LM	UW	LW	Down-ward	Up-ward	Middle	Work-ing
% whose father gambled	30	57	49	40	35	47	39	50
% whose mother gambled	13	23	16	6	12	12	25	16
% where either gambled	37	60	51	41	38	50	44	51
% where both gambled	6	20	15	5	9	10	19	15

(e) TABLE 4.10

| | Gambling – Type I | | | | Gambling – Type II | | | |
	High	Med.	Low	None	High	Med.	Low	None
% whose father gambled	64	46	41	25	61	42	41	11
% whose mother gambled	22	16	10	5	23	13	7	6
% where either gambled	66	49	43	27	67	44	43	11
% where both gambled	20	12	8	4	18	11	6	6

Key: UM, LM, UW, LW — upper middle, lower middle, upper working, lower working.
Down, Up, Middle, Working — downwardly mobile in relation to parental status (in terms of UM, LM, UW, and LW); upwardly mobile (ditto); immobile middle class; immobile working class.

(f) TABLE 4.11

| Middle class only | Gambling – Type I | | | | Gambling – Type II | | | |
	High	Med.	Low	None	High	Med.	Low	None
% whose father gambled	77	43	35	25	69	42	29	20
% whose mother gambled	21	21	15	12	31	16	10	13
% where either gambled	77	50	44	28	81	46	34	20
% where both gambled	21	13	6	9	18	13	5	13

(g) TABLE 4.12

| Working class only | Gambling – Type I | | | | Gambling – Type II | | | |
	High	Med.	Low	None	High	Med.	Low	None
% whose father gambled	59	47	43	26	59	42	48	3
% whose mother gambled	23	13	8	0	21	11	6	0
% where either gambled	62	48	43	26	63	42	48	3
% where both gambled	20	12	8	0	17	11	6	0

Summary   No support whatever was found for the view that gambling is somehow intrinsically part of 'working-class culture' or amounts to a 'way of life' in the working class as a whole. The clear finding that an intergenerational pattern of gambling exists *irrespective* of class suggests that broad, class-based theories of gambling are ill-founded, and that the factors making for variations in involvement in gambling, whatever they are, are permeated throughout the social structure rather than localized in one sector.

(iv) *Structural-functional theory*

Propositions   Devereux's thesis represents the sole attempt to formulate a theory of gambling in relation to the social structure of a major Western society. He viewed gambling, within the structural-functional paradigm, as an essential component of the social structure which contributes massively to its maintenance and equilibrium. In cruder terms, it amounted to a 'safety valve' conception of gambling. He analysed American society in terms of the Weberian model of the Protestant ethic and the rise of capitalism. Protestantism legitimated capital formation, investment and profit. But it did so by venerating asceticism, the 'stewardship' of wealth and the 'calling'. Modern capitalism is based on a degree of inequality, a dysjunction between merit and reward, and a stress on conspicuous consumption, which are at odds with the world-view enshrined in the puritan version of the Protestant ethic. The contradictions built into the fabric of capitalism cannot, however, be exposed without threatening the social and economic fabric. Inequality, injustice and profligate wealth might be exposed and visible: but they must be defined as epidemic rather than endemic in the social structure. The indignation and moral fervour aroused by them must be channelled away from focussing on the economic institutions most central to capitalism, and deflected on to an institution segregated from these pillars but symbolically capable of bearing the brunt of credibility for the errors they represent. Gambling is the perfect scapegoat for the contradictions of capitalism. On to it can be heaped the onus of responsibility for our collective guilts. The Stock Exchange can pillory its speculators as representing the gambling element in investment.

Paradoxically, the assailants must never win the battle. The war must continue indefinitely. Gambling must be tolerated, even allowed to flourish, in practice, since its elimination would leave the contradictions of capitalism untouched and over-exposed. The pretence that we aim to eliminate it must, however, be maintained: otherwise, the credibility of the symbolic crusade would lose force.

Hence the *sub rosa* status of gambling in America, tolerated in practice, illegal in principle. Hence the ambivalences we experience in our attitudes towards gambling, a simultaneous attraction and repulsion. This ambivalence is at its most profound in the middle class, the repository and the legatee of the puritan version of the Protestant ethic. For it is in the Protestant middle-class section above all that these contradictions are most powerfully grounded: and it is in this sector that moral indignation against gambling is most fervently voiced. The predictions from Devereux's theory are that: (a) involvement in gambling is at its lowest among the Protestant middle-class; and (b) that involvement in gambling increases the more one moves away, in any direction, from this sector.

Tests   Gambling by religious affiliation by social class.

Results   The data are inconclusive in regard to Devereux's thesis. This is partly because there are inadequate numbers of non-Protestants to contrast with Protestants. Thus, the data in weighted form refute the propositions (and thus the theory, in part) since they show proportionately more middle-class Nonconformist Protestants to be 'high' and/or 'medium' gamblers than middle-class Roman Catholics. They also show proportionately fewer working-class Nonconformists to be categorized as 'high' gamblers than is the case for middle-class Nonconformists. In unweighted form, however, the thesis is narrowly sustained (see Tables 4.13 and 4.14).

TABLE 4.13   *(middle-class men) (%)*

Involvement in gambling (I)	Weighted				Unweighted				
	High	Med.	Low	None	High	Med.	Low	None	n
Anglican	21	46	12	21	9	42	20	29	(110)
Roman Catholic	2	10	14	73	5	20	25	50	(20)
Nonconformist	19	24	13	44	5	26	16	53	(55)
Other	13	2	2	83	14	7	7	71	(14)
None	8	67	12	13	7	44	25	25	(61)

TABLE 4.14   *(working-class men) (%)*

Involvement in gambling (I)	Weighted				Unweighted				
	High	Med.	Low	None	High	Med.	Low	None	n
Anglican	27	48	11	13	23	51	12	19	(145)
Roman Catholic	46	43	3	8	33	52	5	10	(21)
Nonconformist	6	33	31	30	11	36	18	36	(28)
Other	16	17	16	51	14	29	14	43	(7)
None	28	42	14	16	22	44	15	19	(97)

We would stress, however, that far stronger positive relationships should have emerged between middle-class Nonconformists and 'low' and/or 'no' gambling, and between middle-class Roman Catholics and 'high' and/or 'medium' gambling, for the theory to be sustained. A further test, to compare middle-class Anglicans with middle-class Roman Catholics, shows the former to be more involved in gambling than the latter. One can, of course, modify the theory to allow for this divergency. And one can dismiss the Anglican data as of little social relevance since a formal affiliation to the Church of England is, for the majority, a test of social orthodoxy rather than a testimony to religious conviction. But one is then confronted by the issue of just how 'protestant' must Protestants be to be included in the theory? And how many modifications can a theory take before it loses its distinctive nature as a theory and becomes merely an 'approach'? Indeed, one of the problems with structural-functional theories, as with Marxist theories, is that they are *methods* of looking at problems rather than testable *hypotheses* about them. But it would be premature to reject the Devereux hypothesis on this test alone; and it is worth noting that the data for working-class gambling by religion are more in line with structural-functional theory.

(v) *Decision-making*

Propositions Decision-making theory is rather similar to that of alienation. As propounded by Herman,[11] it is essentially an hypothesis about the priority accorded the decision-making component in gambling by those who lack the scope for decision-making in their work roles. There is in this theory, however, no necessary implication that any process of alienation is involved where the work role restricts decision-making. There is simply an insistence that its absence in work and its presence in gambling are linked. Hence we should predict the strongest relationship between gambling and the claim by gamblers that an element of skill is involved to occur most frequently among those who perceive their jobs as relatively lacking in scope for decision-making on their part. Information on the skill element in betting was available for off-track and on-track horse- and dog-race betters, and to eliminate the occasional punter, we restricted the test to those gambling in this way at least sporadically.

Test Job autonomy by skill element in betting.

Results The data almost preclude any variation emerging which

TABLE 4.15   *Job autonomy*

Betting	Weighted Low		High		Unweighted Low		High	
	1	*2*	*3*	*4*	*1*	*2*	*3*	*4*
(a) % claiming skill element	91	90	83	78	82	68	68	80
(b) % *not* claiming skill element	9	10	17	22	18	32	18	20

could either support or falsify the proposition, since the overwhelming tendency of the more regular betters was to impute some element of skill to their gambling. On the weighted data, however, a slight gradient appears in the predicted direction, but the very small numbers involved make double checking with the unweighted data desirable; and these display no such relationship (see Table 4.15).

Summary   The key fact to emerge is that over four out of five of these betters impute a skill element to their gambling. The test we now need, therefore, is one which will relate *degree of involvement* in this form of gambling to job autonomy, taking the imputation of skill for granted. Such associations appear in Chapter 7, where a strong relationship emerges between betting and the degree of job interest, a different indicator of 'job involvement' to that used in this section.

(vi) *Risk-taking*

Propositions   At odds with the class-based theories of gambling is the view, recently elaborated by Goffman,[12] that gambling is the prototype of that kind of 'action' accorded a very high valuation in the culture and mythology of Western society, but increasingly at variance with its social realities, in that 'action' is progressively 'ironed out' of everyday life by the routinization and bureaucratization of social and economic arrangements. There is a dualism about Goffman's conception of gambling which renders his theorization immune from all but the most sophisticated attempts at falsification. He claims both that gambling operates as a surrogate for the risk-taking ironed out of everyday life but still hallowed culturally: and he also argues that those who are most oriented to action will be so both occupationally *and* in terms of gambling. Miners, steeplejacks, fishermen, sportsmen and members of other 'extreme' and hazardous occupational groups will be heavy gamblers: but so will be clerks, factory operatives and shop assistants who are oriented to action but denied it in their jobs and everyday lives. Perhaps the best way to test Goffman's theory is to take a carefully stratified sample of men doing jobs ranged along the extreme: conventional continuum in terms of the physical risk involved (to allow for metaphysical risk is another matter altogether; as are other components of risk differentially involved in different kinds of job: risks relating to job security, to mobility, etc.). One could then predict (a) that the closer the job is to the 'extreme' end of the continuum, the greater the involvement in gambling, and (b) that *within* each grouping along the continuum, those most oriented to 'action' will be the heaviest gamblers, and vice versa. (The concept of an 'extreme' occupation is not, of course, simply a matter of physical danger: this attribute does appear, however, to be the one most emphasized by Goffman, since it is the qualities of daring, nerve, composure and panache as displayed in the face of physical danger which elicit the highest respect in our (perhaps any) culture. Conceivably, however, he understates the extent to which modern equivalents to physical hazard have come into being and are culturally acknowledged as 'character contests' just as gruelling as a high-wire act or a gunfight: decision-making at the tycoon level, etc., and their apotheosis (spiced with sex) in the novels of such mass-market best-sellers as Harold Robbins.)

As our sample cannot be stratified in terms of risk-taking by occupation, the best we can do is to proceed on the assumption that our sample – on the whole – lacks those involved in 'extreme' occupations. This assumption cannot be lightly made, since *inter alia* the Sheffield sample includes men who work in the steel industry, though it is unlikely that a large enough number work directly in actually casting or moulding (or the other processes involving real physical risk) to affect the emergence of a strong relationship between gambling and orientation to action by those in 'conventional' jobs. This assumption made, we would seek to test Goffman's theory by predicting that *no* relationship will be found to exist between orientation to action and social class. We would also predict the strongest positive relationship to exist between 'high' involvement in gambling and 'high' valuation of 'action'. Our indicator of orientation to 'action' is the degree of preference for risk-taking as elicited by responses to items dealing with the avoidance of risk and ranging to the desire to create excitement in everyday life. The proposition is that those who verbalize a commitment to risk-taking should certainly be expected, given a routinized work role, to opt for gambling rather more than those who prefer 'playing safe': and this relationship should hold *irrespective* of social class.

Tests

(a) Preference for risk-taking by social class.
(b) Preference for risk-taking by involvement in gambling.
(c) Preference for risk-taking by involvement in gambling by social class.

Results   (a) The data confirmed the null hypothesis that no relationship would exist between social class and risk-taking (see Table 4.16). (b) The weighted data failed to sustain the hypothesized positive relationship between involvement in gambling and a preference for risk-taking. The unweighted data reveal a very slight relationship in the expected direction (see Table 4.17). (c) The data fail to sustain the proposition that whatever relationship obtains between risk-taking and gambling will hold independently of social class. They reveal an interesting but fragile positive relationship between involvement in gambling and preference for risk-taking among the middle-class group, along with a higher valuation of risk-taking among *non-gamblers* than among gamblers (whether high, medium or low) in the working class group (see Table 4.18).

Summary   Multivariate analysis of gambling by class and risk-taking preferences demonstrates differences *between* classes in the relationship between gambling and risk-taking orientations that taking class by gambling and gambling by risk-taking separately fail to reveal. The explanation may simply be that middle-class lives and jobs *are*, on the whole, more protected and secure than is the case for the working class; and that, as a result, middle-class

TABLE 4.16   *Risk-taking by social class (%)*

| Preference for risk-taking | | Class | | | |
		Upper middle	Lower middle	Upper working	Lower working
Low	1	30	11	21	24
	2	17	25	24	23
	3	33	34	27	32
High	4	19	30	28	21
		100	100	100	100
		(n = 145)	(n = 110)	(n = 188)	(n = 102)

TABLE 4.17   *Involvement in gambling – Type I (%)*

Preference for risk-taking		High	Medium	Low	None
Low	1	20	21	31	21
Weighted	2	24	22	21	25
	3	34⎫ 56	27⎫ 58	22⎫ 48	40⎫ 55
High	4	22⎭	31⎭	26⎭	15⎭
Low	1	19	24	27	21
Unweighted	2	20	21	20	33
	3	35⎫ 61	22⎫ 55	24⎫ 53	30⎫ 46
High	4	26⎭	33⎭	29⎭	16⎭
		100	100	100	100
		(n = 85)	(n = 228)	(n = 90)	(n = 142)

TABLE 4.18   *Involvement in gambling – Type I (%)*

Preference for risk-taking		High	Medium	Low	None
Middle class only					
Low	1	3	18	25	35
	2	23	18	15	27
	3	52⎫ 74	34⎫ 64	30⎫ 60	23⎫ 37
High	4	22⎭	30⎭	30⎭	14⎭
		100	100	100	101
		(n = 20)	(n = 91)	(n = 52)	(n = 92)
Working class only					
Low	1	25	22	34	9
	2	24	24	23	22
	3	29⎫ 52	24⎫ 55	19⎫ 43	53⎫ 69
High	4	23⎭	31⎭	24⎭	16⎭
		101	101	100	100
		(n = 65)	(n = 137)	(n = 38)	(n = 50)

men in safe but dull jobs, who place a high valuation on risk-taking, resort rather more to gambling as – in part – a surrogate for 'action' in everyday life; whereas working-class men, whose jobs entail tangible risks both physically and in terms of security which are easily overlooked from a middle-class standpoint, gamble for reasons which have nothing to do with the *symbolic* element of risk-taking in gambling, since they either look elsewhere for surrogate forms of action (e.g. sport) or do not need a surrogate for risk-taking as such. However, as the working class shows more or less the same proportion as the middle class scoring highly on the risk-taking, the first of these two explanations is probably more feasible.

(vii) *'Home-centredness'*

Propositions 'Home-centredness' constitutes a set of satisfactions *alternative* to those embodied in gambling. Conjugal role-sharing, the extent to which the husband overlaps in role-playing with his wife, is one indicator of home-centredness. We would predict a negative relationship between this and gambling. Conjugal role-sharing is measured by the husband's participation in any of several forms of work crucial for the maintenance of families and households, such as shopping, washing-up, ironing, etc.

Test Conjugal role-sharing by involvement in gambling.

Results

TABLE 4.19   *Involvement in gambling – Type I (married men) (%)*

Conjugal role-sharing	High	Medium	Low	None	n
Daily	26	44	68	63	238
Weekly	65	42	23	32	200
Less	9	15	9	5	55
	100	101	100	100	493
	(n = 71)	(n = 210)	(n = 82)	(n = 130)	

Summary The data supported the proposition (it hardly constitutes a theory), by showing a markedly inverse relationship between high involvement in gambling and high conjugal role-sharing, and a strikingly positive relationship between low or non-gambling and high conjugal role-sharing (control for social class did not affect this finding).

(viii) 'Work-centred' leisure

Propositions   As with (vii), that work-centred leisure constitutes a set of satisfactions and/or instrumental means alternative to, and possibly at odds with, those inherent in gambling. 'Studying at home' was one indicator of work-centredness in leisure which we tabulated against involvement in gambling for the middle-class group only.

Test   'Study at home' by involvement in gambling.

Results

TABLE 4.20   *Involvement in gambling – Type I (%)*

Study at home	High	Medium	Low	None	n
Weekly	9	19	13	34	38
Monthly	3	15	20	6	39
Yearly	0	2	1	2	7
Less	83	65	66	58	147
	100	101	100	100	231
	(n = 17)	(n = 86)	(n = 49)	(n = 79)	

Summary   An inverse relationship between the tendency to work-oriented leisure and involvement in gambling does emerge fairly strongly from the data. The chief contrast is that between 'high' and non-gamblers, the intermediate groups of 'medium' and 'low' gamblers displaying much the same pattern.

Conclusions

It is customary to enjoin caution in the interpretation of tests such as these, and our findings are certainly no exception to the limitations implicit in survey work on complex social phenomena. In many respects, the tests are either rudimentary or incomplete, or both. And no test is better than the data which comprise it. However, some relationships emerge surprisingly strongly, including one we had not predicted: the finding on intergenerational patterns of gambling. The sequence of refuted propositions which unfolded as we tried theory after theory with at best only limited success, and at worst total failure of the data to match the theories, was itself to be predicted in view of the difficulties involved in constructing theories which go beyond singular propositions. As things stand, we can at least claim to have cleared the ground of a great deal of presupposition and piecemeal theory stitching, and from the few relationships which have emerged, are better placed to get on with building better theory.

Note on job autonomy findings

Our findings on the relationship between job autonomy and social status were the reverse of those commonly cited in the literature. Based as they were on factor analysed ratings, a checking run was made in which the three most crucial components in the job autonomy factor were separately tabulated against social status (see Table 4.21). These produced relationships in the reverse direction to those emerging from the factor analysis. A feasible explanation is that the factor ratings 1–4 had been accidentally reversed in the transformation of the data. In any event, since the factor ratings did not affect involvement in gambling either way, no reassessment of our conclusions on this point is called for.

TABLE 4.21   *Job autonomy (men aged 26–65)*

(a) Does your job give you enough freedom to work as you prefer?					
	UM	LM	UW	LW	S/Ed
% replying 'Yes'	72	68	72	69	56	Unweighted
	77	73	74	70	48	Weighted
	(143)	(111)	(194)	(103)	(16)	*n*'s
(b) Do you have much say in the way you go about your job?					
% replying 'Yes'	97	79	70	48	94	Unweighted
	99	76	62	51	99	Weighted
	(146)	(111)	(193)	(103)	(16)	*n*'s
(c) Does it give you a chance to try out ideas of your own?					
% replying 'Yes'	92	68	46	36	87	Unweighted
	95	62	44	36	74	Weighted
	(145)	(111)	(194)	(102)	(16)	*n*'s

5 The social distribution of gambling

Social concern about gambling invariably centres around the proneness and/or vulnerability of certain social groups which are regarded as especially 'at risk' with regard to inducement to gamble, in particular since the legalization of off-course betting for cash. In this brief chapter we set out our findings on the social distribution of gambling along four key dimensions: age, income, class and sex. The indicator used is mean 'total' gambling frequency[1] over a twelve-month period, the term 'total' comprising participation in pools betting; on- and off-course betting; pub, club and private gaming; gaming-machine betting, and club bingo. The unit whose frequency is measured is the gambling *session*, not individual games within a session. (See p. 102 for age and income groupings.)

Sex: do the same proportions of men and women gamble?

The simple answer is *No*. The overall mean for the frequency of women who gamble per year is about a third to a quarter of men. For women it is 35 sessions per year whereas for men it is 123 sessions per year, or over twice a week. This difference is sufficiently important for us to present most of the rest of our findings for men and women separately.

Age: are the young more gambling prone?

As far as men, but not women, are concerned they are. The mean for the youngest men is 173 times per year compared with 126 and 119 for the middle age groups (see Table 5.1). Elderly men gamble by far the least frequently, with a mean of only 57 times. For women, there is far less variance, though the elderly again gamble less frequently (see Table 5.2).

The young are not uniformly more gambling prone than their elders, even among men and in groups, the poorest and the lower working class, whose characteristics are often assumed to include socialization into patterns of heavy gambling. The youngest and poorest men gambled markedly less than their better-off peers and marginally less than the elderly poorest. Upper middle-class young men gambled least among their own age-group, and less than the middle-aged of similar status. Among young men, the groups *most* prone to frequent gambling were the *upper* working class and the poor with means of 252 and 341 times per year respectively, the highest achieved (with one exception) by any groupings. Other attributes for the youngest men relating to frequent gambling were upward mobility, conventionalism, risk-taking and belief in luck, *both* parents having gambled regularly, being single, affiliation to the Church of England, Sheffield residence, claiming 'not enough' free time, *least* involved in other forms of leisure entertainment, in jobs with good promotion prospects, and individualistically oriented to increase in income. The pattern suggested by this constellation is one of social and economic ambition, of a group struggling to climb out of poverty, but free enough to gamble heavily before settling down, and this is borne out to some extent by the decrease in gambling with each successive age-group both in the upper working class and with poor incomes.

Among young women gambling increases monotonically with decreasing social status, and is heaviest among the poorest where the frequency rate is slightly higher than the equivalent group for men. It appears that extreme poverty correlates with increases in gambling among young women and with decreases in gambling among young men. High scores among the youngest women are principally for having one dependent child, high involvement in performing household tasks, and claiming not enough free time: the correlates, when combined with the poorest household incomes, of economic and domestic constraints from which gambling is an escape? Otherwise young women gamble less than their elders, except the most elderly, and except where they are the most affluent.

Income: are the poor more gambling prone?

The poorest *men* are clearly far *less* involved in gambling than the rest: their mean is 66 gambling sessions per year (adjusted for the impact of area, class and other factors, 58), that is once a week compared with means of over 100 times for higher incomes. Whilst nearly two-thirds of this group are composed of the elderly (whose very low level of income is revealed strikingly), the low mean is not a function of age, since the elderly have the *highest* mean gambling frequency *within* the poorest income grouping: 73 compared to the youngest 71 sessions per year. The poorest have a slightly higher mean gambling frequency than the two more affluent income-groups on the unadjusted figures, but a marginally lower frequency than that for the most affluent group on the adjusted figures. Within this grouping, however, there is striking class variation: the mean for the upper middle-class poor being only 29, that for the lower middle-class being 97, that for the two working-class groups in this income bracket being nearly double that for the latter (188 and 191). Variance by age shows a marked decline from the highest gambling frequency of 341 sessions for the youngest to a mean of only 15 for the elderly.

For *women*, this age gradient (with the exception of the elderly) is reversed, and the gradient for class is not at all marked. In sum, therefore, the most striking relationship is between extreme poverty and very *low* frequency of gambling. Within the working-class groups, rates of gambling among the poor are some three times as high as for the poorest men.

Class: are the lower working class more gambling prone?

The overall means for class groupings for men shows a clear inverse relationship between high social class and gambling, with the non-manual: manual gap larger than that within classes. However, after adjustment for the impact of areas and income the differences in mean frequencies are modified to negligible proportions, both middle-class groups having frequencies of just over 100, with working-class men some 20 per cent and lower working-class men some 40 per cent, more frequently involved in gambling. This relationship holds for the middle incomes, but not for the poorest or the most affluent. In the poorest groups, the lower middle class have the highest frequency; in the most affluent, the upper working class. The lowest mean among the most affluent is produced by the lower working class. Gambling frequencies lessen with age for the lower middle and upper working class. Among the upper middle class, the middle-aged produce the highest mean. Among the lower working class age produces litle variation, except between the elderly and the rest.

Among women, gambling tends to increase with lower social status for the youngest and young middle age; this is also the case

TABLE 5.1 *Men: total gambling frequency: mean sessions p.a.*

		Poorest		Poor		Affluent		Most affluent		[MCA]
		†(65·7)	(117)	†(164·4)	(182)	†(133·3)	(218)	†(111·7)	(223)	[104·8]
Class	UM	32	(20)	29	(18)	48	(38)	90	(107)	[101·4]
	LM	115	(19)	97	(38)	67	(41)	96	(44)	[121·3]
	UW	59	(45)	188	(79)	118	(91)	177	(50)	[144·4]
	LW	68	(27)	191	(52)	226	(44)	55	(14)	[151·2]
	SEd.	40	(5)	115	(3)	417	(1)	138	(5)	
Age	Youngest	71	(19)	341	(27)	107	(36)	120	(37)	
	Young middle age	20	(7)	152	(66)	146	(93)	107	(99)	
	Older middle age	51	(21)	127	(81)	134	(84)	115	(81)	
	Elderly	73	(70)	15	(18)	35	(5)	15	(6)	
		[58·2]		[148·5]		[120·9]		[151·4]		

		Youngest		Young middle age		Older middle age		Elderly		
		†(172·9)	(123)	†(126·2)	(284)	†(119·3)	(299)	†(56·8)	(110)	
Class	UM	75	(33)	34	(79)	96	(70)	42	(18)	†(67·7) (200)
	LM	127	(28)	74	(58)	99	(53)	27	(22)	†(89·7) (161)
	UW	252	(41)	148	(94)	88	(101)	62	(45)	†(130·6) (281)
	LW	140	(20)	188	(41)	175	(62)	68	(21)	†(159·7) (144)
	SEd.	—		258	(9)	81	(8)	9	(3)	(20)

Note:
Incomes unknown were excluded from income tables.
All results are weighted; figures in brackets
beside the mean are *unweighted* population numbers.
+ overall mean = 122·6.

†( ) = Unadjusted mean weighted.
[ ] = MCA adjusted weighted frequencies for a
      category (not available for *age*).

TABLE 5.2 *Women: total gambling frequency: mean sessions per year*

		Poorest	Poor	Affluent	Most affluent
		†(32·1) (321)	†(45·7) (244)	†(32·9) (224)	†(23·7) (209)
Class	UM	23 (36)	46 (24)	7 (38)	16 (90)
	LM	15 (57)	17 (70)	12 (68)	18 (76)
	UW	34 (100)	47 (78)	32 (67)	35 (29)
	LW	43 (100)	66 (54)	65 (46)	26 (12)
	SEd.	6 (13)	26 (14)	40 (5)	96 (2)
Age	Youngest	76 (26)	17 (35)	24 (37)	48 (29)
	Young middle age	28 (28)	45 (84)	37 (117)	19 (107)
	Older middle age	41 (111)	62 (88)	31 (67)	20 (72)
	Elderly	14 (156)	26 (37)	— (3)	— (1)

		Youngest	Young middle age	Older middle age	Elderly	
Class	UM	14 (18)	11 (87)	31 (86)	12 (37)	†(18·7) (228)
	LM	18 (64)	11 (113)	19 (100)	10 (33)	†(14·6) (310)
	UW	46 (30)	36 (96)	36 (108)	28 (64)	†(35·9) (298)
	LW	70 (22)	61 (62)	68 (82)	9 (68)	†(51·6) (234)
	SEd.	—	38 (11)	53 (14)	9 (14)	
		†(40·6) (134)	†(32·7) (371)	†(40·7) (401)	†(25·6) (233)	

+ overall mean = 35·2.

TABLE 5.3 Frequency and expenditure indicator means by type of gambling and for totals

	Frequency: sessions p.a.			Expenditure: turnover in shillings p.a.					
	Men	Women	Both	Men	n	Women	n	Both	n
Pools	22	9	15	106	791	21	1115	59	1906
Betting	33	6	18	392	810	32	1132	195	1942
Gaming	36	7	20	688	782	46	1117	335	1899
Club bingo	13	10	12	162	814	147	1127	154	1941
Gaming machines	13	3	7	143	801	56	1115	96	1916
Total A[1]	117	35	72	1,491	783	302	1062	839	1800
Total B[2]	122	35	75	1,437	(n=783)	307	(n=1062)	809	(n=800)
	(n=816)	(n=1139)	(n=1955)						

A[1] Summation of the 5 component means.
B[2] Derived from the total gambling indicator: it includes means for private betting, cash postal and credit off-course betting, factors affecting men not women, and then only marginally.

for those with middling household incomes. Otherwise, no trend emerges with any clarity.

Conclusion

This bald summary of the mean gambling frequencies of the key social groupings describes the extent to which the conventional wisdom about the social distribution of gambling is confirmed or disconfirmed by one survey. While overall means tend to reflect the conventional wisdom for men, in that the young, the poor (but not the poorest) and the lower working class gamble more frequently than the rest, these differentials are far more modest than is usually assumed, and do not hold uniformly when other factors are controlled. The most striking variation seems connected with a-typically high gambling by the young, single, skilled working-class men in the poor but not the poorest income-group, though this pattern seems age-specific and is not sustained throughout the age-groups.

This social distribution is quite dramatically altered when we examine the components of total gambling (in Part 2). The mean sessions per year as well as spending per year on the key types of gambling are shown in Table 5.3. Clearly the differences between men and women are sustained for all types of gambling save that of bingo. We turn, in Part 2, to a full discussion of these types of gambling, and try to present reasons for the variations.

Part two

Social variations in gambling activity

Introduction

Estimates of the extent and incidence of involvement in, as well as descriptions of the key forms of gambling are presented in the first part of each chapter devoted to them. The second part explores the relationship between form of gambling and the social indicators as a basis for generating hypotheses about gambling. There is no simple continuity between the two objectives of description and generation of hypotheses; and this discontinuity stems from the very different assumptions underlying the *testing* of established theories, and the open-ended exploratory search for unidentified relationships to yield different and perhaps better theories.

The choice of social indicators for the exploration of relationships is more complicated than that for testing established theories. It is 'grounded' on hunch and intuition rather than the sober appraisal of existing evidence. Our survey thus takes on something of a portmanteau appearance, accommodating items based on the broadest of theoretical presuppositions, mainly centred around the sphere of leisure. We assumed that some forms of gambling would have implications for, and possibly be derived from, other aspects of leisure time use, such as an orientation to sport, a low commitment to political and/or community activities, etc. Given the incorporation of these sorts of item we were prevented from exploring other sets of variables; though we also included other potentially useful indicators such as alternative definitions of social class or religious affiliation, they had a subordinate exploratory role.

To explore relationships, AID(2), described in Chapter 3, was deemed an appropriate form of analysis. That it can produce highly problematic results cannot be denied and should be positively stressed. The splitting technique produces sub-groups on the basis of maximum predictive efficiency, but splits frequently occur on unproductive rather than productive predictors.[1] The results of the analysis using this model are only the tip of the iceberg of hundreds of other possible results flowing from marginally different models of analysis. AID(2) makes explicit the problematic nature of interrelationships which other methods of analysis of variance leave submerged but it also falls prey to unproductive relationships which other methods can avoid. AID(2) can be applied to data in a variety of ways. First there is the choice between using the method on the total population surveyed and on as wide a sample of predictors as possible, and using it either on a delimited section of the population, or a limited range of predictors or both; the former is more truly exploratory, the latter more in line with theoretical modification. We chose the first alternative. When modification seemed called for on the basis of the initial results we adjusted the model, and the most usual adjustment was to analyse the data for each *sex* separately.

A second set of choices was about how to use the dependent variable. One could either have a one-stage model asking the question: What are the best predictors of gambling frequency and expenditure *irrespective* of whether or not respondents do participate? The second type of model is to ask questions in two stages: (a) What are the best predictors of *whether or not* people gamble? and then (b) Given that people *do* gamble, what are the best predictors of the *extent* to which they do so? While this second analysis is statistically sounder, it could exclude predictors of intermediate status which would rank as highly effective. Consequently, we have adopted both courses, and present the more sociologically effective analyses for each type of gambling. (See Diagrams, pp. 220–9.)

Exposition therefore takes the form of presenting estimates and descriptions of each form of gambling, as the first part of each chapter, and data of an exploratory character forms the second part, for which some kinds of gambling have had to be grouped together. While estimates and descriptions are presented separately, for example, for pub gaming and private gaming, the exploratory section is on 'gaming' overall. While the results allow us to favour *some* theoretical orientations rather than others, they do not constitute a powerful case for one theory rather than another. In one sense they suggest the need for theoretical particularism (which some would regard as theoretical fragmentation, or the antithesis of theory) in that very different variables achieve prominence in the prediction of different types of gambling. Whether or not these differences can ultimately be accommodated by some more comprehensive theory of gambling, we have at least tried to describe the complex distributions for which any satisfactory theory would have to account. As in other fields of sociological inquiry, high predictive efficiency is not synonymous with adequate theory.

It may well be asserted that this impasse merely illustrates afresh the inductivist fallacy – that the mere adumbration of data will disclose some sort of immanent theory – and that survey work in particular lends itself to such bland empiricism. To this there are two counter-assertions: (i) that what is being attempted is *not* mere adumbration of 'facts' (giving all due weight to the problematic nature of their construction) but their selective ordering in terms of predictive efficiency; (ii) that the absence of any real theoretical yield does not necessarily follow from the methods of analysis of variance adopted, but from the tentative and discursive nature of the input, a state of affairs difficult to avoid when little prior work has been done in a field of inquiry. Had different predictors been chosen, perhaps the yield would have been far greater. Even within our own approach, certain variables could, with hindsight, have been included which would arguably have improved the results: patterns of saving and of household tenure, patterns of shift-work and overtime, and the contrast between short-term and deferred gratification are three which loom large as omissions. Over-concentration on certain *aspects* of the content of the survey entailed neglect of these and other features of potential relevance. At least in future, however, we hope that such constraints will not apply, that our sifting of many possibilities will enable researchers to concentrate on selected probabilities. In the future also, it is to be hoped that this kind of model-building will benefit from exploratory work employing more qualitative methodologies, particularly the kind of sensitive small-scale field research which can concentrate and modify theories by intensive contacts over time with highly selective groups and individuals.

The decision to mount area surveys, rather than a national sample survey, was in part based on the desire to *place* gambling in some sort of recognizable social context, as well as to allow for variations attributable to area as such. In the event, constraints on time ruled out the first aim; and the second proved of little consequence when preliminary runs seemed to show that variables which had their importance at the level of the areas, rather than the sampling unit, were of negligible account. Similarly, in all the AID runs, area was entered, but was not generally powerful enough to split groups. As a result, tabulations were specified for the whole sample, with area entered as an independent variable, rather than for each area sample as well.

Glossary

The following variables are used very often in the descriptions and analyses of types of gambling. We have given each of the categories of the variable names which provide for ease of exposition and are less confusing than the numerical terms that were the original categories. They are:

1 The *age* variable was divided into four categories:

18 to 25 years old	Youngest
26 to 45 years old	Young ⎫
46 to 65 years old	Older ⎬ middle-aged
66 or more	Elderly

2 The (1968) *income* of households also contains four categories:

Less than £612	Poorest ⎫ poor
£613 to £999	Poorer ⎭
£1,000 to £1,432	More affluent ⎫ affluent
£1,433 or more	Most affluent ⎭

3 The *two-generational class mobility* variable contains four categories:

Father middle class and present middle class	Stable middle class
Father middle class and present working class	Downwardly mobile
Father working class and present middle class	Upwardly mobile
Father working class and present working class	Stable working class

4 The dependent variable of *gambling* is usually the *frequency* of the activity per year. The categories used in the questionnaire related to periods of the year:

Weekly or more often	Regularly
Monthly or more often but not weekly	Sporadically
Yearly or more often but not monthly	Occasionally

If the categories refer broadly to all gamblers we shall have occasion to refer to them as:

Monthly or more often	At least sporadically *or* regularly and sporadically
Yearly or more often	At least occasionally *or* annually.

6 Football pools

Distribution and description

Our figures compare with those of the Government Social Survey: both tend to confirm a massive stability about the prevalence of doing the pools occasionally in the population as a whole.[1]

TABLE 6.1 *Proportions 'doing the pools' occasionally*

Sex	1950	1960	
Men	51	52·5	(n = 816)
Women	28	26·2	(n = 1139)

How do we account for this distribution? *Sex* is obviously a most striking feature of pools betting: twice as many men as women bet. But we find few other marked variations in the social distribution. Area, for example, does not account for much variation in doing the pools.

The difference between the areas can be explained by social class,

TABLE 6.2 *Proportions 'doing the pools' by area, at least occasionally*

Sex	Sheffield	Swansea	Wanstead/ Woodford	Total
Men	51·4 (n = 269)	57·5 (n = 310)	44·6 (n = 237)	52·5
Women	26·9 (n = 378)	25·6 (n = 418)	23·0 (n = 343)	26·2

given Wanstead and Woodford's more middle-class character.[2] Nevertheless, we find that pools betting is neither an exclusively working-class phenomenon nor one universally present within the working class:

TABLE 6.3 *Proportions 'doing the pools' by social class occasionally*

Sex	Upper middle	Lower middle	Upper working	Lower working	Self-employed
Men	43·8	47·3	57·9	49·6	38·7
Women	18·3	20·1	32·3	23·8	44·1

To assess the sociologically, as opposed to the statistically significant factors, we need to examine the distributions for men and women separately.

About the same proportions of *men* do the pools regularly as occasionally: between 47 per cent and 53 per cent. There is some area variation and not in the predicted direction. Sheffield falls midway between the others, rather than rating most heavily as its characteristic of heavy industry would imply. Moreover, Swansea's expected Nonconformist conscience (which *is* confirmed by our figures) does not prevent heavy betting among men.

Class cleavages are not as expected. Current social class reveals very little variation, particularly between upper and lower middle and the lower working class. Most variation in fact occurs between the middle class and the 'mobile', with the latter more involved. This supports Tec's similar finding for Sweden.[3] One inference is that mobility within class strata entails less involvement in the pools than mobility – in either direction – between classes, given that 57 per cent of men belonging to 'neither' class in the two-generational variable and only 43 per cent and 44 per cent of the middle and working class are involved. In fact, class only produces a 10 per cent difference at most.

Both religion and education produce clearer associations with the pools. There is a linear effect with pools for type of school: that is, the grammar school is less associated with propensity to do the pools. There is also scope for arguing that an additional inducement to gamble is achievement up to a certain level of part-time further education, basic vocational qualifications, but not beyond. This appears to link with the mobility finding to point to a certain experience of social striving as an inducement to pools betting.

Fewer Nonconformist church members bet regularly than all other affiliates – 23 per cent as opposed to over 48 per cent. Equally, fewer men bet who attend church regularly. Age and income do not much affect the extent of pools betting, confirming another of the Government Social Survey's findings, both that betting is highest among the middle-aged and the middle incomes. (Direct comparisons are not possible because we used different income categories.) The poor and the poorest and the most affluent are less involved; namely 31 per cent, 44 per cent and 48 per cent are regular, and 35 per cent, 52 per cent and 51 per cent are occasional betters.

The experience of marriage and family life does have some slight connection with betting, since a rather higher proportion of married men (and women too) bet than the single or those whose marriages are over. Moreover, among married men, those with two or three dependent children seem markedly more prone; 61 per cent being regular betters as opposed to 44 per cent of the others.

For *women*, almost the same proportions bet regularly, 22 per cent, as occasionally. Area has no impact on doing the pools, whereas age does. Only 6 per cent of the youngest participate regularly whereas 23 per cent and 29 per cent of the two middle-aged groups do, suggesting the effect of marriage. But class is also important. The mobile are as involved as the stable working class – all about 24 per cent – but only 9 per cent of middle-class women bet regularly. This is accentuated by intra-class mobility: then only 8 per cent of the middle class participate as opposed to 27 per cent of the working class. Education appears to enhance these links: those with no further education or qualifications being the most prone and a clear linear relation obtaining between education and propensity to bet. Moreover, attitudinal factors produce variations as expected: low conventionalism and risk-taking or belief in luck matching low involvement in the pools.

These data therefore are broadly in line with an interpretation which sees the pools as a form of gambling which has, since the Second World War at least, gained general acceptance as a modestly respectable activity in all social classes.

Its promise of large winnings relative to small regular outlays appears to hold great attraction for the middle-aged, the middle-income, the married and family men rather more than the poor, the single or the young or elderly. There are signs that it is just as attractive to those experiencing social mobility in any direction, as to those relatively fixed in a working-class position. The only real diminution in pools betting seems associated with middle-class anchorages which have remained unchanged over two generations, and either with contact with Nonconformist religion or regular church-going, or with a degree of success in education above the vocational and basic skills associated with most middle-income jobs. Among the minority of women who do the pools, a belief in luck, a desire to take risks, and a belief in a relatively fixed social order, seem associated with propensity to bet on the pools, whether regularly or occasionally.

Pools spending

The data show that only relatively small amounts of money are used on the pools and at infrequent intervals, for about 35 weeks of the year.

TABLE 6.4   *Spending on the pools – 1968*

Sex	Gross annual expenditure		Net profit or loss
	mean	median	
Men	£10·9	£6	− £7·1
Women	£4·5	£4	− £4·0
Both	£8·6	£5	− £6·0

N.B. Weighted data only.

We cannot examine in detail these figures since two examples of extreme expenditure – spending over £100 – distort the distributions. It is more appropriate to examine the components of expenditure, such as that of stakes.

Social relations and the pools

The pools can be done alone or together with others. In fact, about 40 per cent of men and 60 per cent of women who do the pools at least sporadically share the stake: married women do not simply take a share in their husband's coupons. Sharing for men occurs most among the young – 70 per cent – and least among the elderly – 11 per cent, probably simply reflecting availability of friends and its obverse. Among women, sharing decreases slightly as incomes rise and with class. Whether pools are shared or not seems little affected by the key socio-economic variables. Sharing is probably of little consequence in the initial decision to do the pools, but it may affect other facets of pools betting: the amount staked, time spent, etc.

(i) Doing the pools alone

Those who do the pools alone usually do them at home.

TABLE 6.5   *Place for doing the pools at least sporadically*

Place	Men	Women
Home	85·2	95·4
Work	11·6	4·6
Other	3·1	0
	100%	100%

Social class makes no difference but age does: nearly a quarter of the younger men fill in coupons at work. But the pools do seem to be home-based rather than rooted in work-place associations and networks.

Is doing the pools a solitary pursuit? It could at least have been a topic of conversation; that is not generally the case.

TABLE 6.6   *Pools discussion*

Out of last five times	Talked about matches		Talked about permutations	
	Men	Women	Men	Women
None	81	89	72	87
1–5	13	6	21	8
Not known	6	5	7	5
	100%	100%	100%	100%

About three-quarters of the men and almost all the women did the pools entirely alone. Young men account for most variation: the youngest discussed both matches (31 per cent) and permutations (59 per cent). Sufficient interest attaches to the activity for these young men to discuss both choices with friends or relatives perhaps in the desire to maximize payoff and from a sense of relative inexperience.

(ii) *Sharing the pools*

Is the major form of sharing for men the syndicate at work, whereas for women the share with her husband? Certainly the data confirm this, but there are interesting differences. Whereas a majority of men (63 per cent) share with workmates nearly half of the women share solely with their spouse and not a group. Middle-aged men are most involved in sharing – 77 per cent, but it is not a particularly working-class characteristic since the same proportions of the middle and working class share. The question of who fills in the coupon rests largely on the number sharing. Stakes are lower than for those filling in the coupon alone, but age and income still have the same effect. Most important is the fact that the middle class are just as, if not more, likely than the working class to bet through syndicates of half a dozen or more workmates, albeit for smaller stakes. It is without a great deal of personal involvement since 60 per cent of men and 57 per cent of women did *not* help to choose the matches on any of the previous 5 occasions on which they had staked money.

Stakes and winnings

The nature of any form of gambling is, as Goffman has elucidated,[4] reducible to four stages or dimensions: 'squaring off'; 'determination'; 'disclosure'; 'settlement'. In the case of pools, the process between the first and the last of these stages is relatively protracted temporally and diffused spatially, in that the 'action' takes place well away from the better's milieu, and it lies totally outside his or her power to influence the outcome of any of the complex set of events that must be seen through before disclosure can take place. As a result, pools betting is an unusually passive form of gambling, the 'action' on the whole being limited to filling in the coupon ('squaring off') by choosing the appropriate permutation(s), and sending it off. This stage may be as limited as paying your share of the stake to others who will do this job for you. Nothing then happens (nothing *can*) until the announcement of the results on Saturday at 5.00 p.m., and while this can be for many a highly charged experience, for others the result will not be known until the beginning of work on Monday. Hence, while immense variation is possible as to choices of matches and permutations; as to the choice to choose by proxy; as to mood, expectancy, or degree of sharing the experience, the one feature common to all pool betters, given the decision to bet at all, is the need to part with, put up or invest a 'stake' – the larger the stake, the larger the possibilities afforded for maximizing chances of winning via the more expensive permutations available.

The data seem to support the view that a relatively simple relationship exists between income and stake in stage one, and stake and winnings in stage four. The data for the last stake confirm those for usual stake that men stake more than women. Doing the pools alone or sharing makes little difference – over 70 per cent stake less than 5s. The stakes are not high and range from 1s. to £1; only 5 per cent of men and less than 1 per cent of women who bet on the pools stake more than 11s. and 68 per cent of men and 91 per cent of women stake 5s. or less. In 1950 the average stake was 3s. for men and 1s. 8d. for women. It appears that age and income are important for high stakes – 10 per cent of the youngest bet over 11s. whereas 96 per cent of the elderly stake less than 5s. Equally the higher the income the higher the stake: none of the poorest staked over 11s. whereas 6 per cent of the poor and most affluent did. High stakes are not a function of sharing or lone betting.

TABLE 6.7 *Last stake by income (%)*

| Income | Men and women | | | Women only | | |
	Less than 6s.	6s. or more	NK	Less than 6s.	6s. or more	NK
Poorest	86	10	4	90	8	2
Poor	82	14	4	91	6	3
Affluent	77	20	3	99	1	0
Most affluent	63	33	5	82	14	4

The trends are roughly the same for men and women though the differential is sharper for men, and affluent women stake least.

The amount staked as indicated by last stake is a major determinant of payoff, whether winnings over the last year or the largest single amount ever won. For example, of those whose stake was small, less than 11s., the vast majority had won under £2 for an outlay that ranged between £2 and £6. Thirty-five per cent of them had never won at all.

By comparison, only 44 per cent of those staking 11s. or more had won either nothing or less than £2 in the past twelve months, and only 4 per cent had never won at all. Outlay here was of course substantially higher: some £20 a year or more. Seven per cent of this group had won sums of £100 or more in the preceding twelve

TABLE 6.8 *Last stake by largest win (%)*

Largest win	1s.–3s.	Men and women 4s.–5s.	6s.–10s.	11s. or more
No win	35	21	8	4
Not known	*	3	*	0
Under £2	29	31	16	4
£3–5	13	11	9	7
£6–10	8	10	9	2
£11–99	14	22	57	50
£100 or more	1	2	1	33
	(n = 277)	(n = 251)	(n = 84)	(n = 22)

* Indicates less than 1 per cent.

months, and 33 per cent had 'most ever won' sums of over £100: compared with less than 1 per cent and 1 per cent who bet in the 6s. to 10s. range. Although betters who share stake slightly less than those alone, payoff is very similar for the two groups, presumably because the far greater range of permutations open to 'syndicates' made up of small shares is bound to pay off more frequently, if only for amounts in the range below £100.

What should have been a relatively simple relationship, that age increases (assuming that the older a pools better is, the longer his or her career of pools betting) with size of largest single amount won, is not borne out through the age spectrum.

Use of winnings

In the mythology that has built up around gambling, pride of place should go to the image of the gambler who, even when he wins, blues his winnings in mindless sprees or ploughs it all back onto a bet which fails to come off. What basis in reality does this conception have? For pools, we asked how respondents spent what they'd won, relating to the largest amount. In categorizing the open-ended answers we tried to isolate the possibilities of rebetting, spending on a spree and saving or spending on goods for the home or family. In practice, this proved very difficult, since many answers were multiple (i.e. people bought things for the home *and* gifts for the family, etc.) and the major tendency was quite simply to merge winnings with spare cash. This was the case with 43 per cent of the men and 46 per cent of women. Another third of the men and quarter of the women either saved or spent their winnings

TABLE 6.9 *Winnings and their use (men only) (%)*

| | | | Most ever won | | |
Use of winnings	Up to £2	£3–5	£6–10	£11–99	£100 or more
Pocket	47	50	41	40	16
Rebet	26	23	2	2	0
Gift/spree	8	7	15	13	4
Save/home	20	20	42	45	80
	(n = 74)	(n = 55)	(n = 43)	(n = 114)	(n = 19)

on the home, presumably buying goods for which they had not other sources of cash available. Of the remainder, 10 per cent of men and 21 per cent of women used their winnings either for gifts or for a spree, ranging from holidays to buying drinks. Finally, 11 per cent of the men and only 6 per cent of the women rebet their winnings.

Plainly, the amount in question is likely to influence very heavily the direction in which it is spent (Table 6.9). For example, an unexpectedly large win opens up possibilities for unplanned consumer spending. On the other hand, winning a small sum of, say, under £5 is much more likely to be treated as of little account, and be merged with spare cash or used to buy gifts for family or friends. For men, for example, the tendency to pocket winnings sharply declines only when the amount exceeds £100. Sums below £5 were rebet in almost one in four cases, but winnings over £5 were hardly ever spent in this way. Where the sum in question is moderate rather than either very low or very large, the tendency to give gifts or spend the sum on, say, a party, rises somewhat. Winnings between £5 and £15 do not enable the winner to simply pocket the sum quite so readily, nor to contemplate buying goods normally well outside his range. This tendency is, however, slight. Most interestingly, the tendency for the winnings to be used on the home, or for savings, or for repaying debts grows sharply with the amount won, from 20 per cent in the range below £5 to 80 per cent in the range above £100. In other words, the larger the win the greater the tendency to avoid both rebetting and short-term expenditure, rather than the reverse.

The same analysis on women's spending of pools winnings varies this pattern somewhat (Table 6.10). The tendency to pocket winnings *does* diminish with a rise in the amount won, once that amount exceeds £5. 'Rebetting' is almost entirely confined to winnings of

TABLE 6.10 *Winnings and their use (women) (%)*

Use of winnings	Under £2	£3–5	Most ever won £6–10	£11–99	£100 or more
Pocket	50	51	30	28	15
Rebet	11	0	0	1	0
Gift/spree	27	3	52	16	32
Save/home	12	46	18	55	53
	(n = 61)	(n = 29)	(n = 14)	(n = 18)	(n = 8)

N.B. Weighted data.

under £2. But the tendency to spend the money on gifts or sprees is not affected directly by the amount won, nor is that for saving or spending winnings on the home or family.[5]

It is interesting to note with either social class indicator, the more middle-class men are proportionately *most* likely to rebet their winnings. Men belie the class stereotypes, for current class, with lower working-class men appearing most likely to save or spend their winnings on the home and family – 51 per cent as distinct from 35 per cent, 30 per cent and 34 per cent. Women, however, accord to almost a caricature of class stereotypes, with a declining tendency to save or spend winnings on the home as one descends the class hierarchy, from 52 per cent among upper middle to only 14 per cent among lower working; and with an increasing tendency to spend winnings on short-term satisfactions likewise, from zero among upper middle class to 50 per cent among lower working class. A puzzle remains as to why the patterns of behaviour should differ so markedly between men and women of the same social class. Among the men, those who shared the coupon were three times as prone to rebet winnings as those doing pools alone: whereas with women, those doing pools alone appear six times as likely to rebet as those sharing, the difference being apparently accounted for by the gift/spree category. No neat trends obtain but some of the differences which have emerged over use of winnings should set sharp limits to the notion that all pools winners automatically blue their winnings on drinks, parties or further gambling: the grain of truth that attaches to the myth seems to accord with social class stereotyping as far as women are concerned, but certainly not men, who are, after all, both the more frequent and heavier betters – since in their case the social class stereotyping comes close to being falsified if not reversed.

Method

One of the most frequently voiced criticisms of gambling is that it encourages irrationality – people follow it blindly, without rational grounds for their choices. Gambling is *inherently* irrational, its essence being the uncertainty of future events against whose outcome money or goods are staked. The professional gambler testifies by his very existence to the fallacy underlying this view,[6] but professional gambling is located in fields other than pools betting. It deals with events which are too various to permit the calculated risks of the professional. (Fixed odds betting was an exception to this pattern.) How far do pools betters attempt to systematize, and how far do they do so on bases other than luck or chance? Treble chance betting yields least scope for rationality, but whilst this accounts for the overwhelming majority of bets cast, we do not have data against which to measure how far it accounts disproportionately for luck- and chance-based bets, since we cannot differentiate data on home- and away-win betting.

The distinction between luck and chance, and skill elements are tenuous in that the latter can be imputed by the respondent to reliance on, for example, tipsters. This lacks any substantive basis in rational calculation and is as much based on chance as the archetypal better who selects his team by use of a pin. Yet we have measured *imputations* by respondents of their methods in terms of luck, chance or skill – or a mixture of all three. Luck selection denotes reliance on attitudes invested with supra-rational significance, e.g. lucky numbers, names, personal associations, dreams, etc. Chance denotes selection by resort to random sampling, whether by a pin, taking every *nth* team, or another arbitrary device. Skill denotes the attempt to maximize choice potential by means which include the study of form, reliance on tipsters, assessment of good betting prices, personal judgments, etc. Some respondents, of course, simply replied in terms of the categories themselves – luck, chance, skill. We further differentiated between match choice and perm choice, since the elements of choice behind the one may not underlie the other.

The data show a tendency for the skill element to obtrude increasingly with the increase in the size of the stake: 44 per cent of those staking 11s. or more claim some basis in skill, compared with 20 per cent of 4s. to 5s. betters, and only 7 per cent of smaller (1s. to 3s.) betters. This chimes with the greater claims to skill among men than women (20 per cent: 5 per cent) and the greater acknowledgment of resort to luck among women than among men (35 per cent: 24 per cent), in terms of match choices. In terms of permutation choice, a rather higher percentage of both sexes claim a basis in skill – and this is in line with objective possibilities, since permutation range and scope can be closely aligned with the number of draws forecast and the desired relationship between stake and possible permutation. The finding that of the 11*s.* and above group who claimed most resort to skill in match choice, 79 per cent claim no skill in permutation choice is probably accounted for by the likelihood that a very high percentage of this group left the choice of permutation to another person. Reliance on luck in match choice is inversely related to social class, and on chance and/or skill is directly related to it. But using current social class reveals that among men a higher proportion of upper middle-class betters stated that they relied on luck, and a lower proportion on skill, than was the case among lower working-class betters. For women, however, the luck gradient remains strong as in the two-generational class variable, and skill-based choice – though claimed by a tiny majority – emerged more strongly among lower working-class than among upper working-class women.

Budgeting

Some importance has been attached in at least one theory[7] to the idea that gambling is acceptable to a crucial segment of the community – the lower middle class – only under certain symbolic constraints of budgetary zealousness. That is, as long as a small amount of money is budgeted for, minor incursions into gambling – which is defined as having a flutter for purely entertainment purposes – can be made; resolving the conflict between a strictly rational world view and the desire to gamble. Our data show little support for this view since among men there is little variation by social class. One main variation is by sex – only 40 per cent of men budgeting for pools betting, compared with 56 per cent of women betters. Surprisingly *as many as* two in five men and nearly three in five women set money aside *at all* for what are, after all, relatively small stakes. It could well be that Devereux's thesis on this point has relevance for *all* pools betters, not only those from any one status group: that pools betting is kept carefully under control, represents expenditure which is not simply thrown away, but kept under surveillance, and that a ritual of putting money aside operates both to legitimize what might otherwise be too problematic a decision if one had to make it afresh week by week, and to keep under control what might otherwise escalate into larger amounts at risk.

Finally, *summer* pools represent that element in pools betting which can most clearly be separated from a vaguely expressed interest in football, and anchored in a set of personal and local associations; summer pools are based on results of Australian soccer matches. One would expect, therefore, only the most habitual betters to persist in doing the pools in the summer, when the subtly engineered rhythms of English life have moved away from a focus on the game to more enticing forms of betting. It is perhaps noteworthy that nearly a third of men, and almost a fifth of women, pools betters still bet on summer pools: that, moreover, proportionately more middle-class than working-class pools betters do so, and that for men this applies to both present and two-generational class indicators. As a finding this corroborates earlier impressions that the traditional image of the pools better as typically working class needs substantial revision.

Pools in a leisure context

We anticipated *some* causal connection between leisure orientations to life and involvement in gambling. Both leisure and gambling are viewed as superstructural phenomena, which are heavily constrained by major structural attributes such as age, class, income, sex. Hence, analysis of the extent of gambling compared to leisure activities needs to be rooted in these attributes. We assume that, despite the limitations of confounding, clear enough relationships exist between leisure orientations and forms of gambling activity. If no relationships of any clarity emerge, *this does not mean* that no relationships *exist*, only that our limited tabulations may have failed to reveal them.

For the pools, we assumed *some* positive relationship between involvement in football in particular, or sport in general, and doing the pools – the rationale being that out of the patterns of gambling choices available, some predisposition to the pools via an interest, however marginal, in football at least was likely. The data on *playing* football do not really nourish this view. Those men, young and middle-aged, who played football regularly had only very slightly higher rates of participation in pools than those who did not play at all. *Watching* football as a spectator and doing the pools is slightly related for men, but not for women. *Following* football reveals a stronger link between sport and the pools (for both sexes), but the definition of *following* is such as almost inevitably to include the activities essential to doing the pools. In terms of playing, watching and following *all* sports (including football), the data for *playing* and *watching* do *not* suggest any overall relationship between sports-orientation and pools betting, whereas that for *following* is subject to the constraint mentioned above. Finally, watching races (as a spectator) and betting on one or both of the two biggest races of the year (the Derby and the Grand National) *are* positively related to pools betting, though not unambiguously, since those betting on big races only every two or three years, and not during the last twelve months, bet slightly more heavily on the pools than those betting on these races *during* the last twelve months. However, the relationship between a propensity to watch racing and to bet either every year or every two to three years on the big races and do the pools is stronger than that between either a specifically football or more diffuse sports orientation. Only with groups rated as 'most active' in terms of political and community involvement is there a marked differentiation – which curiously operates in opposite directions for men and women. Among men, a very low proportion indeed, 19 per cent, do the pools at all and they are of the stable middle class and Nonconformist religion. Among women, 30 per cent of the most active political and community groups do the pools. One possible explanation is that men's involvement in the community is assumed, women's involvement represents a search for satisfactions which are also expressed in pools betting.

Factors predicting variation in doing the pools

Sex was the best predictor, from the thirty-eight social indicators, of how often people do the pools, men doing them almost three times as often as women, measured by frequency of involvement over a 12-month period (Diagram 1, p. 221). Very different factors then combined to produce greater variation for men and women. For men, the most interesting combination of factors was the interaction between very infrequent pub-going and no history of regular parental gambling, which produced a grouping (1:22) of some size and with an average pools involvement less than half that for men as a whole. No comparable grouping emerged to predict frequent pools participation,[8] and this is in line with our conclusion from the descriptive data that the relatively mundane and low-key form of gambling entailed in the pools renders it normative, so that only strong inhibitory influences from background socialization make much difference. One exception to this occurred on the analysis of spending on the pools. A small grouping (2:11) gave the highest annual expenditure, over £25: this grouping combined middle-aged affluence with a high orientation to risk (Diagram 2).

For women, the factors which interacted to produce the most striking variation were belief in luck and number of years spent in the same job. Women who had spent ten years or more in the same job and who expressed a strong belief in luck (1:15) produced a frequency some three times that for women as a whole. Those with a low belief in luck (1:10) bet on the pools the least often. A similar combination emerged in the analysis of only those women who do the pools (Diagram 3). One small grouping (3:31) emerged which linked very high proportions doing the pools (83·7 per cent) with spending ten to twenty years in the same job and perceiving nil prospects of promotion. Those findings suggest that women with a negligible belief in luck, or who disbelieve in it, are strongly disinclined to bet on the pools. Given a belief in luck, however, high rates of involvement are associated with the sameness of experience, and closure of ambition, entailed in holding the same job for a decade or more.

7 Betting

Distribution and description

(i) *Betting: off-course*

Betting shops were set up as a direct result of the 1960 Betting and Gaming Act, and since then they have been the subject of controversy over the extent to which they have increased off-course betting. The fact of increase is assumed, and the evidence, albeit distinctly impressionistic, tends to support the assumption. Reliable turnover figures have only been available from 1967 through the regularization of Customs and Excise data. The demand for betting shop licences far exceeded expectation, rising from an initial 8,802 in 1961 to a 'plateau' of 15–16,000 in 1964–8, the increase being checked finally by the trend towards the elimination of the smaller shop (see Appendix 3). While no real data exist to compare the pre-Act and post-Act situations, it is believed that this mushroom growth of licensed betting offices was much more than the rapid legalization of previously undisclosed business. The trade itself, moreover, confirmed these impressions. William Hill (then Britain's self-styled 'largest bookmaker') asserted that there was a vast increase in off-course betting in terms of both clients and turnover, as a result of licensing. Using his lay-off business as an indicator, he asserted a fourfold increase had taken place in the space of a few years.[1]

There are also other grounds for the view that legalization has substantially increased off-course betting. First, it was previously difficult to lay more than one bet a day; post-Act, the first bet could be followed by further betting: *continuous* betting became feasible. It is *this* that is likely to have caused the bulk of the increase. Second, the Act is hardly likely to have deterred people accustomed to bet *illegally* from doing so *legally*, but for those previously deterred at the 'invitational edge' of gambling by the existence of legal prohibitions it would remove the symbolic obstacle of illegality. Third, the sheer availability of betting shops, offering full and ready access to facilities for betting on both horses and dogs, must have captured at least some 'passing trade'. A substantial increase in off-course betting, therefore, did not require generation from any subtle transformations of social attitudes towards gambling as a result of its legalization: the trade simply capitalized on the *existing*, and partially repressed, demand, and on such marginal increments as might ensue from the side-effects of legalization.

While our data can contribute only indirectly to the debate on the effects of the 1960 Act, which itself is based on the sketchiest suppositions about gambling turnover before 1967, it is worth summarizing different viewpoints on the extent of substantial and sustained increases, since the pivot of the debate is off-course betting. Otto Newman[2] has recently compared gambling turnover in 1947, 1962 and 1967, and argues forcefully that the increase in turnover is very modest when due allowance is made for inflation and for comparable trends in different forms of consumption. Betting on horses and dogs amounted to £700m. in turnover in 1947 (as estimated by the Churches' Council on Gambling); £1,176m. in 1962[3] and £1,209m. in 1967 (Customs and Excise data).[4] This comparison suggests an increase in betting between 1947 and 1962 in line with inflation and the rise in GNP and what amounts to a *decline* in betting between 1962 and 1967 if allowance is made for these factors.[5]

The Churches' Council on Gambling were criticized by the Royal Commission of 1949–51 for giving too high an estimate of betting expenditure for 1947. They subsequently changed their policy to give estimates which erred on the side of caution, and this led Newman to accept their 1947 figures as probably accurate. Their estimates from 1946–60, however, now suggest relative stability in the volume of betting on horses' turnover from a minimum of £350m. to a maximum of £450m. per year,[6] against which betting on dogs declined from a high of £450m. in 1946 to a low of £130m. in 1952. Total turnover figures, therefore, dropped sharply between the immediate post-war period and the mid-1960s, from nearly £1,000m. to £520m. by their estimates. They would argue, therefore, that the correct comparison is between the mid-1950s position and the post-Act period, not 1947 and the same. Both they and Newman agree in assuming relative stability from the mid-1960s on in the volume of off-course betting; though the Churches' Council would argue for a lower figure for 1962 than that given by the New York investigators. In sum, Newman cites data which *minimize* the pre- and post-Act differences; the Churches' Council emphasize trends which heighten the same comparison.

Our own data can be compared with that gathered in 1950 for the Government Social Survey, but the latter was based on a national sample not local surveys, so they are not truly compatible. Also, our own data *can* be assessed against the *bona fide* figures produced by Customs and Excise, 1967–8. When this is done, a considerable shortfall by comparison appears in our data. Taking off-course betting for 1967–8 as the mean of the years 1967 and 1968, approximately £950m., and deducting 9 per cent as Newman's proportion for lay-off betting, we are left with a total of some £864m. Our own survey data, if generalized from the areas studied to the nation as a whole, can account only for some £630m., or roughly 70 per cent of the total. The difference can be accounted for in a variety of ways: (1) The three areas studied may lead to underestimates of the nation as a whole since they include a London suburb which may over-represent the middle class. (2) A household survey fails to tap the heaviest betters. (3) Respondents in general understated the true extent of both the frequency and the average amounts of their gambling. (4) The survey failed to tap betting by proxy, in particular for women.

A combination of these factors would certainly account for a difference of the magnitude described. The first point may be less important than the rest, since the population of Wanstead and Woodford did not loom large in the aggregate totals. Points 2 and 3 were shared in all probability by the 1950 survey, which estimated the total for off-course betting on horses as at least £130m. and at most £180m. against the Churches' Council estimate of at least £350m. for horse-racing as a whole. If we assume, as a result, that (4) is the most serious source of underestimation, then we can assume that our data for men betting regularly are adequate. If we make that assumption, our data tend to support Newman's contention that the net effect of legalization has been small. At the same time, legalization can still be seen as having an immediate effect on the volume of betting, since the decline in betting on *dogs* meant that the 1947 position was not sustained. From 1947, betting turnover first declined and then stabilized until 1960; rose sharply in the 1961–3 period, since when it has (net of inflation, etc.) largely stabilized again. We deal with comparisons between the 1950 data and our own at a later stage in this chapter, for it is only by charting the social distribution of betting through betting shops and other outlets, that the constraints governing such a comparison can be made clear.

One incontestable result of the 1960 Act was to enable betters to gamble through the long-withheld facility of licensed betting offices. Their creation and proliferation within a remarkably short period of time led to their virtual monopolization of off-course betting. Credit betting and cash postal betting declined throughout the 1960s. The proportion of betting in these ways was negligible in our survey: less than one per cent for both men and women. Newman, asserts that 95 per cent of all wagers and 90 per cent of all the money staked on horse- or dog-racing is channelled through betting shops. He states that they are by far the principal arenas of gambling activity in Britain – which is certainly so for com- mercialized gambling, though gaming in pubs may exceed them in terms of sheer turnover. Logically, at least, we should expect analysis of their activity, more than that of any other single outlet, to yield some insights into the social variation in gambling.

(ii) *Betting shops*

The most striking variation over the use of betting shops is that of *sex*: 17 per cent of men and only 2 per cent of women bet at betting shops regularly. Men are over eight times as likely as women to bet regularly in this way. This finding may underestimate the actual extent of women's betting, since women may share their husband's bets or may place a bet through a neighbour or friend. The Government Social Survey showed this proxy betting to be the preferred mode for 36 per cent of women who bet, though this was in the era of illegal off-course cash betting. It may well be, however, that so powerful a stigma attaches to the commercially provided outlet of the betting shop that even now a large minority of women prefer to bet via their husbands, friends or some other form of proxy. For men, however, betting by proxy was much slighter in the 1950 survey, and there is less need to suspect that betting shop outlets are not the major locale for betting on horses and dogs. But there is no doubt that our data are incomplete over channels other than the commercial for betting on horses and dogs. Our only check on this 'hidden' betting derives from three big races –

TABLE 7.1 *Proportions using betting shops*

	Men	Women
Regularly	17	2
Occasionally	27	7

the Derby, the Grand National and the Ascot Gold Cup. The first two are events which attract people who bet on no other races in the year and we cannot take their volume to be representative of proxy betting regularly. For men, therefore, we assume near-total coverage, since use of betting shops and runners, credits and cash postal and on-course betting tap all the known institutional outlets. Our data for women are more suspect.

The data for betting shops should also be more accurate for regular rather than occasional betting since a weekly pattern implies a degree of institutionalization which is likely to involve the better directly rather than by proxy. As such, the data on men who use a betting shop regularly confirm the assumption that this is primarily a class-based institution, the actual betting in which is in turn class-based, though less so. There is little variation by area which is not explicable in these terms.

TABLE 7.2   *Use of betting shops by area (%)*

| Cumulative frequency | Sheffield | | Swansea | | Wanstead/ Woodford | |
	Men	Women	Men	Women	Men	Women
Regularly	17	2	17	1	11	0
Occasionally or more	27	7	28	8	25	7

The middle-aged use betting shops the most – 23 per cent – compared to the elderly as the least – 9 per cent – and the young and youngest with 14 per cent each. The stable working class use betting shops between five and twelve times as frequently as the stable middle class, with the mobile between. Moreover, use of betting shops increases as one descends the current class hierarchy – from 4 per cent in the upper middle to 32 per cent in the lower working. The downwardly mobile are almost as involved as the stable working class, about 20 per cent. Income also differentiates with the poorest and the most affluent using betting shops less than those with middle incomes (about 10 per cent each). The class bias is repeated for education with sharp differentials over type of school, qualifications and further education. The Roman Catholics bet three times as much as Nonconformists and 'other' affiliates and nearly twice as much as Anglicans and non-affiliates. Church attendance is slightly inversely related to use of betting shops: slightly presumably because of the Roman Catholics. In summary, the data support the principle underlying the 1960 Act that a considerable disproportion of off-track cash betting on horses was located among

123

the poorer and more working-class sections of the community who would take advantage of legalization to bet via commercially provided outlets. Class bias in use of betting shops cannot be taken as a direct indicator of that in all betting. Other available outlets like credit, postal and on-track betting itself need to be looked at.

Spending

TABLE 7.3   *Expenditure in betting shops*

	Gross yearly spending	Profit/loss
	£	£
Men (n = 178)	111	−3·8
Women (n = 70)	5·8	−0·8
Both (n = 248)	85	−3

N.B. weighted data.

Spending per year even by occasional betters is higher than for the pools. Men spend on average eleven times more than on the pools whilst women spend about the same. Profit/loss data reveal an average loss less than that for the pools.

But here the different methods of accounting profit/loss must be stressed. For pools and bingo, we elicited an assessment of the number of times per year in which the respondent took part, and the last stake, and multiplied them to produce an overall turnover figure. We also asked for a statement of actual winnings over the past twelve months, since they tend to be infrequent and more memorable. This winning total was then deducted from the total yearly outlay to give us a figure for profit or loss.

For all other gambling, we thought this method inappropriate, and instead asked the respondent to assess whether he or she had won, lost or broken even over the past twelve months. We then asked, if they had won or lost, how much they thought they had won or lost. We found a majority claiming to have 'broken even', flattening the profit/loss figures. While we were only too aware of this danger, we hoped that subjective assessments would prove rather more accurate than has been the case.[7] That they are very inaccurate indeed can be demonstrated by the calculation that our profit/loss figures would yield a net gain to the betting-shop industry of not more than £30m. per year! In 1968 terms, at least £150m. was needed to maintain the capital and current costs of the betting-office business and pay the duty.

Social relations and the use of betting shops

Three-quarters of those men and women who use betting shops at least sporadically did so near home rather than work.

TABLE 7.4 *Location of betting shop (%)*

| | | Regular betters | | Sporadic betters |
	Men	Women	Total	Total
Near home	73	76	75	57
Near work	14	12	13	21
Other	5	9	5	12
Not known	8	2	7	9

Regular betters also rely on facilities near home rather than work, probably indicating a tendency for regularity to depend on sheer proximity. Three-quarters of those betting use shops near home which in two-thirds of cases are within five minutes walk. It is most appropriate to assess this activity in a leisure rather than a work context. Do people bet alone or in company? Seventy-five per cent of the men bet alone whereas the preference for a minority of women is to bet in company, preferably family and presumably husband.

TABLE 7.5 *Betting company (%)*

| Out of last five visits | With family | | With friends | |
	Men	Women	Men	Women
None	88	70	80	86
1–5	10	30	18	14
Not known	2	0	2	0

$$(n = 118) \quad (n = 22)$$

Men tend to prefer friends to family if they choose company; the reverse is true of women. Seventy-five per cent of the mobile and 66 per cent of working-class betters go alone, compared with only 28 per cent of the middle class who bet at least sporadically. Most middle-class betters were less likely to use betting shops alone, though their company was not family at all. Forty-two per cent did go on at least one out of the five occasions with friends. The norm, however, seems to be that regular betters use shops on their own rather than in company, except for the very small minorities of women and middle-class men who prefer company: women with the family and men with friends.

Patterns of betting

The stereotype of the man who uses the betting shop is of one who 'hangs about' for hours placing a succession of bets for fairly high stakes. This picture cannot be sustained for the majority, who are petty betters, staking less than 5s. on average and staying only for the few minutes necessary to place a single bet.

TABLE 7.6   *Usual number of bets for sporadic or regular betters (%)*

Number of bets	Men	Women
1	51	81
2 or 3	32	16
4 or more	18	3

TABLE 7.7   *Time spent in the betting shop (%)*

	Men	Women
Under 5 minutes	48	88
6 to 29 minutes	15	0
30 or more minutes	36	*
Not known	1	11
	(n = 118)	(n = 22)

Women, then, usually bet only once and stay for a very short time. Men on average do not spend a long time and the majority place a small number of bets. There is a link between length of stay and number of bets.

The fact that the length of stay is longer the more bets are placed is presumably linked to the time-lag between races, and the preference for seeing the results of one race before betting on the next. Also being paid the winnings of a race counts for subsequent betting too. Regular betters tend to place more bets than the sporadic: 18

TABLE 7.8   *Time spent by number of bets (%)*

| Stay | Number of bets | | |
	1	*2–3*	*4+*
Under 5 minutes	66	32	23
6 to 29 minutes	10	19	22
30+ minutes	23	47	54
Not known	2	1	0
	(n = 60)	(n = 37)	(n = 21)

per cent place four or more bets compared to 4 per cent, and to stay longer – 39 per cent stayed for over 30 minutes or more compared with 8 per cent.

It is the mobile who place most bets whereas the upper working class place more than one bet per visit only slightly more than the lower middle and lower working class. Only 2 per cent of the youngest placed more than four bets whereas of all those older 20–25 per cent did so. The poorest and the most affluent also bet most often per visit.

There seems however to be little connection between number of bets and size of stakes – save a slight link between very small stakes of less than 3s. and making two to three bets a visit. But those regular betters who make more than four bets tend to stake over 10s. per bet compared to the 2 per cent of the sporadic. The poorest men *all* bet less than 5s. compared to 43 per cent of the most affluent. The relation between stake and income was the most marked – 50 per cent of the more affluent male punters staking over 10s. on each bet. This may be related to age: of the elderly only 14 per cent bet more than 3s. per bet. Area also affects stake: Sheffield betters tend to spend more – 60 per cent staked 4s. to 5s. compared with 44 per cent in Swansea and 30 per cent in Wanstead and Woodford. The only group where a sizeable minority bet more than 10s. are the younger, where 23 per cent did so among men; and the upper working class also tend to stake more than 10s. most, 18 per cent compared to about 3 per cent of the other class groupings. If one tried to identify the group most prone to high stakes, it would be the more affluent, skilled working class, young, but not the youngest, men.

One independent check for the reliability and validity of our data is offered by figures issued by the Mark Lane Group (a leading betting-office chain) as to the average stake per *slip* for 1968.[8]

Average stake per slip	*1967*	*1968*	*1969*
	13s. 4d.	15s. 4d.	16s. 4d.

Two points should be noted: (a) the Group's average stake per slip *increased* by 2s. between 1967 and 1968, a period when off-course betting turnover *fell* from £969m. to £938m. That this Group was *expanding* its average stake at a time of slight recession may mean that its clientele was placing stakes rather higher than the average nationally; (b) average stake per *slip* is not the same as average stake per *bet*, since several bets can be recorded on one slip.

Due to (b), it is obviously not appropriate to compare the average stake per *slip* for the Group with our data on average stakes per *bet*. A better comparison, in the absence of data on slips in our survey, is to compare the Group's data with average stakes per *visit* in our data. Again, the comparison is flawed, since one *visit* can accommodate more than one slip. But since 51 per cent of the men, and 81 per cent of the women (at least sporadic betters in our sample) made one bet only per visit, and of the remainder, a certain proportion making more bets would do so on one slip only, we might assume that for two-thirds of the sporadic betters at least, the amount stated per slip and amount stated per visit are the same. To be reasonably adequate, our figures for average stake per visit would need to be at least 50 per cent higher than those of the Group for average stake per slip, a proportion which is almost attained:

TABLE 7.9   *Average stake per visit to a betting shop*

	Men		Men and women	
	Weighted	*Unweighted*	*Weighted*	*Unweighted*
Stake*	£1 1s. 6d.	£1 5s.	£1 0s. 2d.	£1 2s. 9d.

* = Number of visits by last number of bets per visit by stake on the last bet, for at least occasional betters, divided by their number.

The appropriate figure for comparison is £1 0s. 2d. and if we compare it with the Group's 1967 figure, the comparison seems adequate, though the 1968 figure is perhaps a slight underestimation, except that the Group's figures are apparently higher than the norm.

The Mark Lane Group's figures also offer one historical comparison of great interest. In his evidence to the Select Committee on Betting Duty in 1923, Supt. Frederick Denton, of Sheffield City Police, described the arrest of a street bookmaker 'on Saturday at 1.30, that is before any race was over. Up to that time he had taken

164 betting slips, and they related to bets on 829 horses running in that day's racing. The amount of money that the punter had put on in those bets was £34 14s. 6d.', adding that this was 'chiefly taken from women and children' in a very poor quarter of the city.[9] The police strategy which engineered this *coup* testifies to the complexity of collaboration between the bookies and their clientele, but it also affords a glimpse of the economic realities of betting in very hard times. The average stake per slip was then 4s. 3d., as compared with the 1967 figure of 13s. 4d. for the Mark Lane Group. The 1967 equivalent to 4s. 3d. in 1923 is roughly 12s. But it should be emphasized that the 1923 slip represented betting for the whole day, whereas this is not necessarily so for the 1967 figure.

Aspects of betting

Such versatility as there is in the extension of off-track betting to events other than horse-racing is virtually confined to men and is associated with size of stake and frequent betting.

TABLE 7.10   *Betting at least occasionally (%)*

	Men	Women
Only betting on horses	91·1	99·8
Betting on dogs and other events: e.g. boxing	8·9	0·2

The overwhelming tendency for both men and women who bet is to concentrate exclusively on horses. This in itself is a major clue to the character of betting in our society. It plainly is not simply the manifestation of an 'impulse to gamble' which settles randomly on any event staged for gambling purposes or capable of yielding such a set of purposes. If this were the case, horse-race betting would simply be one of many competing attractions, along with dog-racing, boxing, wrestling, and so on. The near-total monopoly enjoyed by horses in the off-track betting sphere, its dominance over dogs, and its virtual exclusion of any remotely comparable rival, must relate profoundly to the mainsprings of Western culture in general, and English culture in particular. It is, of course, the only sport in which men and animals combine to make the contest particularly rich in symbolic connotations, more so than contests between men or between animals. Backing the horse or the jockey is less creative than backing the combination between the two (and taking into account the host of relevancies

129

E

such as the trainer, conditions at the course, etc.). At the height of professionalism, betting on horses can become almost an actuarial exercise, with due account given to all these factors plus the odds at which a worth-while profit becomes a distinct possibility. At the extremes of amateurism, the punter makes a guess and backs it. But in the middle ground the majority of betters, and the regularities they display in their patterns of betting, may tell us a little about its appeal.

It is worth seeing if the tendency to bet exclusively on horse-races is spread randomly throughout the different age, income and class groups within those using betting shops. The 9 per cent of all men using betting shops for events other than horse-racing, either as well as or instead of it, becomes 16 per cent for the younger, 11 per cent for the 'mobile', 14 per cent for the upper working class (compared to only 6 per cent for the lower working class, popularly supposed to be the main supporters of dog-racing in particular) and so on. Variation is not marked except by stake – where it is much larger in that 28 per cent of those last staking over 10s. bet on events other than horse-racing. Thus, betting on events outside horse-racing seems most strongly associated with the most regular and the heaviest betters. This makes sense in terms of 'gambling impulse' theory – the heavier the gambler, the more prone he is to bet on anything that moves – but not in terms of 'rational' gambling theory – where specialization is the hallmark of the trade.

Method

TABLE 7.11   *Methods of betting (%)*

	Men	*Women*
No method, not known	4	*
Luck or chance	27	48
Skill	65	21
Mix of skill or luck or chance	4	30

A major difference between men and women emerged over method. Two-thirds of men claiming skill in choice of horse – even if this related only to 'form' or 'record' – compared with only a fifth of women. By contrast, nearly half of women and just over a quarter of men who bet backed their choice on grounds of luck or chance alone. More women covered both options, and did not give priority to either luck/chance or skill. It might well be argued that women are simply more alert to the inevitable components of luck and/or chance in any betting decision, whereas men played up the skill element disproportionately. But even this tells us something about different orientations of men and women to the process of choice, i.e. that men stress the element of rationality, however small, in the betting process, while women discount it.

This emphasis shows up also in the patterns of type of odds preferred: favourites, outsiders or horses with odds lying between the two (see Table 7.12). 'No preference' meant that respondents chose none of these three options, and it is of some interest that so few replied in these terms – only 7 per cent of the men and 16 per cent of the women. To back the favourite is consistent with various styles of approach; but it implies the reliance on form and a willingness to risk the stake for relatively small return. The exact reverse can be held of backing outsiders. The fact that a quarter of the men and only one in twenty-five of the women preferred the former, and that only 14 per cent of the men and just over a third of the women preferred the latter, are indicators of the greater respect paid by men to form and the willingness of women to ignore it in the hope of outstanding returns in comparison with outlay. The most rational choice of all is 'in between' – since it is there that the greatest scope lies for a choice which is both realistic and might 'beat the odds'. Over half the men and only two-fifths of the women do this.

Whether the bet was usually each way or to win clearly discriminates men from women, over three out of four women preferring 'each way' as compared with 47 per cent of the men (see Table 7.13). Only 17 per cent of the women back 'to win' compared with 42 per cent of the men. Acknowledging that 'each way' bets are the majority preference, it points to one further distinction between men and women – for if we assume that bets on a horse 'to win' represent greater faith in one's judgment than 'each way' bets – which ensure some return if the horse is placed first, second, third or – in large races – fourth, then men are much more inclined to the total risk of betting 'to win' whereas women prefer to hedge their bets. Two contrasting modes of betting are emergent here: that (by men) on favourites 'to win', and that (by women) on outsiders 'each way'. The first represent total risk of the stakes on the basis of form 'rationally' appraised; the second a temporizing with the far greater risk inherent in a choice made against the 'rational' dictates of form. In speculating about these 'ideal types', however, remember that the majority prefer 'in between' odds, irrespective of the 'each way' or 'to win' options.

A further difference emerges over the type of bet preferred, a

TABLE 7.12 *Type of horse chosen (%)*

	Men	Women
Favourite	24	4
Outsider	14	36
In-between	54	40
No preference	7	16
Not known	*	4
	(n = 185)	(n = 73)

TABLE 7.13 *Betting risk (%)*

	Men	Women
Each way	47	77
To win	42	17
No preference	7	6
Not known	4	*
	(n = 185)	(n = 73)

TABLE 7.14 *Combination of bet (%)*

	Men	Women
Single	40	61
Double	30	19
Treble/accumulators	18	7
Not known	11	12
	(n = 179)	(n = 73)

higher proportion of women (61 per cent) prefer single bets to men (40 per cent) and the difference increases as the risk implicit in the bet mounts (see Table 7.14). But the large proportions saying 'don't know' reflect the extent to which respondents did not know such terms at all. Men are nearly three times as likely as women to choose the most risky types – trebles, accumulators – in which the stake is tied to a sequence of races, all of which must be correct for the bet to succeed while the odds multiply. Forty-eight per cent of men preferred these compared to 26 per cent of women. This complicates the 'ideal typical' possibilities outlined above – for it renders possible a 'stretching' of the total risk for men over between two to several races, compared with the women whose greater preference is for curtailment of risk to a single event once their choice is cast. The contrast is now between the possibility of making two or more 'rational' choices, based on form, the basis for an extension of the odds by linking these choices into a multiple bet; and rendering one 'irrational' choice against form as riskfree as possible in betting 'each way' and on a single race only. Again we must enter the *caveat* that at least half the men and three-quarters of the women do not fulfil the prerequisite for the first 'ideal type', since they bet only on singles, but men seem much more likely than women to correspond to it. The fact that more than twice as many men as women read the racing pages daily, and a racing paper at least some time during the year, strengthens this view. But can it be sustained against the interrelationships between the indicators in which we are interested?

To sustain them, clear lines should exist between, on the one hand, the elements of skill, backing the favourite, betting to win, and likelihood of multiple betting; and, on the other hand, the elements of luck or chance, backing outsiders, betting 'each way' and making single bets. In the event, the chief link – between skill and the favourite, and luck/chance and outsiders – is not sustained: men basing their choice on luck and/or chance are no more likely to back outsiders than those basing their choice on skill; though the latter are nearly twice as likely to back favourites as the former, that is really not a convincing enough difference to sustain the ideal type (Table 7.15). Interestingly, the small (4 per cent) proportion who insist on a mix between luck/chance and skill plump overwhelmingly for the 'in between' category of odds (85 per cent) and those 4 per cent who deny any habitual method (hardly an irrational choice) plump heavily for outsiders (61 per cent). This link broken, it is still worth noting that the rest of these data support the ideal-types rather more – 'luck/chance' betters bet 'each way' more than 'skill' betters (63:41 per cent) – and the reverse applies to bets 'to win'. Also, 'luck/chance' betters are twice as likely to make single bets only, compared with 'skill' betters (60:34 per cent); and half as likely to make treble bets (13:23 per cent). Again, the ideal-types appear to be only slightly borne out by the finding that whether favourites or outsiders are habitually backed, the choice of 'each way' or 'to win' bets is pretty much the same. Hence if we can ignore the imputations of luck, chance or skill by respondents to their methods, the relationships between the elements which comprise the ideal-types do hold – but these remain

TABLE 7.15 *Betting methods by types of bet (men only) (%)*

| | | Method | | |
	None	Luck/ chance	Skill	Mix	Total
Odds preferred					
Favourite	31	16	29	0	24
Outsider	61	13	12	4	14
In between	1	60	53	85	54
No preference	7	10	5	11	7
Don't know	0	2	0	0	*
Each way or win					
Each way	47	63	41	46	47
To win	46	30	46	47	42
No preference	7	2	9	7	7
Don't know	0	5	4	0	4
Type of bet					
Single	20	60	34	39	40
Double	31	22	33	38	30
Treble etc.	3	13	23	1	18
Don't know	46	5	11	21	11

(n = 7) (n = 49) (n = 117) .(n = 12) (n = 185)

contrasts between extremes, while the majority of men, at least, back 'in between' odds rather than either 'favourites' or 'outsiders' taken separately.

The gambling specific variables, stake and frequency, produce most variation in method. The young claim a greater degree of skill compared to others (81 : 53–67 per cent), as do the stable working class (76 : 50–60 per cent). The upper middle class confess to a greater reliance on luck or chance than all other classes (50 : 20–29 per cent). But again, the group staking over 10s. has a far greater proportion claiming skill than any other (95 : 54–67 per cent) and a linear effect linking regularity to skill emerges.[10] The explanation could simply be that a large component of attributions of skill resides in resort to 'expert' tipsters and racing page 'form': and the more heavy and regular the better, the more he resorts to these touchstones.

The data on the odds preferred break this pattern. The elderly and the poorest are most prone to back outsiders (51 per cent and 37 per cent respectively). The middle-aged and the poorer are most prone to back favourites (37 per cent and 36 per cent respectively). Social class, moreover, differentiates 'favourites' from 'outsiders'. Our original assumption here was that working-class betters (short-run hedonists to a man) would be far more prone to back outsiders while the cautious and prudential middle-class betters would plump for favourites – exactly the *reverse* is true. One in four upper middle-class betters back outsiders compared with only one in twenty or so lower working class. The reverse holds true for backing favourites. And it should be stressed that 'in between' backers were the majority of the middle class, just under a majority for working class. Those preferring the lowest stakes backed outsiders (significantly more than other groups) and the highest stakes were slightly more often on favourites. Preference for favourites increased with frequency of betting, but this factor had no impact on preference for outsiders.

'Each way' or 'to win' bets did not vary over age, income, stake, area and social class. Current social class was directly and decreasingly associated with bets 'to win', inversely so with 'each way' bets, a pointer to the greater prevalence of what we have termed as 'rational' gambling among working-class betters. The same holds for frequency of betting – the more regular the better, the more likely he is to bet 'to win', the less likely he is to bet 'each way' – these gradients are quite strong on both sets of data.

The most complex relationships emerged in the types of bet preferred by different groups. Our assumption was broadly that the more risky multiple or sequential bets would be associated quite strongly with poverty, small stakes and working-class betters. This pattern is certainly present, but has to be taken in conjunction with another pattern which in certain respects links the most complex bets with very high stakes, determined in part by the irreducible minimum under which some of these bets would be impossible. The elderly and the stable middle class tend to make multiple bets half as often as the other groups. A large difference emerges between current classes, multiple bets being preferred most by the lower working class – over twice that of the upper middle and almost twice the middle (61 : 25 : 34 per cent). The double bet seems to be that of the poorest (42 per cent); the most affluent go for the most complicated bets, but the single bet is still the most preferred.

Finally, do betters assess 'form' and take 'professional' advice? What are the patterns of reading (a) the racing pages of daily newspapers and (b) racing papers, those exclusively devoted to racing information and betting advice?

There is an increasing orientation, but slight, to betting literature with age – save that the elderly were less inclined to consult a racing paper than the middle-aged. The middle class are much less likely

TABLE 7.16   *Reading about horse racing (%)*

	Men	Women
Racing pages		
Read racing pages daily	66	30
Read racing pages weekly	17	14
Read racing pages sporadically	8	30
Used to/never read racing pages	9	26
Racing papers		
Read racing paper occasionally	28	14·5
Used to/never read racing paper	72	85·5

than the working class to read racing pages, though the major (and statistical) difference in readership of a racing paper is between the lower working class and the rest. The heaviest betters stand out as twice as prone to such readership as the rest: those betting sporadically are much more likely to read racing pages daily; those betting regularly to read a racing paper. Method differentiates readership: those claiming a skill element are almost twice as likely to read both papers.

To sum up, these indicators of betting involvement hang together in ways which are explicable in gambling specific terms. They confirm the relatively low involvement of the middle class in betting and – more unexpectedly – reveal that those from the working class are least likely to make rash bets on outsiders, most likely to base their bets on form, and then to attempt the longer odds of sequential betting to maximize pay-off.

Winning and budgeting

The frequency of betting should heighten the likelihood of winning irrespective of the size of the stake; but the latter should primarily determine the amount won. In fact, the relationship seems more complex: both factors have an impact on whether or not the better wins at all. Frequency of betting has the expected relationship with most won throughout the year: among men, 10 per cent of the regular, 18 per cent of the sporadic and 33 per cent of the occasional won nothing at all. Uniformity exists for those whose stakes ranged from 1s. to 10s., only 3 per cent of those staking 11s. or more failed to win at all, compared with 16–21 per cent of the rest. This could point to a skill factor in those staking 11s. or more. There seems to be a pay-off for more regular betting if only in terms of a rather higher proportion winning amounts under £2. It should be stressed that while the 10 per cent or so of regular betters who do not win at all throughout the year might even be classed as incompetent, to say the least, the fact that the *most* won in the last twelve months is under £2 does not denote incompetence. This is compatible with regular winnings of never more than £2 at any one time. In terms of stakes, the same might be said of the distributions between the smaller stakes – there is little here to suggest that the size of the stake makes more than a slight difference to the largest single amount won in the 1*s*. to 10*s*. range. Only when the size of the stake goes above 10*s*. does propensity to win large amounts increase dramatically – 73 per cent of those staking 11*s*. or over win as much as £11–98 in the year compared to around 10 per cent of those staking less. The bulk of these larger wins are at the lower end of that range but this does not explain away the large differences.

The odds also play a part in determining the amount won. Those who back outsiders or play trebles, when they win, may win larger amounts on shorter odds but probably less often. This does not show the tendency for shorter odds to produce a lower rate of 'no win' over the year.[11]

TABLE 7.17   *The effect of type of bet on winnings (men and women)*

Type of bet	No win	Up to £2	Most won in the year					
			£3–10	£11–99	£100+	Not known	%	N
Single	20	44	18	11	0	7	100	136
Double	18	21	53	7	1	*	100	64
Treble	25	12	20	24	6	13	100	41
Not known	22	18	48	13	0	0	101	17

How do betters use their winnings? The sheer size of the amount won is assumed to be the chief determinant of its use; very small sums are simply pocketed or rebet; the larger amounts go on debts, gifts or minor sprees which would otherwise be low priorities; the largest sums make possible unusual consumer spending. Only two respondents won more than £100, ruling out analysis of really large wins. One in two betters simply pocket their winnings where these are less than £2, one in three where they are over £2, the size of the amount thereafter making little difference to this pattern. There is, however, a direct link between size of win and the tendency to save or buy household goods with the proceeds. While only

TABLE 7.18   *Use of largest win in the year (men and women) (%)*

Use	Up to £2	Most won in the year £3–5	£6–10	£11–99
Pocket	54	32	28	28
Rebet	13	16	0·5	6
Spree/gift	9	11	22	14
Save/home	25	40	50	52
	(n = 44)	(n = 25)	(n = 29)	(n = 29)

8 per cent of men rebet their winnings, this trend is greater for wins of under £5.

It should be emphasized that money that was merged with spare cash may well have been rebet subsequently, but we were only concerned with what happened at the time of winning, especially whether the win was earmarked for a purpose. Rebetting occurs only among the regular betters, and they also prefer the spree or gift option, supporting the often imputed connection between regular betting and 'spontaneous gratification'. But what should be stressed is the fact that three times as many regular betters save or spend their winnings on household goods as rebet them. One would infer exactly the reverse from a great deal of polemic on gambling. It is interesting to note that no women rebet their largest win and for men the overall proportion was only 8 per cent. The group most prone to pocket any winnings, nearly most prone to spend on sprees and least on the household or save are the upper middle class.

The pattern of budgeting seems all too clear: 80 per cent of

TABLE 7.19   *Class differences in use of winnings (%)*

Use of winnings	Socio-economic group Upper middle	Lower middle	Upper working	Lower working
Pocket	69	19	40	31
Rebet	0	18	11	5
Spree/gift	25	0	9	26
Save/house	6	63	40	38
	(n = 19)	(n = 24)	(n = 60)	(n = 38)

men and 85 per cent of women simply staked money that they had spare at the time, the remainder – less than one in five – using money they had set aside for the purpose (Table 7.20). Devereux's suggestive model was that the lower middle class could reconcile gambling with an ascetic world view (a) by only gambling in moderation and (b) by incorporating outlay into a rationally based budgetary scheme of earmarking small sums for the enjoyment derived from betting. Yet we find the reverse to be true – the overwhelming tendency for both men and women was to lay out ready cash.

TABLE 7.20   *Cash for betting (%)*

	Men	Women
Spare	80	85
Set aside	17	15
Not known	3	0
	(n = 185)	(n = 73)

But the poorer, the elderly and the working class tend more to eke out their spending by setting money aside for betting.

(iii) *Other forms of betting on horses and dogs: off- and on-course*

One of our principal aims was to acquire as comprehensive a coverage as possible of all kinds of betting among the population aged eighteen or more. We therefore covered other forms of betting off-course such as credit, cash-postal and agents or runners and also on-course horses and dogs, as well as betting on the three major races. But this has not led to a full coverage: we omitted to include those who bet by proxy and did not take account of the Government Social Survey finding that a minority who do in fact bet on horses and dogs do not acknowledge the fact unless prompted by *specific* instances.[12] We had hoped that betting on three races – Derby, Grand National and Ascot Gold Cup – would be sufficient. We summarize our findings and then compare them with those of the Government Social Survey for 1950.[13]

There is an aspect other than proxy betting in which underestimating seems to have occurred. We expected a higher proportion to have bet by credit or post. We find that only 1 per cent of the population bet this way. Our approach may be responsible.

We asked: 'Do you ever make a credit bet on the horses or dogs?' which may miss out those who think of credit bets in terms of betting by telephone. In the event we will not analyse these data. The proportion of the population betting on- or off-course in any one of these ways is less than one in ten.

TABLE 7.21 *Betting on-course or off-course through agents/runners (%)*

Cumulative frequency	On-course dogs		On-course horses		Agent/runner	
	Men	Women	Men	Women	Men	Women
Regularly	2	1	0	*	4	1
Occasionally or more	4	1	9	3·5	8	5

The most interesting finding, if we compare this with the Government Social Survey, is that there has been a slight but noticeable decline in on-course betting:

TABLE 7.22 *On-course betting (%)*

	1950		1968	
	Men	Women	Men	Women
Horses – occasionally or more	11	5	9	3·5
Dogs – occasionally or more	5·5	1·3	4·1	1·0

a. *Betting through agents or runners*, in which the bet is placed through an individual acting on behalf of a bookie, usually occurs in the work context in 1968 though the context may be recreational (say a pub or a club) in which a runner operates. Its incidence is far more marked in the industrial areas of Sheffield and Swansea than suburban Wanstead and Woodford (9:3 per cent), and among the middle-aged men and women. The downwardly mobile and the stable working class appear to be those betting regularly, with those currently in the lower working class having the highest involvement (6 per cent). The upper middle class and the upwardly mobile make much greater impact on occasional betting: which may indicate only that, in the context of the workplace, the bosses occasionally place a bet on the same network more regularly used by the workers.

b. *Betting at the dog-track* is more clearly stereotyped as the resort of the 'rough' working class revelling, after a day's hard grind, in the raw and short-lived pleasure of the thirty-second race. The higher involvement regularly is in the stable working class

(7 per cent) among the middle-aged and those without any qualifications, being skilled (4 per cent) rather than the unskilled working class (1·5 per cent). No Roman Catholic or Nonconformist bet regularly at the dog-track compared with 3 per cent of the Anglicans and non-affiliates; also no sporadic or regular church attender bet regularly. Sheffield, with a long-established dog-track at Owlerton, had a higher rate of dog-track betting than the other areas. But while the data support the view that on-track dog-race betting is most characteristic of stable working-class men, the rates are *twice* as high for the skilled and *as* high for the lower middle class as the unskilled.

For women, whose involvement in dog-track betting is slight, the mobile and those currently of upper working-class status rate slightly higher than the other groups. The only surprising finding is that those educated at grammar school or equivalent yield a slightly higher proportion than those in other types of school.

c. *On-course horse betting* is also stereotyped: and thought generally to be the preserve of the more affluent race-goer, and of those living near race courses. In fact, area shows little variation, and income, save for the poorest (and by definition the most elderly) differentiates barely at all, as far as men are concerned. The immobile and lower working-class men are most prone to bet at horse-tracks (17 and 14 per cent respectively). Perhaps this is connected with the very high rate of on-track horse betting for Roman Catholics (one in five) and for those regularly attending church (one in ten).

Cumulatively the data may point to a substantial degree of occupational and educational under-achievement as linked with betting at the horse-track. The findings for women are somewhat different; the socially mobile make much more impact.

There has been a shift in the income distribution of those betting at the horse-track. In 1950 the Government Social Survey found that the prevalence of such betting increased with income; our data do not show this. Thus, while in 1950 *at most* 10 per cent of the group earning the equivalent of *under* £1,000 per annum bet at horse-tracks compared with *at most* 11 per cent of the same group in 1968, 22 per cent of the group earning over £1,000 per annum in 1950 did so compared with at most 10 per cent of the group in 1968.[14] The income change does seem a real one, and – if reliable – indicates a *disappearance* of the link between increasing income and on-track betting above the poorest. This in a sense vindicates the logic of the 1960 Act, but at the expense of on-course bookies: since one interpretation of what has occurred is that whilst *before* the Act the better-off did in fact bet rather more than the rest on-track,

TABLE 7.23   *Incomes of those betting on-course (%)*

Incomes per annum	1950 – Men and women				
	Up to £150	£150–250	£250–375	£375–500	£500+
Horses	3	8	9	10	22
Dogs	0·4	2·9	7	5·8	4·3

	1968							
	Poorest		Poor		Affluent		Most affluent	
	Men	Women	Men	Women	Men	Women	Men	Women
Horses	3·5	5	11	4	9	3	10	2
Dogs	0	1	5	2	3·5	*	6	1

since the Act they have resorted more frequently to off-course betting, and the less well-off have not increased their tendency to bet on-track with rising incomes. The Act has therefore operated not only to enable the poorer better to bet off-course; it has enabled the richer better to do so as well, thereby reducing the proportion of bets on-track, most significantly among the affluent betters. On-course bookmakers have been lamenting this falling away for some time: it is interesting not only to confirm it, but to see which group it has affected most.

Spending at the horse- and dog-tracks These figures are also comparable with those of the Government Social Survey:

TABLE 7.24   *Spending at the races*

1968	Mean annual outlay*			Profit/loss		
	Men	Women	Both	Men	Women	Both
Horses	£23·5	£3·5	£16·5	− £3	*	− £2
Dogs	£140	£236	£153	+ £21	*	+ £18
1950 (adjusted)						
Horses	£30–44	£6–8				
Dogs			£100			

N.B. Weighted data.

* Expenditure data are based on the product of the frequency of betting over the past twelve months by the average stake in the case of regular or sporadic betters or the last stake in the case of occasional betters. On-track betters' outlay is also the product of the above by the numbers of bets staked on the last visit.

Even if we take the lower figure of £30 for men, and £6 for women, horse-track betters, they are still higher than those for 1968. And even if we take the lower unweighted figure of £119 for dog-track outlay, the 1968 figure is still higher than that for 1950. The horse-track figures back up the point made earlier: it is not only that proportionately less people are betting at horse-tracks than in 1950; they are spending less *per capita* than in 1950. (Considerably less if the upper rather than the lower figure is taken for 1950.) For dog-track betting this is not the case: proportionately fewer are betting at dog-tracks than in 1950; but those that do are betting more *per capita* than in 1950. In both 1950 and 1968, the mean outlay at dog-tracks is far higher for both men and women than at horse-tracks, primarily because – while attendance is far more regular at dog-tracks – average stakes *per visit* are about the same.

Betting through agents or runners produces an average yearly outlay of £29, somewhat lower for men than is the case for betting shops, but considerably higher for women in the same comparison: £16 for women via agents, £4 for women on average in betting shops. As there appears to be no great difference in the mean *frequency* with which women bet via these different channels, the excess must presumably be accounted for by higher mean *stakes* in the case of women betting by agents or runners.

Social relations and on-track or agency betting[15]

Betting through bookmakers' agents or runners was overwhelmingly a workplace activity, for men betting sporadically or more. Dog-track betting was in seven out of eight cases limited to nearness to home, whereas horse-track betting took place for two out of three well away from the home: this points up the localized character of dog-track and the expeditionary character of horse-track betting. For all three modes of betting, *company* is involved on some occasions, in that clear majorities have, out of the last five occasions, *talked with* family or friends about the bets cast via agents or *gone with* family or friends to the track. In the case of betting via an agent, friends (mainly in the workplace) rather than family predominate; in that of dog betting, both assume equal weight; in that of horse-track betting, friends predominate slightly more than family – though the difference is too slight for more than passing mention. One bet at a time is the pattern for betting via an agent; on the last five visits to a track, by contrast, over two-thirds of the betters placed four or more bets on average. Stakes were lower for betting via an agent than was the case for on-track bets. Seventy-five per cent of the former were 5s. or under compared with only 24 per cent at the dogs and 18 per cent at the horse races. People spent less time at the dogs than the horse races; only 24 per cent stayed over two hours at the dogs compared to 77 per cent at the horse races. These findings are broadly corroborated by those for occasional betters.

Aspects of betting The type of bet placed suggests that those preferring singles fared best on-course but that those placing doubles fared best with agents or runners.

TABLE 7.25 *Effects of bets on winnings*

Most won in the year	Horse track			Type of bet Dog track			Agent/runner		
	Single	Double	Treble	Single	Double	Treble	Single	Double	Treble
No win	40	62	86	11	0	0	54	44	62
Don't know	0	0	0	0	0	(1)	13	0	27
Up to £2	10	0	0	41	0	(2)	13	35	0
£3–10	29	39	14	21	(3)	(3)	20	12	11
£11–98	21	0	0	27	0	(1)	*	4	0
	100% n = 46	100% n = 14	100% n = 9	100% n = 13	n = 3	n = 7	100% n = 30	100% n = 7	100% n = 5

N.B. ( ) used for actual numbers and not percentages.

Dog-track winners are rather more ready to 'blue' their winnings on gifts or 'sprees' than the others, but this was mainly a function of the very low proportion of dog-track winners who simply pocketed their winnings; one-fifth saved or spent their winnings on the home in each case. Budgeting for bets was uniform throughout.

TABLE 7.26 *Use of winnings (%)*

	Horse-track	Dog-track	Agent/runner
Pocket	42	11	37
Rebet	0	8	18
Spree/gift	37	60	25
Save/home	21	21	20
	(n = 15)	(n = 15)	(n = 18)

Dog-track betters backed the favourite far more than horse-track betters, and both on-track betters did so far more than those betting through an agent. The small field at dog-tracks is probably crucial here. Compared with those using betting shops and agents, on-track betters back more often 'to win', slightly more claim a 'skill element' in their bets, and fewer bet on 'outsiders': these differences may reflect the greater opportunity on-track betters have to see the preliminaries to the races, or to their greater skill, or both.

d. *Betting by proxy*. In an attempt to cover those who nevertheless bet, although not answering positively and who possibly used family or friends, we included questions about the three major races. Two of these – Derby and Grand National – are unsuitable as indicators of anything except the very occasional bet and would provide only a clue to the absolute limits of the appeal of betting in the population. The third – Ascot Gold Cup – is a major event but one which does not attract many non-betters and is probably quite a good indicator of more regular betting by proxy, since betting on this race either annually or every two or three years can be assumed to indicate a tendency to bet moderately on other races in the calendar than the Derby and Grand National. We still cannot allow for those (i) who bet by proxy but for some reason do *not* bet even every two or three years on the Ascot Gold Cup or (ii) those who are reticent about admitting to betting, and would admit to it if specific instances were named, but do not bet on the Ascot Gold Cup. In view of the legal status of off-course betting we should not expect this population to be very large – about 1–2 per cent – and for it to be smaller the more regular the better.

We found that 7 per cent of the men and 5 per cent of the women bet either annually or every two to three years on the Ascot Gold Cup, but did *not* reply in the affirmative to other questions on forms of betting. The differences between these reticent betters and men using betting shops were fairly marked – age; social mobility; income; religion; marital status and number of dependent children. On other factors, the *trend* of the distributions was broadly similar. The reticent Ascot betters were twice as likely to be either young or elderly than in middle age; they were far more likely to be downwardly mobile or stable working class than upwardly mobile or stable middle class; the very poorest were (age-linked) at least twice as likely to be 'reticent' than the more affluent; they were least likely to be Roman Catholic or 'other'; those whose marriages were over were twice as likely to have bet in this way. Hence the obvious distributions of proxy betting – that it would occur more among women than men, that it would affect the middle class disproportionately, and that its prevalence among the working class could be negligible – are not borne out. It should be stressed, however, that two quite different patterns are at issue here; first, betting by proxy, which would not be tapped by questions on betting in person; second, 'reticent' betting, where the respondent does not admit to betting in person in various ways, but *does* admit to betting *every year* on a specific race. The extent to which the data on a ᴗingle race tap either of these sources is unfortunately a matter for conjecture.

Data for 1950 and 1968: a comparison

Comparison between 1950 and 1968, on the basis of pools, dog and horse race betting only, cannot provide a valid comparison for *all* gambling in those years.[16] In 1950 some forms of gambling were illegal and so not covered. Other forms such as bingo, casino gaming and gaming machines operate in 1968 as *alternatives* or additional forms of gambling to those available in 1950. Nevertheless, we can compare certain forms of on-course and all off-course betting with a fair degree of assurance.

TABLE 7.27   *Off-course betting on horses (%)*

	1950 Men	1968 Men	1950 Women	1968 Women	1950 Both	1968 Both
Occasional betting or more at shops, cash, credit, agent, runner		29·8		11		19·6
Ascot Gold Cup only at least every 2–3 years		7·2		5·4		6·2
Off-course betting except major races	36	37	22	16·4	29	25·8

The trend revealed is one of little or no increase in overall off-track horse betting by men, and of a decrease for women. In the 1950 survey 16 per cent of the men and 36 per cent of the women who bet (in a context of illegal street betting) used a friend. It is still likely to be the case that women bet by proxy proportionately far more than men: and if one assumes that the Ascot data for 1968 are a good indication of proxy betting, then the figure for proxy betting for 1968 is represented by the ratios of 7·2:37 for men and 5·4:16·4 for women: about 19 per cent and 33 per cent respectively, roughly comparable to 1950. Even if the ratios of proxy betting were rather higher, the increase of 1968 over 1950 would still not be substantial for men, and would have to be very high indeed for that to occur for women. On this indicator, therefore,

TABLE 7.28   *Off-course betting regularly (%)*

| | Horses | | Dogs | |
	1950	1968	1950	1968
Men	16·0	18·1	3·2	4·6
Women	5·5	2·4	0·3	0·8
Total	10·8	9·6	1·6	2·5

our conclusion would be that off-course betting is no more prevalent now than it was in 1950.

The figures for 1950 are from answers to the question: 'Have you had a bet off-course during the last seven days, excluding today'. It was found that 10·8 per cent had so bet, but – since the survey was carried out in March/April 1950, and preceded the heavier betting which the authors estimated took place during the summer another 2–3 per cent was added on to the 10·8 per cent total to allow for those who had bet on between eight and twelve major races throughout 1949, to gauge the extent of regular betting more accurately. 'On this basis the proportion of regular betters could be estimated as between 10 per cent and 13 per cent of the adult population.'[17] The 1968 figures were culled from summation of answers to the question: 'How often do you . . .', followed by reference to the various betting outlets. We have excluded from the total for regular betting in 1968 the Ascot betters whom we included in the annual total. This is because even betting every year on the Ascot Gold Cup does not seem sufficient to warrant inclusion as regular betting. It must be admitted, however, that the 1968 figure for women does seem suspiciously low, and this is probably due to our missing out on proxy betting which looms *relatively* larger for women than for men. In conclusion, we can treat indicators as tentatively suggesting that for men the increase in regular betting has been contained to a slight increase only in the 1950–68 period; and, even more guardedly, that the data for women are compatible with a slight *decrease* in regular betting.

The figures in Table 7.28 for off-course betting on dogs indicate a slight rise in the prevalence in line with the greater facilities available. In conjunction with on-track dogs data, however, the trend *overall* is one of a slight *reduction* in betting on dogs for men, and an equally slight increase for women.

There has been an increase in at least two cases of betting on major races: the Grand National and the Ascot Gold Cup.[18] The sharp rise in popularity of the Grand National compared with the Derby is certainly noteworthy. But more interesting still is

TABLE 7.29   *On-course betting on dogs, at
            least occasionally (%)*

	1950	1968
Men	7·0	5·3
Women	1·5	2·25
Total	4·1	3·65

TABLE 7.30   *Betting on the major races*

| | | Per cent betting | | Average stake* | |
		1950	1968	1950	1968
Derby	Men	46	44	11s. 6d.–13s. 2d.	10s. 4d.
	Women	31	27	5s. 6d.–6s. 4d.	3s. 4d.
Grand National	Men	35	46	9s. 6d.–10s. 10d.	9s.
	Women	21	28	5s. 1d.–5s. 10d.	4s.
Ascot Gold Cup	Men	13	20	15s. 4d.–17s. 6d.	15s. 10d.
	Women	5	10	5s. 7d.–6s. 4d.	4s. 2d.

* 1950 prices have been doubled to allow for changing money values. It is
possible that a multiplier of 175 per cent as distinct from 200 per cent
should be used: this would bring the 1968 stakes into line with those of
1950.

the apparent rise in popularity of the Ascot Gold Cup: by the
1968 estimate, one in five men and one in ten women bet every
year on this race, compared with one in eight men and one in
twenty women in 1950. But the number of races for which this
information is available in 1968 is too few for this trend to be
generalized to regular betting or even to major race betting in
general. It could well be that the Ascot Gold Cup has quite exceptionally increased its magnetism for the occasional better.

It is also worth noting that the relative amount staked on the
major races is strikingly similar as between the two years, with the
average stake for the Ascot Gold Cup remaining markedly higher
than those for the Grand National and the Derby. Average stakes
on these races for men are slightly lower than was the case in 1950;
for women, the average stake is markedly lower. These decreases
in the amounts staked do not seem to be linked with the broadening
of the appeal of these races to a larger section of the public, since
the same relative decrease applies to the Derby, which has under-
gone a slight falling-away in popularity on our data.

Finally, a comparison is possible between betting turnover per week in the 1950 survey with the 1968. The 1950 survey had asked people how much they had bet on horse-racing off-course during the week preceding interview. 'In all, 228 men and 86 women had bet ... with an average bet in the week of 19s. 8d. for men and 3s. 10d. for women.'[19] To get comparable figures, we have taken the mean yearly total betting shop expenditure for men and women and divided by fifty-two. The weekly total for men comes to £2·13 and for women slightly over 2s. The figure for men is slightly higher than that for 1950 translated into 1968 purchasing power; that for women is consistently lower, almost certainly for reasons summarized above. The inclusion of off-course bets via other outlets would probably slightly lower the total for men, but increase it for women, since the mean yearly outlay for betting via agents and runners is only £29 for men but £16 for women.

Conclusions

With the exception of data on the Grand National and the Ascot Gold Cup, our data do *not* support the view that there has been a sharp increase in the prevalence of betting – particularly *off-course* horse-race betting – as a result of the 1960 Betting and Gaming Act. Unfortunately, we cannot present a comprehensive comparative assessment of the 1968 situation *vis-à-vis* that of 1950. We have attempted to fill the gap, on ways which overlap with, but do not match, the contours of either 'reticent' or 'proxy' betting. However, and particularly for regular betting by men, we expected a sharp increase to have been reflected in our figures. Finally, with these qualifications in mind, we are inclined to accept the trend in regular betting by men as having risen from 16 per cent to 18 per cent between 1950 and 1968, and on an annual basis from 36 per cent to 37 per cent, as reasonable; the trend for women from 5·5 per cent to 2·4 per cent and from 22 per cent to 16·4 per cent, for the same year, seems more likely to be unreliable, since the extent of 'proxy' and 'reticent' betting by women in the 1950 sample was so much larger than for men, and which – as a result – our 1968 data are likely to have underestimated.

(iv) *Private betting*

The friendly bet or wager probably best embodies the distinction between betting and gaming, for it ideally maximizes the element of skill and knowledge in the former by contrast with the pure chance character of the latter. That money is staked on one's opinion or knowledge naturally brings it within the domain of gambling, but it accommodates an almost infinite variety of possibilities. For example, whereas gambling is *in general* linked with the outcome of a future and uncertain event, friendly betting can just as readily be based upon a past event, the only outcome left to the future being the correctness or otherwise of the better's knowledge – about, say, a sporting event, the commonest subject of friendly betting.

The extent to which private betting, unsullied by commercial pressures, is undertaken by people might stand as an index of the prominence that the vocabulary of betting has attained in their everyday life, were it not for the finding that friendly betting is not especially highly associated with any other betting. It may well be that those who resort to private betting to settle an argument over, say, which team won the 1934 Cup Final, are revealing far more about their involvement in football than their immersion in betting: it serves as a handy form of conflict-resolution for dis-agreements in spheres where vital interests of a cultural rather than an economic kind are at stake.

About one in fifty men claimed to make this kind of bet as frequently as once a week, and as many as 16 per cent at least once a year: the figures for women, in comparison, are a negligible less than 1 per cent, even for the year. The only other trend of any note is that by age: a decline in rates of both regular and occasional friendly betting with advancing age for men.

TABLE 7.31   *Private betting proportions*

Cumulative frequency	Men	Women
Regularly	2·3	0·1
Occasionally or more	15·7	0·7

The very high incidence of a form of gambling – this time not attributable to commercial pressures – among the young points to some quite powerful connection between coming of age and the 'impulse' to 'wager' as well as to 'gamble'.

These trends are consistently not sustained for expenditure. Turnover figures are low even for the more regular betters: £9·4 is the mean figure for those betting sporadically or regularly; £5·5 for those betting occasionally. The higher turnover figures (though £16 is the largest for any group) occur for the stable and lower working class; the older; the poor; and the single: but differences are so slight as to make interpretation very speculative indeed. The overwhelming tendency was also for respondents to claim either breaking even or winning: giving a mean profit of £6·5 overall.

Our expectation was that a high sports-orientation should have been associated with friendly betting, sport being the major topic of friendly bets and a general 'games' orientation seemed the most appropriate attitude-set within which friendly betting would occur. This idea also seemed to fit the sex and age trends noted above. The data for leisure indicators do support this view as far as 'watching' as a spectator, football, racing and sports in general, but not 'following' or playing sports, are concerned. Nor is there any link with annual betting on the major races. There does seem to be some link between friendly betting and pub-going: 78 per cent of those making friendly bets regularly also went as frequently to pubs, compared with 51 per cent, 47 per cent and 35 per cent for sporadic or occasional betters and those not betting at all. By contrast, an inverse relationship appeared between friendly betting and involvement in do-it-yourself and political or community activities, though these trends may chiefly reflect the age trend noted above. Friendly betting, therefore, seems primarily a young, male, sports and pub-orientated activity, possibly denoting a need to assert or establish one's authority in a field to which an unusually high commitment has been made in terms of personal character.

Factors predicting betting

(i) *What factors predict how often people bet and how much they spend?*

We have grouped together as the dependent variable the four major forms of off- and on-course betting – using betting shops, agents or runners, on-course betting on horses and dogs.[20] As with pools, for both indicators of participation – frequency or times and expenditure (turnover) per year – *sex* proved the best predictor. The extent of the differences may have been exaggerated by under reportage of women's proxy betting. As regards frequency (Diagram 4) men bet five times more frequently than women; and men spend annually *ten* times more than women.

For men, frequency of betting was best predicted by social class and job specific factors, whereas for women the first split, over social class, was unproductive. The split on *men's* social class distinguished between the lower working class and the rest, rather than the manual/non manual differences that apparently emerged in the descriptive data (Table 7.32). Two predictors of lower working-class betters (4:5) emerged, with degree of job interest being the stronger. The other was type of school attended, distinguishing elementary only from all types of secondary education. This seems to indicate the age-specific nature of the group's frequency of betting. The predictive split on job interest does not reveal an age difference; it distinguishes interest from lack of it.

TABLE 7.32 *Men*

Current social class	Betting mean times per year	s. d.	n
Upper middle	4·4	21·4	200
Self-employed	6·5	40·1	20
Lower middle	14·2	51·1	161
Upper working	30·3	28·3	281
Not known	38·2	39·7	10
Lower working	67·5	119·2	144

TABLE 7.33 *Lower working-class men*

Job interest	Betting mean times per year	s. d.	n
Not applicable	9·3	25·3	8
High	38·0	73·1	51
Very high	40·2	105·5	32
Medium	43·7	95·2	24
Low	136·5	146·0	22
Very low	254·2	149·3	7

It should be stressed that this interest refers to the intrinsic content, rather than the extrinsic interest brought to it by the subject. However, it is clearly impossible to disentangle the two empirically. Clearly also, there is no simple causal link between dull jobs and frequent betting, however satisfactory it would be to establish that link. The reverse is equally plausible: that frequent betting leads one to define one's job as dull. The two obviously interact, and it would need a different methodology to sort out causal priorities.

But the establishment of this *association* is of the utmost importance, none the less.

Job-specific factors seem more than usually important here, as the next best predictor to job statement is job preference:

TABLE 7.34   *Lower working-class men*

Preference for last rather than new job	Betting mean times per year	s. d.	n
Not applicable	16·2	30·9	4
No	34·6	35·9	86
Yes	114·7	142·6	54

The ratio of those who *had* had a job they liked better to the rest was 3:1 in those with past (4:7) and 1:2·5 in those with present preferences (group 4:6). In the former it is plausible to suggest that frequent betting is coupled not only with active dislike for one's present job but also with the comparative dislike which stems from memories of better jobs held in the past.

For those men of lower working-class status who rated their jobs as more interesting, and whose mean frequency betting was little higher than that for all men (4:5), their best predictor was risk-taking (see Table 7.35).

TABLE 7.35   *Lower working-class men who rated jobs as neutral-positive interest*

Risk-taking	Mean betting frequency	s. d.	n
Not known	0	0	4
Very low	12·9	22·7	16
Medium	20·4	34·2	28
Low	30·0	71·3	34
High	86·4	140·1	33

The main contrast is between those with high risk-taking and the rest. High risk-taking therefore seems a strong incentive for this group, though again the statement could equally well be reversed to the assertion that frequent betting is a strong incentive to a self-image which incorporates high risk-taking.

Variations in *men's spending* was best predicted by attitudes to free time, an unexpected result. The link between heavier spending on betting and claiming to have enough free time, and the reverse, cannot be explained in terms of any of the other indicators used, since particularly in the case of those concerned with other uses of leisure, there was little variation between those claiming to have 'enough' and those claiming to have 'not enough' free time. The most plausible explanation is that of rationalization. Gambling is more readily legitimized if one can discount any other pressing claim on one's time. Those less prone to gambling are less in need of accounts to justify the time thus spent, and may also be more involved in activities which demand a clear-cut leisure context.

(ii) *What factors predict whether people bet?*

In this analysis we looked separately at men and women. The analyses provide very different results from the frequency and expenditure analyses and from each other. For men, the most effective predictor was parental gambling (Diagram 5) clearly distinguishing those at least one of whose parents gambled regularly from those with parents who did not. For women, age is the best predictor (Diagram 6), distinguishing the elderly who do not bet from the others. The rest of the analysis is much like that for doing the pools, but here a very high belief in luck interacts with low job interest to produce high proportions of women who do bet (6:9). About 73 per cent of the grouping of men whose parents had gambled regularly participated in betting. The other predictors of this grouping are having no regular hobbies, being more affluent, not belonging to the lower middle class, having attended an elementary only or secondary modern school. Some of these factors, such as the latter, chime in with the analysis of frequency. The final grouping (5:13) produces even higher proportions who bet – around 80 per cent – and its characteristics are being lower working class *or* downwardly mobile *or* claiming free time *or* rating low on conjugal role-sharing.

These results are very much in line with commonplace stereotypes of betting behaviour. The highest proportions are produced by a combination of parental example, lack of regular hobbies alternative to betting, and a relatively poor education. Where parents bet sporadically or not at all, high proportions of betters are still associated with a combination of low conjugal role-sharing and low job interest. Low means are associated with lack of parental gambling, high conjugal role-sharing and élite education. While a simple deprivation model does not seem in order – the poorest, for example (5:6), are less involved than the other income groups – these data are in line with theories which see betting in either compensatory or protest terms, or both.

Men whose parents had not gambled at all regularly (5:2) divided initially over conjugal role-sharing, differentiating those with high from low scores and the non-married.[21] Perhaps the safest way of summarizing this result is to conclude that those who lacked the parental stimulus to gambling *and* who orientate themselves heavily to familial bonds in leisure have far less inclination to bet than those who lack either of these characteristics. An even lower proportion bet when those not educated at secondary modern were eliminated, producing a mean of as low as 5 per cent.

Given parental non-gambling *and* low conjugal role-sharing, the best predictor was job interest (5:9), those evaluating their jobs negatively producing a mean participation of 57·8 per cent.

8 Gaming

Distribution and description

(i) *Pub gaming*

Gaming in licensed premises was illegal, until the 1960 Betting and Gaming Act, though the Royal Commission of 1949–51 admitted that betting and gaming such as playing darts for drinks or money were widespread, but major breaks of the law were very rare. They upheld the prohibition, arguing that the combination of drink and gambling was too explosive to contemplate. The 1960 Act, however, legalized the playing of certain games 'for small stakes' and it is with this form of gambling that we are now concerned.

Our data suggest that pub gaming remains a popular pastime: yet it must be stressed that our definition is the broadest, including such 'bets' as the loser of a darts game buying the next round of drinks. The surprisingly high figure of 16 per cent of men compared with only 1 per cent of women participate regularly in pub gaming. However, only 8 per cent of these *men* bet 'usually' on drinks: 60 per cent bet in cash, with 12 per cent either drinks or cash, and about 20 per cent unable to say which form they usually chose. Pub gaming is clearly an activity engaged in regularly *or not at all*, since only 3 per cent of the men participate in pub gaming less frequently. Moreover, 37 per cent of the men go to the pub regularly so that practically one in two of those who visit pubs, play games there.

While the formal legalization of gaming on licensed premises 'for small stakes' probably did little more than enable players to bet quite openly, instead of surreptitiously, there is little doubt that pre-war, if not pre-Act, the practice of pub gaming in certain areas was severely curtailed by local licensing pressures. In their

'Worktown' study, the authors of *The Pub and the People* wrote:[1]

The whole autocratic control of licenses by the licensing justices working in conjunction with the police, makes it everywhere possible for these authorities to go beyond the law and intimidate publicans into obedience to any regulation. Arbitrarily and without appeal, a pub can have its license taken away. That is a permanent disaster for the publican and his family.

Social control of pub gaming could be drastic, arbitrary and severely enforced. However, 'gambling and raffling, though theoretically prohibited, takes place among drinkers generally . . . and in addition to the betting that takes place (in the pub) with bookmakers'.

Involvement in pub gaming varies considerably especially by area, age, class and formal education. The rate in Sheffield was almost twice that in Swansea, and almost seven times that in suburban Wanstead and Woodford. One in four of the youngest participated regularly, five times the rate for the elderly – yet pub

TABLE 8.1 *Gaming proportions*

Cumulative frequency	Sheffield	Swansea	Wanstead/ Woodford	Total	
				Men	Women
Regularly	20	11	3	16·5	1·1
Occasionally or more often	23	14·5	8	19·5	1·9
	(n = 269)	(n = 310)	(n = 237)		

gaming is strongly associated with the image of men in retirement or near-retirement mulling over dominoes and cribbage. (This is not incompatible with our data: we are discussing here gaming for money or drinks, not the playing of pub games without stakes at all.) Only the stable middle class seem strongly averse to pub gaming (0·5 per cent participate): the mobile and the stable working class appear to participate over fifteen times their rate. But the lower middle class participate at roughly the rate of the working class (15 per cent), which is twice that for the upper middle class. Education almost certainly reflects this class-based differential; just as income does that of age. More single men participate than married or those whose marriages are over, so that the highest rates probably occur amongst young, single men (except those from the upper middle class). We cannot, however, assert that it is an exclusively working-class pastime, since as many lower middle class play games as regularly as working class for money or drinks.

Mean expenditure on pub gaming appears to run in 1968 at about £148 a year for the men and £26–£31 per year for the women: but this figure drops to around £67 a year for men when two freak cases of expenditure totalling over £1,000 are eliminated. Even this appears large by comparison with mean pools and expenditure in a betting shop: but these are *turnover* figures, assessed by taking the product of the average stake per game and the average number of games per visit. Actual mean profits or losses are derisory: a profit of rather less than £1 in the case of men, and a loss of slightly over £1 in the case of women. Although the profit/loss figures are very suspect, they accord with the common-sense expectation of a lot of small stakes circulating amongst a group of regular players.

Pub gaming is only weakly associated, either positively or negatively, with a few of the leisure possibilities. The view that those most oriented to sport would be more inclined to participate in pub gaming than those who are not is confirmed: but this is unequivocally so only if one compares 'high' with nil sports-orientation. That those who are 'achievement-oriented' in leisure will have less propensity to gamble is shown by the inverse relation with do-it-yourself and political activities. Pub gaming is also weakly associated positively with family visiting. As a check on our data we compared frequency of visits with pub gaming. The finding that 34 per cent of those who visit pubs regularly also take part in pub gaming, is offset by the discovery that 6 per cent of those who *never* go to pubs somehow continue to game in pubs regularly. This apparent discrepancy stems from the question on pub-going which focused on *evenings* and *weekends* (in order to exclude those going to pubs for mid-day meals). Questions on pub *gaming*, however, did not have this limitation. Not surprisingly, data on pub *going* reveal a similar, though more diluted, distribution for its incidence to pub *gaming*.

Social relations and gaming in pubs The traditional view of pub gaming is of a small group of friends meeting in the 'local' on a fairly regular basis and playing games of cards, darts or some other local favourite pastime for small stakes. Do we need to modify this view at all substantially in the light of our data?

We have already established the regularity with which pub gaming is normally played. Do people also frequent local pubs, near home or work? Two-thirds of the men, and all of the women (namely seven being regulars) used a pub near home; and for nearly two-thirds of the men this pub was within ten minutes' walking distance.

The only significant exception to this pattern occurred among the youngest who were much more inclined to go further afield for their games, and who preferred a pub near work as frequently as one near home.

TABLE 8.2   *Visiting pubs (men only)*

Pub near:	18–25	Age (%) 26–45	46–64	65 or more	Total
Don't know	1	0	3	0	1
Home	25	85	87	100	69
Work	56	9	0	0	19
Other/both	18	6	10	0	10
	(n = 24)	(n = 37)	(n = 25)	(n = 4)	(n = 90)

The women always played pub games for a stake with family; men tended overwhelmingly to choose the company of other, presumably men, friends. Over two-thirds of the men had not played in family company on the last five occasions but over 90 per cent had played with friends. This pattern was most marked for the youngest. Well over half the men, and all the women, usually played in the evening, but a third of the men usually played during the day.

TABLE 8.3   *Gaming: company at pubs (men only) (%)*

Out of last 5 visits:	Family	Friends
0	68	5
1–5	23	92
Don't know	9	3
	(n = 90)	

The type of game usually played obviously affected the nature of the gaming. The largest minority among the men (37 per cent) usually played card games, other than cribbage: a quarter habitually played cribbage, and another dominoes. Only 12 per cent played darts, whose popularity does not seem tied to the playing of a game for stakes. Dominoes was clearly most popular for the older men. The youngest clearly preferred other card games more than the rest. Sheffield alone gave a high preference for dominoes, which were not played at all in Swansea and the London surburb, where cards other than cribbage took preference. Card games were played most by the more affluent.

The small minority who had staked over 5s. on the last visit did so mainly on cards other than cribbage. The numbers involved are far too small for meaningful comparisons to be made on the weighted data. All four respondents who had staked 11s. or more, and two of the eight who had staked between 6s. and 10s., did so on card games (other than cribbage); three of these eight did so on darts, one on dominoes and two on cribbage.

Only 6 per cent of the men, and none of the women, saw their aim as the desire to make, or gamble for, money. The majority motive in each case was stated as either an interest in the game or in the exercise of their skill (54 per cent). The rest gave social or enjoyment reasons, a trend most marked among the younger men. Only the youngest saw gambling for money as a motive, and then only 13 per cent. The game, in fact, seems more central than the gaming for all the players, who play primarily to demonstrate skills and derive enjoyment from the social ambience of the group, and only secondarily invoke money as an element in the play. Nearly all instrumental replies were given by the more affluent, upper working class – those playing card games other than cribbage: interest/skill predominated for dominoes and games other than darts and cards; social/fun responses predominated for darts and cribbage. Surprisingly, a higher proportion played darts for money than for drinks, a pattern which is said to have produced, in the North at least, some legendary games for stakes of over £100. The norm, of course, is for darts to be played without any stake at all.

TABLE 8.4   *Age (men and women)*

Why that game?	18–25	26–45	46–65	66+
Gambling/money	11	5	0	0
Interest/skill	41	53	68	84
Social/fun	46	42	29	16
Not known	1	0	4	0
	99%	100%	100%	100%

The usual number of rounds played per 'gaming' session varies considerably, one-fifth of the men play only three rounds or less, and almost one-third of the men play eleven rounds or more (the amount of time taken per round obviously varying considerably by type of game). The heaviest players by this criterion were the lower middle class rather than the working class.

While a small minority play for stakes above the norm of a few shillings per game, the majority clearly play within regular limits of that norm, only exceptionally going more than a few shillings above it. This is reflected in the pattern of winnings. Strangely, a quarter of the regular players and a half of the occasionals claimed that they had never won at all. This may reflect the wording of the question as to the 'largest' win – where winnings are uniformly of a small amount, respondents may have not considered these worth stating as their 'largest' win. Half had never won more than £2 at any one time: of the remainder, 4 per cent claimed to have won over £10, which also applied to the last twelve months. Winnings of this amount are difficult to account for in terms of normal small stakes, but become a possibility where the stakes per game exceed 10s. We should add that one in five of the weekly players 'set aside' or budgeted for their game: and nearly 90 per cent had either pocketed their largest win in the last twelve months or spent it on 'sprees' or 'gifts' – in this context, almost certainly a round of drinks for the group.

(ii) *Casino gaming*

Compared with pub gaming, casino gaming has been the subject of a great deal of press comment and public anxiety since its accidental legalization in 1960. Partly because it lent itself so readily to gambling for high stakes, partly because it became associated with the danger of 'protection' rackets and the infiltration into this country of American criminal entrepreneurs, and partly because it embodies, for many, the archetypal setting for moral decline on the part of the individual, casino gaming was subjected to particularly sharp scrutiny and control by the government, and modifications of the legal status, ownership and operation of casinos were made within a decade of their initial legalization. A particular cause of anxiety was the fear that the habit of casino gaming would quickly spread and a taste for it, once acquired, would be difficult to eradicate. To this fear the casino operators replied that there was a strong 'natural' demand for gaming facilities and that to deny it legal expression would encourage 'underground' casinos operating outside any legal constraints, but on a larger scale than existed prior to 1960. 1968 is an interesting year in which to have conducted a survey on casino gaming in the country at large, since the casinos had had several years in which to build up and maintain a demand, and the 1968 Bill which limited the operation of casinos to a certain

F

number of licensees, applications for which were then subject to very careful screening by a newly created Gaming Board, had yet to reach the statute book. It should have been a year in which casino gaming was in full spate.

TABLE 8.5   *Casino gaming*

Cumulative frequency (%)	Men	Women
Regularly	0·1	0·3
At least sporadically	1·6	0·7
Occasionally or more	3·5	1·5

As a result, it is interesting to note that no more than 3½ per cent of men and 1½ per cent of women participated in casino gaming at least occasionally and of that total, the majority in each case did not do so regularly: these amount to 1 in 500 of the population which, of course, if generalized nationally, would mean some 80,000 regular participants in casino gaming. Our analysis, however, will focus on the larger minority who visit a casino only occasionally.

The distribution of this population does not seem to vary significantly by area or by religion; but on other variables some interesting features emerge. The first of these is age: the propensity to take part in casino gaming is highest for the youngest (7·3 per cent of men and 3·3 per cent of women) and declines progressively. The youngest in 1968 were those to attain their majority in the period immediately following the legalization of casino gaming, and it is possible that their greater exposure to the idea of legal gaming explains this greater propensity. However, one should note that exactly the same age trend holds true for pub gaming, which – although it was also legalized at the same time – seems more rooted in local cultures than in commercial pressures. And the age trend also holds for the older age-group, whose ideas about gaming were formed in the days of the prohibition of gaming. The fact that the age trend occurs for over-26-year-olds as well seems to suggest an association between youth and the 'gaming impulse' which transcends the question of its legal or illegal status in society at any given time.

Another strong association is that between income and casino gaming. It was traditionally the view that casino gaming was the rich man's form of betting, and the most luxurious casinos have always incarnated reverence for wealth as the supreme goal and value, mimicking the splendours of aristocratic baroque. The casinos which, in America and now in Britain, have come into being to promote gaming on a 'mass' scale may strive to retain that association with the glamour of wealth – but the ambience wears thin in some of the seedier clubs. However, even though casinos and gaming clubs sprang up to meet the 'natural' demand for gaming at every social level, they attracted far fewer men in the poorer than the more affluent income-groups, almost 10 per cent of whom participated in casino gaming at least occasionally compared with 3–4 per cent in the affluent, just over 1 per cent in the poorer, and only 0·2 per cent in the poorest.

This trend is corroborated since the highest figure for casino gaming obtains among those educated either privately or outside the mainstream state system – 13·4 per cent, and this figure almost corresponds with that for the current upper middle class – the next highest being only 6·3 per cent for those educated at grammar schools. Those with sub-professional or professional qualifications, and who stayed on at schools for two years or more above school-leaving age, also rated considerably higher than the rest. The upwardly mobile and the stable middle class are also much more prone to casino gaming than others: 6 per cent and 3 per cent compared to less than 1 per cent. Perhaps the middle-class link explains the findings that a higher proportion who go to church sporadically also participate in casino gaming than among those who go to church less frequently.

In conclusion, the social distribution of casino gaming for men – an occasional indulgence for an unexpectedly small minority – seems patterned still upon lines traditionally associated with the pre-1960 situation, though obviously modified by its extension beyond the tiny minority who had access to legal gaming then: it is proportionately much more prevalent among the young, the upwardly mobile, and the expensively educated upper middle class than among the rest of the population (this does *not* mean that, in terms of absolute numbers, they will predominate). The distribution for women, being small, has no seeming consistency. Our figures for expenditure on casino gaming turnover are probably a gross underestimate, but are presented in Table 8.6. The overall figure for profit/loss may, ironically, be rather more accurate, since it is based on respondents' own estimates, gathered quite independently of the turnover data material.[2]

The turnover figures do point to the lower and the stable middle class and the London suburb as producing exceptionally high means (£420, £399 and £336 respectively) which suggest that metropolitan casinos may draw this group slightly more than others.

TABLE 8.6   *Casino gaming expenditure*

| | Turnover | | Profit/loss | | |
	Weighted	Unweighted	Weighted	Unweighted	n
Men	£56·1	£142·9	+ £1·1	+ £23·7	19
Women	£20·9	£13·4	− £77·8	− £26·2	15
Both	£41·8	£85·7	− £26·3	+ £4·8	34

Social relations and casinos   Since only 16 people in the sample participated regularly or sporadically we have only looked at the data on *company.*

Is casino gaming a solitary affair, or one undertaken with friends or family? The latter seems to be the case in 14 of the 16 cases – on *none* of the last five occasions did they play alone. On no occasion had any of the five women been without family or friends, though half the men had participated without accompanying family, and a quarter without accompanying friends. The lone gambler, even in this context of regular casino-going, is a-typical.

It is clear that casino gaming for many is a fleeting as well as a very occasional occurrence, about half of the sample staying for two hours or less on their last visit, playing only ten games or less, and staking in four out of five cases no more than 10s. on each game. A fiver for an evening out is not cheap, but these days as much could be spent on a meal, an evening at the pub, or a trip to the theatre. At the other extreme, of course, and apparently irrespective of the amount of time stayed, a sizeable minority spent over 10s. per game and played over ten games on their last visit: the scope for escalation is obvious. So far, the contrast between pub and casino gaming is none too marked in terms of time stayed, average stake and number of games played, save that casino gaming is far less common and more infrequent a pursuit. Rather higher proportions in casino gaming bet higher average stakes, but the differences are not large. It is only when we look at the *most spent* per game that real differences emerge. In pub gaming the gap between the average spent and the *most* spent per game was slight. In casino gaming, it is very marked, half of the men and about a fifth of the women, compared with 8 per cent of the men and none of the women in pub gaming, had staked a £1 or more at some time: and this gave an approximation of the elasticity of expenditure in casino as compared with pub gaming.

About a fifth had never won at all, irrespective of size of stake, though two-fifths claimed to have won at some time sums of £11 or more, most of this latter falling into those using higher stakes.

TABLE 8.7   *Most staked per game at casinos and pubs*

Stakes	Men		Women	
	Casinos	Pubs	Casinos	Pubs
1s.–5s.	18	64	60	81
6s.–19s.	35	23	22	15
£1 or more	47	8	16	0
Not known	0	5	2	19
	100%	100%	100%	100%
	(n = 27)	(n = 98)	(n = 15)	(n = 10)

Note: (Weighted data).

Only one respondent stated that she had rebet the largest single amount she had won in the last twelve months. Of the other winners, three of the nine women had saved their winnings or spent them on the home. About a third of the men had done the same, the rest pocketing or spending their winnings on gifts or treats.

Roulette appeared to be by far the most popular single game. Almost as many men preferred cards to roulette, but no single game emerged out of all the alternatives as clearly the favourite, while craps was preferred by only one woman player.

TABLE 8.8   *Game most played at casinos (%)*

	Men (n = 27)	Women (n = 15)
Roulette	54	38
Cards	43	2
Craps	0	5
Not known	3	55

(iii) *Private gaming*

'We had a very pleasant game of cards, though I lost four shillings and Carrie lost one, and Gowing said he had lost about sixpence: how *he* could have lost, considering Carrie and I were the only other players, remains a mystery.'[3] Mr Pooter's description of his game of cards speaks volumes about the problems of enquiry into what is *a priori* a casual pastime, occasionally indulged in and given a little spice by the addition of small stakes to the game. Especially when we approach the questions of stakes, winnings and losses, the possibility of accurate information becomes remote, largely because – one suspects – the participants themselves either just do not *know* the answers or because they conceal them from *themselves* as part of the role-playing involved in the enactment of the game. But the description also reminds us of another point: the extent to which friendly gaming must have been a routine source of entertainment in middle-class and artisan homes in Victorian and Edwardian England. (Whether or not stakes were involved is another question: the prohibition against playing *any* game for money may have been more strongly felt in those days.) While the actual *extent* of friendly gaming at that time remains unknown, one *assumes* it to have been fairly widespread, either on a regular or on an occasional basis.

To the extent that this holds true, our figures – Table 8.9 – seem surprisingly low – only 7 per cent of men and 4 per cent of women played games of cards with friends for money – regularly. It may well be that private gaming of this kind is in decline, a casualty of TV, shorter working hours, greater mobility and the rise of the 'leisure industry' in other forms, plus, of course, the far greater availability of the mass gambling industries for those who primarily want to *gamble*. However, rather higher proportions of both men and women played cards *without* stakes than with them: 10 per cent of men and 6 per cent of women regularly. *For men*, the principal variation is, again, by *age*:

TABLE 8.9 *Private gaming by age*

	Men (%)					Women (%)				
	18–25	26–45	46–65	66+	t	18–25	26–45	46–65	66+	t
Regularly (stakes)	14	5	6	5	7	6	4	5	2	4
Occasionally or more often (stakes)	33	13	13	5	15	8	10	10	4	9
Regularly (no stakes)	10	11	8	13	10	5	4	5	11	6
Occasionally or more often (no stakes)	35	24	18	14	24	24	24	20	14	21

The youngest men are more than twice as likely to gamble both regularly and occasionally as the older. Only 5 per cent of the elderly participate even occasionally. The Anglican and the non-affiliates participate regularly more than the Roman Catholic, Protestant Nonconformist and 'other religion' group: but the trend disappears for occasional gaming. Only the stable working class seem *less* involved than the rest, though the *lower* middle class emerge as substantially more involved. For women, the age trend as such does not hold true, but the elderly participate least: nor does that for class, but friendly gaming increases with income.

In sum, patterns of 'friendly' gaming differ by sex, reflecting different milieux. The greater participation by men, especially the young, and the popularity among the lower middle class, may derive from a combination of the card-playing habit for men in breaks at work (which occur as much in offices and staffrooms as in factories) and the residue of the slightly more suburban convention of card-playing among the lower middle class. For women, the convention of card playing in the home seems far weaker than might have been assumed, since in the home (as distinct from the work context) a plethora of competing alternatives for leisure-time-use have appeared in the last two decades.

Gaming in a leisure context Figures for card-playing *without* the money element redress these trends somewhat. More elderly men play cards regularly than younger and twice as many elderly women play as younger. There is a clear trend for women to play less the more children they have of dependent age. With very few exceptions, the trend of participation increases, the *higher* the respondents' educational attainment. More of the stable lower middle class, men and women, play cards occasionally than the other classes: and the privately educated men again show far higher rates than the rest. Generally, however, card-playing *not for money* follows much the same trend as private gaming, except that the elderly emerge as most prone to regular card-playing where the money element is absent, presumably as either a reflection of sheer economic hardship, of traditional frugality, or both.

In view of this line of speculation, the association between friendly gaming and other leisure is particularly relevant. If, for example, a clear inverse relationship emerged between friendly gaming and TV, we could assume that the growth of the latter had to some extent displaced the former as a leisure pursuit. In only one respect is this borne out: 22 per cent of men watching TV only every two to three days occasionally game with friends, whereas 14 per cent of those who watch TV daily play. Otherwise, the relationship tends in the opposite direction – the regular TV watchers are most likely to play cards. There is also an inverse association between regular visits to a social club and friendly gaming, but this 'finding' is suspect, since the *raison d'être* of many 'social' clubs is card playing of one sort or another – though the money element may not obtrude. There are then no grounds at all for supposing that friendly gaming primarily occurs where people do not use other leisure alternatives or outlets. Spending on private gaming, like that for pub gaming and friendly betting, looks far larger in turnover than in terms of profit or loss. Turn-over for men averages out at £60 p.a., for women at £20 p.a., with average profits of just under £1. Stakes are very low for the majority – between two-thirds and three-quarters state the average stake per game is 1s. or less. Half the men and over two-thirds of the women had *never* staked more than that.

A large majority play for two hours or more (76 per cent) yet hardly any for less than half an hour per session – suggesting that players habitually settle down for a lengthy session rather than snatch a quick game or two when time allows; the vast majority (70 per cent of the men, and 84 per cent of the women players) had *never* won more than £1 at any one session. The 'gambling' motive is expressly invoked by less than one per cent of the players as their chief reason for playing; and winnings are for the majority (over 60 per cent) simply merged with ready cash rather than used for more specific purposes. A tremendous variety of card games are played, with no clear 'national' favourites emerging, and the seven most frequently preferred games failing to account for even half the total volume of card-playing involved. Only 2 per cent of the men, compared with 14–15 per cent of the women, *most often* played *bridge*; 8 per cent of each most often play *whist* or *solo*; one in five men and almost as many women played *rummy* or *crib* most often; and 7–8 per cent of men and 9 per cent of the women played *poker* or *brag* most often: the remainder either could not state their usual preference or it was one of a variety of other games – e.g. Newmarket, variations of pontoon (twenty-one). Bridge was clearly a middle-class game for both men and women: but whereas among the middle-class men players, bridge was the game played most often by only 14 per cent, for women it was the game most played by 41 per cent. And whereas for men less than 10 per cent of the mobile group played bridge most often, 22 per cent of this group among the women did so, maybe indicating that for *women* bridge-playing is a status-conferring activity. Bridge was played over-whelmingly for small stakes at sessions usually exceeding two hours and on a regular basis in most cases. Whist and/or solo appeared games for the more affluent, rummy and/or crib for the less affluent. Expressed motivation by most bridge and whist/solo men and women players stressed skill and/or interest as distinct from 'social' or 'fun' reasons. Rummy/crib players' motives divided for men between skill/interests and 'fun' reasons, whereas the poker/brag players for the most part gave 'social' reasons for playing. This result is rather at odds with the expectancies associated with the games themselves – poker and brag, for example, are 'hard' gambling games, depending on chance more than bridge or whist, and the skills drawn on in poker and brag are principally those of calculating risks and odds for and against particular *combinations* of cards being held by other players, rather than both *this* and the need to play out one's own cards in a carefully calculated sequence as is the case with bridge and whist or solo. The generally *static* situation in poker and brag is the basis for bidding, and the skills involved here are – apart from those involved in a rational appraisal of the strength of one's hand – an ability to assess shrewdly the psychological make-up and sources of vulnerability in other players. Hence, the skills of poker and brag are – in a sense – more purely based on interpersonal skills than is the case with bridge and whist or solo, where the socio-psychological dimension is less important than the sheerly *technical* skills of the players. Even a nervous player at bridge, whist or solo – given *technical* skill – can happily survive. But in poker and brag, the technical skill is more narrowly based, therefore greater consequentiality flows from the *interpersonal* skills – 'bluff' and the 'poker face' are caricatured instances – which underpin the strategies of bidding. In this sense, 'social' reasons constitute an intelligible response to the questions about motive in the case of poker and brag players as distinct from the rest. This said, taking all card-players together, men and women, 'social' reasons predominate more, the more occasional the player; 'skill/interest' reasons predominate, the more regular the player. As for men the majority preferring poker and brag played regularly rather than less, the results for them are against the trend for card-players as a whole, though the exact magnitude of the difference is blurred, since due to small numbers and the effects of weighting, we cannot really isolate poker/brag players from the rest of the regular players and still tabulate by motivation.

While *stakes* at poker/brag were substantially higher per game than for any other games, this can partly be accounted for: the men, the 8 per cent staking 4*s*. or more *per game*, almost all fell into the category playing three games or less on their last session: the stake probably applies to the session. Those women spending 4*s*. or more per game generally play between eleven to twenty games per session. Middle-class spent longer per session than working-class players, probably because games of bridge generally lasted longer than two hours. The 'most staked' data show that high spenders among men were scattered throughout the socio-economic and income groupings, whereas among women they were almost all the most affluent *and* of working-class background. Eight per cent of the men and 22 per cent of the women set money aside for friendly gaming: among men, this was especially so among the poorest and the lower middle-class players – the only instance in which Devereux's proposition has been fulfilled – whereas among women the practice was almost entirely confined to the Sheffield

TABLE 8.10   *Stakes per card game*

	Bridge	Whist/ Solo	Rummy/ Crib	Poker/ Brag	Other	Not known
1s.	70	79	86	27	58	88
2s.–3s.	0	2	1	37	21	1
4s. or more	30	3	12	33	5	2
Not known	0	16	1	3	16	9
	100%	100%	100%	100%	100%	100%
	(n = 5)	(n = 16)	(n = 11)	(n = 18)	(n = 32)	(n = 13)

area and spread throughout income- and class-groupings. Another odd finding was that answers which amounted to a 'don't know' response, were more frequent for men, the more regular the player, in the case of questions about the game most played and the reasons for playing: this may simply mean that when more than one game is played regularly, no answer is possible, and that when asked *why* a particular game is played most regularly *avoid* a clichéd response. But for both men and women, the outstanding feature of replies to the question on motive was that skill-oriented reasons prevailed, and sociably-oriented reasons receded, the more regular the player. Finally, the bulk of the (usually small – under £1) winnings were pocketed – but in the case of nearly one in five women, they were rebet, and this happened proportionately most often among the poorer; and one in three players used their winnings on some form of celebration or other – in the small numbers of cases where winnings exceeded £2, they were spent in special ways, either in celebration by a minor 'spree' or by gifts or by expenditure on the home – and this raises a new question, central to any consideration of gambling, especially petty gambling, as to how far this is the only device which 'frees' people (however temporarily) from the constraints which typically operate to curb largesse in expenditure.

Predicting gaming

(i) *What factors predict how often people participate in gaming?*

The runs for pools and betting, on both frequency and expenditure indicators, selected sex out of the thirty-eight independent variables as the most powerful predictor of variance. This was not the case for gaming. Sex was the third most powerful predictor, the strongest being the extent of pub-going, the next strongest being attendance at soccer matches. Since the dependent variable of gaming as a whole comprises pub gaming, casino or club gaming, and private gaming, the link with pub-going is to a large extent circular.

Yoking together such diverse milieux for gaming as pubs, casinos and private contexts[4] was intended as a basis for isolating variations in expressions of the 'gaming impulse'[5] as a phenomenon *sui generis*. Some credence attached to this attempt from the finding that the interconnection between participation in these three activities does override that between them taken separately and other gambling activities.[6] For example, 16·5 per cent of men in our sample took part regularly in pub gaming. The figure for those who go at least occasionally to a gaming club is 51·7 per cent, and for those who take part regularly in private gaming, 51·4 per cent. While participants in all forms of gambling show figures higher than the mean for pub gaming, these are by far the highest, and the interconnection is repeated where club gaming and private gaming are the objects of comparison. A substantial part of the variance will stem, therefore, from people who engage in gaming in all three contexts.

Despite these considerations, the runs carried out under this section, though not entirely unproductive, were exceptionally difficult to interpret. Overall, there was the strong, partly circular, link with pub-going and an interest in sport: links which emphasize that gaming implies gregariousness and a heightened interest in play as an arena for character contests. Given this framework, and placing more emphasis on the frequency than the expenditure runs,[7] the sets of tabulations for men produced three groupings of some homogeneity with high gaming propensities: individualistically-minded working class; upwardly mobile, conservatively-minded lower middle class; and downwardly mobile, or stable working class who had experienced 'forced' job change, and whose perception of increasing income followed more collective lines. Two groupings of women were selected: those in full-time work, who were still single, or whose marriage was over, and who were stuck in dull jobs; and (mostly) young women who scored low in terms of conventional leisure pursuits.

The chief pervading factors overall were parental gambling; a mixture of levels of job indifference or low job interest; and an individualistic approach to increasing income. One tentative conclusion is that gaming seems (irrespective of class) most compatible with individualism in the work sphere combined with the search for gregariousness and scope for character expression in leisure: a background of parental gambling, and the contingency of negative job experience, may strengthen the correspondence between the two.

Finally, the key feature of most of the runs, of the earlier material which looked at the forms of gaming separately, and the data on gaming machines (see p. 193) is that for men, though far less so for women, age is inversely related to gaming. To say that the 'gaming impulse' is strongest in youth, or that men mature out of it, is simply to shift the root question one stage further back. It would be tempting to see it as an expression of *machismo*, given the link with sport and drinking; but in our analyses, other facets of the cult of masculinity – such as low conjugal role-sharing – were absent from those groupings which linked gaming most strongly with sport and pub-going. The more suggestive association was between individualistic perceptions of how most easily to increase one's income and regular gaming, the inference being that the kind of competitive individualism which is best asserted in a group context declines with age.

(ii) *What factors predict whether or not people participate in gaming?*

Far and away the strongest predictors for men were parental gambling, age and income. Income is the least interesting predictor, since the most striking feature is the lack of variation by all income levels save the poorest, a grouping which overlaps heavily with the elderly. Otherwise, the direct relationship between the extent of parental gambling and gaming, and the inverse relationship between age and gaming, confirms analyses described above (Diagram 7).

The grouping thus formed (7:5) – men whose parent(s) had gambled and whose household incomes exceeded the poorest – next split on the 'hobbies' predictor, those with none (and a very small, n = 6, group of those with very high frequency scores for hobbies) achieving the higher mean (7:7). *Both* resulting groups (7:6 and 7:7) then split on the social mobility predictor, with most variation stemming from the interaction of the indicators of upward mobility and the differential pursuit of hobbies. Those pursuing hobbies and rated upwardly mobile (7:24) produced a very low mean of 3·2 per cent; those *not* pursuing hobbies (ignoring the half dozen who scored unusually highly) produced a mean of 62·5 per cent (62·1 per cent when combined with those whose social mobility could not be ascertained) (7:9). The two remaining groupings (7:8 and 7:25) produced much the same means (34·0 per cent and 37·1 per cent) despite their stemming from parent groups of very different means. The upwardly mobile, with a background of parental gambling, thus produce very different means for gaming depending on whether or not they rate themselves as hobbyists.

TABLE 8.11 *Percentage participating in gaming (men)*

		n.	*s. d.*
Parental gambling			
Neither	15·4	434	36·1
Either	32·3	276	46·8
Both	45·5	106	49·8
Household income (net)			
Not known	3·6	66	18·7
Poorest	9·8	117	29·7
Poor	29·2	192	45·4
Affluent	32·1	218	46·7
Most affluent	32·4	223	46·8
Age			
66+	5·8	110	23·4
46–65	20·1	299	40·1
26–45	31·2	284	46·3
18–25	45·0	123	49·7

One inference is that the spirit of competitiveness that makes for upward mobility spills over in leisure *either* into hobbies *or* into gaming.

In other respects, the run failed to confirm the apparent importance of job factors as was the case in the frequency runs, nor does it produce other findings of interest. The frequency run (not reproduced here) for those who participate in gaming (and excluding the rest) did select 'increasing income' as the best predictor, corroborating the link between economic individualism and gaming, especially for those who did not receive an élite education.

The runs for women were least productive, due to the selection of extent of watching TV as the best predictor, a variable whose relation to gambling is tenuous, to say the least, but which was included as a possible indicator of the degree of privatization in leisure. Parental gambling was among the next most powerful predictors, though it should be stressed that, as with other forms of gambling, this is generally the best predictor of whether or not people gamble at all, but a weaker predictor of variations of gambling within the gambling population.

9 Club bingo

Distribution and description

Bingo has come to occupy rather the status of a joke in British social life. In song, parody and social comment, it has come to epitomize the 'dead end' use of leisure to which a newly 'affluent' working class have resorted in the absence of any ability to do something better with their time. Since its sudden rise in popularity in the immediate aftermath of its legalization in the 1960 Betting and Gaming Act (though its status before the Act was not so much illegal as anomalous), bingo has also come to be associated with *middle-aged women* in particular, so much so that its attraction has been held to have something (usually unspecified) to do with the 'crisis' of the menopause. But whatever the origins and functions of these views, they are not confirmed by our data:

TABLE 9.1   *Proportions playing bingo*

Cumulative frequency		Sheffield	Swansea	Wanstead/ Woodford	Total
Regularly	Men	13	9·5	2	11
	Women	12	9	1	10
Occasionally or more	Men	18·5	18	5	17
	Women	18	16	4	16

First, the alleged near-monopoly by women of bingo is not corroborated. Instead, proportionally just as many men as women play bingo, and this holds whether one looks at the regular or more occasional participation. Other surveys tend to find women predominating. See, for example, the Gallup survey *Gambling in Britain* (January 1972) which gives a 15 per cent figure for women compared with 6 per cent for men, the criterion being 'ever' playing bingo 'these days' at places 'where an admission charge is made'. The figure for women matches our data for playing club bingo at least occasionally. The discrepancy for men is probably due to our survey explicitly including working men's clubs as one of the locales for this. Second, proportionately more of the young than middle-aged play bingo, and this is *especially* so for women, where rates of participation decline monotonically with age. Third, those of the most affluent households play *least*, and this finding is not entirely accountable for by class. In only one respect is the conventional view of bingo sustained: it is, *almost exclusively*, a working-class pastime, and its appeal does seem inversely proportional to degree of success in terms of formal education. This variation apparently explains the area differences shown above.

Since bingo is no more constituted on 'irrational' or 'non-rational' lines than any other game based almost entirely on chance, such as the pools or roulette, one is tempted to ask why this of all gambling forms should be singled out not so much for moral as for purely social censure – 'mother playing bingo' as not so much feckless as feebleminded. Is it simple snobbery? If so, the origins of the game as *tombola*, an upper-class pastime, have either been conveniently forgotten or rendered inappropriate by the social context in which the game is now played. The latter explanation seems the more potent – for unlike the smooth negotiation of the mechanics of roulette, with the hushed tones of the croupiers, the retention of French phraseology, and the ritualistic control of emotions, bingo calls for an expressive gusto from the participants which is played up by the caller and which is essential if players are to claim their 'line' or 'house'. And, once established as a game for the 'low-brow', the processes of social selection sustain the pattern.

Whilst differentials of class and education are marked, they are not absolute, and operate chiefly to exclude the stable middle class from bingo. The downwardly mobile participate more than the upwardly mobile, whose involvement is intermediate. Married men are only half as likely to participate as the single or those whose marriage is over, but married women are slightly more likely to play. Finally, regular church attendance is *inversely* associated with bingo, which may explain why the Roman Catholics have a surprisingly low rate of participation. There is possibly slight under-recording of their involvement, for bingo club membership does

TABLE 9.2 *Expenditure on bingo*

Frequency		Mean turnover p.a. Weighted	Unweighted	Mean profit/loss p.a. Weighted	Unweighted
Sporadically	Men	£49	(£44)	−£41	(−£36)
	Women	£65	(£58)	−£51	(−£46)
Occasionally	Men	£44		−£32	
	Women	£52		−£37·5	
	Both	£52		−£34·5	

not cover that contained in church gaming, although we found only 3 per cent involved here.

Expenditure and profit and loss figures for bingo are more likely to be accurate than for any other form of gambling except pools. Turnover figures are calculated by taking the product of the annual number of visits, the last number of games per visit, the number of cards per game, and the cost per card. Profit/loss figures simply take this figure and deduct from it any winnings over the year. Technically, profit/loss would be zero if blanket or truly representative coverage was obtained for all members at any one club or for all clubs in the areas concerned, since stakes must by law be *all* returned in the form of winnings, ultimate losses being made only from entrance money. Our figures show how individuals can be and are affected within that total picture.

The largest mean turnovers for men are for the single, secondary modern educated and youngest: next the nonconformists, the upwardly mobile and those with two to three dependent children. Otherwise, high turnover (and profit/loss) occurs among the elderly; the regular church-goers; the group who left school one year after minimum leaving age; and those educated in grammar or comprehensive schools. All these groupings had spent over £100 at bingo (in the case of the elderly over £200). The next highest expenditure figures for women occurred in the upper working class – some four times higher than for the other classes – and the upwardly mobile.

Bingo in a leisure context

For men there are direct associations between bingo and watching football, pub and club entertainment, and negative associations with bringing work home and involvement in political or community activities. These on the whole reflect the class differentials already noted. Women display much the same pattern, with family visiting and betting on major races proving more sharply associated with playing bingo than was the case for men.

Social relations and bingo

It appears that for roughly one in two players bingo is a very localized activity indeed, the club usually visited being within ten minutes' walking distance.

Half the men and four-fifths of the women *never* play alone. For roughly two-thirds of the players at least one out of the last five visits had been with family, and at least one with friends for about a third. The only clear trend was that the older the women the less they went with friends: one in four women aged over twenty-five had been alone to bingo on at least one of the last five occasions. But there are few indications here that bingo exists pre-eminently to fend off 'alone-ness' – in the majority of cases people seem regularly to go with pre-arranged company of families and/or friends. This is not to preclude the possibility of bingo providing a context in which fresh contacts are made: two-thirds of the players talked to people they did not know at all on some of their previous visits.

By far the largest proportion played only five games or less on their last visit and only 5 per cent played eleven games or more: more women than men played between six and ten games per visit. Among the men, surprisingly, more of the regular players had played five or less games on their last visit than the less regular players. One would naturally expect the reverse: that does in fact occur for women. Two-thirds of the players play only one card per game, and only 5 per cent play three cards or more per game. Among the men, but not the women, the tendency to stick

TABLE 9.3 *Company for bingo (%)*

Out of last 5 visits	Sex	
	Men	Women
None alone	58	81
1–5 alone	40	19
Not known	2	*
	(n = 67)	(n = 87)

TABLE 9.4 *Number of bingo games per session, by area (%)*

Number last visit	Men				Women			
	Swansea	Sheffield	W/W	t	Swansea	Sheffield	W/W	t
1–5	40	75	20	64	44	49	13	47
6–10	46	7	23	18	25	38	51	34
11 or more	0	9	0	6	0	6·5	0	5
Not known	14	9	57	11	31	6·5	36	14
	(n =39)	(n =41)	(n =10)	(90)	(n =54)	(n =48)	(n =13)	(115)

TABLE 9.5 *Sessions per visit (%)*

Number last visit	Frequency of bingo					
	Men			Women		
	Regular	Sporadic	Occasional	Regular	Sporadic	Occasional
1–5	78	43	34	40	62	57
6–10	10	34	35	37	21	35
11 or more	0	17	20	7	0	0
Not known	12	6	11	16	17	8
	(n = 52)	(n = 13)	(n = 25)	(n = 65)	(n = 22)	(n = 28)

to one card only increases with age. Regularity of play is not linked with the number of cards per game, and since greater frequency of play is likely to be associated with the skill required to keep up with the caller on more than one card, we can infer strong social rather than 'compulsive' reasons for playing bingo. The length of time stayed was for the majority over an hour (but less than two). The most ever staked per game was, for the vast majority, 5s. or less – a sign that expenditure on bingo is inelastic relative to other forms of gambling, since the number of games per visit is strictly limited. The cost is uniform, and the number of cards one can manipulate is also strictly limited. It may well be this awareness of a 'ceiling' which renders bingo attractive to many players with small incomes or margins for leisure expenditure, since the possibility of a win exists in a context which precludes the risk of escalating stakes. Among the men, indeed, a third of the regular players set aside money for bingo though this link between budgeting and regularity of play does not occur among women, nor is it especially linked with household income.

In terms of *winnings*, very nearly half the sample had not won at all in the previous twelve months, and almost a quarter had *never* won at all. Frequency of play did not impinge on this result for men, though for women the more regular the play the less the

TABLE 9.6   *Use of bingo winnings by frequency*

Uses	Men				Women			
	Regular	Sporadic	Occa-sional	Total	Regular	Sporadic	Occa-sional	Total
Pocket	21	47	69	34	51	46	62	53
Rebet	0	0	2	*	*	0	0	*
Spree/gift	55	10	2	39	9	36	12	12
Save/home	24	43	27	27	41	18	26	35
	(n = 34)	(n = 7)	(n = 10)	(n = 51)	(n = 48)	(n = 11)	(n = 15)	(n = 74)

proportion who had not won in the last twelve months (as was to be expected all round). Largest winnings over this period for the remainder fell principally in the £3–£10 range, though some 10 per cent of men and 7 per cent of women had won at least one prize of over £10 in the year. Under 1 per cent had won over £100 in the year, though 5 per cent of the men claimed this large a win as their largest win ever. For women, though not for men, the proportion who had not won at all in the previous year decreased as income rose, the poorest winning least. The groups playing more games per visit tended to win proportionately more of the larger amounts, a result which was to be expected as was the case for those playing two cards rather than one. These winnings were simply merged with other cash by a third of the men and half of the women. A rather higher proportion of the men than the women spent their winnings on 'sprees' or gifts. A quarter of the men and a third of the women saved or spent their winnings on the home or family. An interesting result for women was that saving or spending winnings on the home, was associated with the lower household income – and with regular rather than less regular participation, a finding which is at least compatible with an instrumental approach to this form of gambling (see Table 9.6). For women also this trend broadly increased with the size of the amount won, whereas no such trend appeared for the men for whom the larger the amount, the greater the tendency to spend the sum involved on 'sprees' or gifts, especially for the regular players. Taken together, these results suggest a real contrast between men and women in the motivation underlying playing regularly.

Predicting bingo playing

(i) *What factors predict how often people play and how much they spend on bingo?*

Bingo was the one form of gambling which we expected to be

confined to women. The outcome has been that, of all forms of gambling considered, it alone produces virtually no initial variation by sex. While sex was not a useful predictor of frequency of playing or expenditure on bingo as such the runs nevertheless seemed to sort out homogeneous groupings which predominantly comprised either men or women. Here, *social class* was a very effective predictor: *not* being working class was practically enough to predict virtually no bingo playing. The two groupings of men only emerged after four variables – pub-going, football, family size and interview situation – which split unproductively, had been removed from the analyses. (Regular pub-going was the best predictor of how often people played.) A job factor, as in the betting and gaming runs, but this time that of job change, emerged as the best predictor of frequency. The frequent bingo players, playing three times that of all the sample, were those who preferred a previous job, had a very low or medium belief in luck and put a lot of effort into their job (Diagram 8). This group (8:11) mainly comprised men of the skilled working class with low job interest, a combination of characteristics which, *inter alia*, suggest that ambitious working-class people who see themselves as putting in a lot of hard graft for little reward, who are not at all politically inclined and who do not like using the home for leisure, find club bingo an attractive pursuit. The extent to which frequent participation by the young or middle-aged goes with being a man or a woman in this grouping is impossible to gauge, however; and this renders any inferences tentative in the extreme.

The other main grouping (8:7) derives from a split on current social class, isolating as frequent bingo players manual workers who were either women in full-time paid jobs or men whose wives came into that category. Other predictors here are those conventionally associated with bingo – middle-aged married women, stable working class and in full-time jobs, bereft of responsibility for children now grown up, in jobs to which they attach some interest but which carry no promotion prospects, with a collectivist approach to increasing income, seeing themselves as having 'enough' free time, conjugally role-segregated, not among the poorest members of the community but not well-off either, with strong conventionalism and belief in luck, who attach importance to religion but are not church-goers, whose education stopped at the elementary level, whose home life no longer takes up the slack in their leisure-time, and who have no hobbies.

Finally, extremely efficient prediction of *not* playing bingo flows from the initial majority job-change category via non-working-class membership (a residual group 8:4) which almost split over promotion prospects, those with either no paid job at all, or whose jobs have even the slightest promotion prospects producing a mean of almost zero, whereas those defining the promotion prospects as non-existent produced a mean almost as high as the population average.

In brief, non-working-class membership combined with jobs that offer even slight promotion prospects (or housewife) seems virtually to rule bingo out.

These patterns are elaborated in the analysis of bingo spending. The first predictor is social class, differentiating again manual workers from the rest (Diagram 9). The strongest predictor for these manual workers is the extent of TV watching, with those who watch least (less than alternate days) being those with a high mean expenditure. Nearly as powerful were the three job factors, as in the frequency analysis – a preference for a past job, having changed jobs voluntarily and low interest, but the next split was finally over religious affiliation, which appears to have little in common with these characteristics.

The combination which finally emerged (9:11) suggests the middle-aged and elderly respectable working class, but lacking the traditional working-class appetite for pub-going, football and hobbies, and perhaps finding in bingo the community and mild excitement others find in these contexts. The means for this grouping were by far the highest.

A second residual grouping (9:13) emerged from the more predictable splits entailing working-class background, TV-watching at least every other day, regular pub-going and a background of parental gambling, with a final split between those with very low *job autonomy* and the rest. High scores on bingo spending in this residual grouping were linked with Sheffield and were almost all accounted for by the youngest and young men. A medium or high belief in luck, high rather than low job effort, poor income, no or one dependent child only, stable working class or upward mobility, and no hobbies also produced high spending scores. This appears to overlap with one of the groups (8:17) differentiated in the frequency model, but distinguishing more clearly the impact of low job autonomy on participation in bingo.

Third, the non-working class grouping again proved residual, indicating the class-linked nature of bingo playing, and again the category of non-existent promotion prospects was quite a strong indication that would account for some of the remaining variation.

A residual grouping of some interest (9:6) is working-class people who watch TV at least daily but whose pub-going is infrequent. Mean bingo spending is only about half that for the population as a whole, but *within* the grouping higher means are associated with women rather than men, and a small grouping who have been educated at grammar school achieved by far the highest bingo mean as did the grouping who claimed they had too much free time. This suggests that better educated housewives in the upper working class who otherwise have few *leisure* outlets open to them find some attraction in playing bingo – they may well constitute the group who qualify for the bored housewife label that became commonplace in the rather patronizing commentaries on the popularity of bingo in the 1960s. Otherwise, however, the higher means (9:6) are associated with a large group of the elderly and the very poor.

(ii) *What predicts whether or not people play bingo?*

In this run the pre-eminence of social class as a predictor of bingo confirmed the previous analysis, especially since we did not separate men from women (Diagram 10). The next most powerful predictor was the one that has emerged consistently in pools, betting and gaming, that of parental gambling, which emerged as the most powerful predictor for the working-class grouping.

It is of interest to note that the difference in the mean proportions playing bingo between those both of whose parents gambled and those only one of whose parents gambled is as great as that between the latter and those whose parents did not gamble. Where this occurs, one might infer real cultural continuity in gambling, since neither parent arguably had opted out of a pro-gambling way of life. This kind of intergenerational continuity is not unique to the working class: parental gambling was also the third most effective predictor of participation in bingo for the middle class and self-employed group, with the split between those both of whose parents gambled and the rest. Here, in fact, the predictor which split the groups was belief in luck, a variable markedly associated with the working rather than the middle class. Since the belief in luck, and the fatalism that implies, appear to hold more sway among working class than among middle class, it may well be that what variance exists in playing bingo among the non-working class is explicable in terms of working-class *origins*: the results for social mobility, though predictively weak, give some credence to this. These findings are most compatible with that perspective on gambling which views it as one component in a working-class culture substantially at odds with the mores of middle-class life. They also illustrate the fallacy of generalizing such a perspective to forms of gambling which lack such clear-cut class associations. More than one interpretation of this perspective could find support, however, from the variance which flows from these initial splits. Given the attributes of being working class and parental gambling, the most powerful predictor is income, the poorer having a mean *twice* that of the most affluent. The poorer then divided over job factors – effort and interest. A combination of economic impoverishment and occupational dissatisfaction predict the extremely high mean participation of 72 per cent for those of working-class status and a background of parental gambling. Club bingo, therefore, seems to have a particular appeal for those who are badly off economically and occupationally within the working class. It could well be that its appeal is to recreate, via its combination of live entertainment and gambling, the ambience of working-class community whose loss this group in particular feels very heavily, for they especially have not benefited from the upheavals which have dismembered their communities.

Summary

Overall, then, being working class and sharing working-class leisure such as pub-going and football seem the most powerful predictors, with parental gambling again playing a definitive role in separating the heavy spenders from the rest. Within this framework, different groupings appear to exist which depart quite markedly from this pattern. The data reveal at least three groupings for men, and two for women, which possess some homogeneity. Among men, a relatively high recourse to this form of gambling seemed firstly to involve recent voluntary job change and high ambition that was thwarted in the job sphere; secondly, a grouping involving low job autonomy; and thirdly, one involving the middle-aged and elderly inversely associated with TV watching, which may indicate that club bingo is in some sense a way of resisting the pull to 'privatized' leisure, and which offers a clue to the more positive aspects of what has become the most exclusively working-class form of gambling.

Among women, two groupings emerged with high propensities for playing bingo: one which stemmed from full-time paid work, and which possibly involved the absence of a busy 'housewife' role in middle-age; and one of housewives whose education perhaps involved frustration at too domesticated a role, and who claimed to have 'too much' leisure. The latter of these groupings did not have a particularly high mean, but scored relatively highly in the context of a low-mean grouping.

10 Gaming machines

Distribution and description

Before 1960 gaming machines – colloquially known as fruit machines – were almost entirely confined to amusement arcades and a limited range of social clubs. The 1960 Betting and Gaming Act made possible their introduction on a far wider scale – so that within a few years of the Act a far greater number and variety of premises had installed them, generally by renting them from a vending company for a share of the profits. Along with club bingo, gaming machines have probably been the outlet for the main *extensions* of gambling since the Act.

In 1968, in terms of our sample, almost one in ten men – though only one in fifty women – played fruit machines regularly. Nearly one in three men and one in five women played them at least occasionally. For both men and women *age* stands out as the major factor in the variations: one in five of the youngest men played regularly compared with one in ten of the younger and one in twenty-five of the older group. The trend for the other indicators

TABLE 10.1 *Proportions using gaming machines*

	Cumulative frequency	Sheffield	Swansea	Wanstead/ Woodford	Total %
Men	Regularly	7	13	7·5	9
	Occasionally	27	30	37	29
		(n = 269)	(n = 310)	(n = 237)	
Women	Regularly	2	2·5	2	2
	Occasionally	15	21	23	17
		(n = 378)	(n = 418)	(n = 343)	

was of roughly the same order. Given this age-trend, one can probably rule out any idea of the group who came 'of age' in the 1960–8 period being socialized uniquely into pro-gambling behaviour and attitudes. It appears, rather, that the attractions of fruit machine playing, whatever they are, are inversely associated with growing older. These machines might be associated with the type of game Caillois[1] termed 'vertigo', i.e. games involving a sense of disequilibrium, temporary loss of control and producing a sense of chaos – only for order to be restored, 'normalcy' to be rendered more welcome, at the close of play. 'Vertigo' finds its major expression in the fun fair, the horror film, the thriller, the pursuit of certain sports. The 1960s have enriched its repertoire in the field of youth culture – strobe lights, psychedelic drugs, 'heavy' electronic sound – all can be said to produce a vertiginous effect, in Caillois's sense of the term. Playing a fruit machine is a far cry from these, but it *can* be seen as answering to the same tenets of experience: the drums speeding round *do* have a slightly dizzying effect, the player *is* temporarily out of control, the check given to each spool in turn does have the apparent outcome of order plucked from chaos. The possible bonus of a pay-off roots the game quite literally in the small change of everyday life. The game might be said to represent the routinization of vertigo, and as such to be inherently more attractive to the young. For with 'growing older' comes a distaste for vertigo, a preference for *uninterrupted* order and at least the illusion of control.

Speculative as these notions are, they must at least accord with the difference in rates of gaming on fruit machines between men and women. At the level of occasional play, these differences are not large, but in terms of regular play there is a 1 to 5 difference. This *could* be accounted for in terms of *opportunity*: women do not regularly frequent the milieux in which machines are available to anything like the same extent as men. In that event, the difference can be explained away, leaving age as the only major variable calling for explanation. For on other variables, it is the *lack* of variation which commands attention. Social class could hardly make less impact, for all the men fall within the range of between 6 to 11 per cent regularly using gaming machines.

In terms of *spending* more variation emerges, though subjective estimates of profit/loss produced derisory and almost certainly underestimated figures (but it only needs one in four of the adult population to lose an average of £4 p.a. each on fruit machines to produce a £40m 'take' for the vendors and proprietors – roughly the figure suggested by the Churches' Council in Gambling) (see Table 10.2). Men and women tend to stake on average roughly similar amounts occasionally; the more regular figures are difficult

TABLE 10.2 *Expenditure on fruit machines*

| | Turnover p.a. | | | Profit/loss p.a. | |
Frequency	Regular or Sporadic		Occasional	Sporadic	Occasional
Men	(n = 94)	£40	£26 (n = 137)	− £2	− £1
Women	(n = 34)	£125	£20 (n = 102)	− £1	− £0·4
Both	(n = 128)	£62	£23·5 (n = 239)	− £1·5	− £1

(Unweighted)

to interpret because of a few freak cases of turnover exceeding £1,000. Age does discriminate as with participation, amounts declining from £37 for the youngest to £7 for the elderly, yet the highest mean turnover occurs, surprisingly, among men whose marriages are over − £136. Expenditure (unlike participation) also tends to decline with increasing formal education, from £34 for those who left at the minimum school-leaving age to £8 for those who stayed on for two years or more beyond that point. The affluent men staked more; the poorest and the most affluent women staked more than the intermediary. Whilst upper middle-class women staked as little as £3 p.a., the other social classes were uniform in their stakes. The mobile men spent more than the stable, whereas the stable middle-class women (1 per cent only) spent £53 on average. Roman Catholics spent less by far than the other religions or non-affiliated. In sum, the only safe conclusion seems to be that the groups usually associated in theories of gambling with both higher participation and higher expenditure than the norm, i.e. the stable working class and Roman Catholic − are amongst the lowest participants in this form of gambling by the two major indicators − participation and turnover.

Fruit machines in a leisure context

Do any items clarify the age distribution of playing fruit machines? Our indicators are probably too broadly conceived to show up any three-way link between age, playing fruit machines, and uses of leisure. Frequency of playing sport seems directly associated with fruit machine play, as is to be expected given the greater involvement of the young in sport. The more passive inducement in sports which we have termed 'watching' and 'following' show little by way of consistent trends in relation to playing these machines. Involvement in racing is certainly *not* associated with playing fruit machines: the group most prone is that betting only once every several years on the major races, rather than those betting more regularly. Indeed, the most consistent links with fruit machine playing emerge with 'entertainment', where regular playing is associated with regular involvement in all forms of entertainment including pubs and clubs. The latter is to be expected, since they are the main locations of fruit machines. The former – which brackets together such forms as 'eating out', cinema-going, theatre-going, etc. – is not so obvious in itself, though it becomes so given the greater involvement of the young in those forms of leisure pursuit. By the same token, we can account for the slight inverse relationship between fruit machine play and 'do-it-yourself' activities. The inverse relationship with political and/or community activity is not so sharply accounted for, and provides further support for the view that this orientation tends to be incompatible with a gambling orientation. There are slight but interesting direct associations between fruit machine play and 'bringing work home'; and also family visiting. It seems that the 'work' and 'family' orientations in leisure are quite compatible with the constellations of interest underlying fruit machine play. But without controlling for age, we can do little more than note these trends.

Social relations and playing fruit machines

Playing fruit machines is apparently an activity which takes place nearer home than work. By far the majority normally played on machines near their home. The only exceptions were the youngest men who played near their work: this may reflect a greater detachment from the home as a base for leisure and a corresponding propensity for leisure activities to centre on the workplace. It

TABLE 10.3 *Location of fruit machines (%)*

Near	Sex	
	Men	Women
Home	56	65
Work	23	4
Both	5	0
Town centre	*	1
Out of town	4	14
Other	4	14
Not known	11	16
	(n = 115)	(n = 50)

chimes with that for betting. The *sorts of place* in which machines are usually played are enormously varied, but pubs, social clubs and working-men's clubs account for about three-quarters of the range. Amusement centres account for a surprisingly low percentage – 3 per cent, though our survey preceded the sudden emergence of many more amusement centres, at least in London, in the last two to three years. Even so, the availability of these machines in the places to which people resort regularly for entertainment seems far and away the main determinant of their habitual use for the vast majority of players – the amusement centres, whatever their impact initially and environmentally, are unlikely to make much of a dent on these figures unless their growth continues at an astronomic rate. Only 3 per cent of men who regularly played the machines in Sheffield gave pubs as their usual location, compared with about 40 per cent in other areas; in Sheffield the majority probably use working-men's clubs. This was not, however, the case with women, one in four of whom in the Sheffield area gave pubs and working-men's clubs alike as the usual location. Men in the stable middle class play machines almost entirely in golf clubs (42 per cent), social clubs (29 per cent) and gaming clubs (24 per cent). Fruit machine vendors seem to have been almost as successful as sanitary engineers in installing their conveniences in just about every public location except work.

Playing fruit machines seems ideally designed for the solitary player whiling away a few minutes in the pub or club, and, *lacking* company, killing time over a drink or whilst waiting for friends to turn up. Our data show the rather different picture of 80 per cent of the regular men and over 90 per cent of the regular women playing alone on no occasion out of the last five sessions at a machine. Of those who *had* among men, regular were three times as likely as sporadic players to play occasionally on their own – 18 per cent as compared with 6 per cent – and these were more likely to be middle-aged than young. Three-quarters of the men and two-thirds of the women had played on at least one occasion in the past five with *friends*; a third of the men and over half of the women with *family*. The kind of company in which men play fruit machines is, therefore, far more likely to be friends than family; whereas for women either family *or* friends are equally likely. With both men and women, the family orientation grows with age, and vice versa for friends. The main point is that people who play fruit machines regularly do so in company rather than on their own. This seems to rule out the simple 'pathology' view of fruit machine play. If there is any element of compulsion or addiction involved, it is *group* compulsion rather than individual, a somewhat unlikely explanation; and though almost one in five of the regular men players had *at least once* of their last five sessions at a machine played it alone, a far smaller minority would habitually do so.

For men, over half those playing occasionally compared with only 5 per cent of those playing regularly could give no assessment of the last number of times they played the machine. A high percentage of those who claimed to have had only one game on their last session – a dubious figure since the question was ambiguous – would have also claimed to have spent over 3s. on that session. In fact, only 12 per cent of the 23 per cent of men claimed to have spent that much on a single game, compared with 28 per cent of those playing six times or more on their last session – 28 per cent in fact spending over 5s. on the session. The finding that 54 per cent of those playing six times or more often spent 3s. or less *per session* can only be explained by assuming that replies took into account incidental winnings, which are fairly frequent in any session at a fruit machine. Our attempt to elicit replies on the simple-sounding issues of how many times players play per session, and how much they *spent* per session, failed to make certain crucial distinctions which, *even if they had been made,* would still have presented respondents with formidable problems of recall and calculation. As things stand, all we can really say is that our data show that, for *men* who play regularly, a third played the machine only once in their last session, almost half played between two and five times, and about a fifth *only* played six games on their last session and almost half spent *over* 3s. on that occasion. The amount of time spent on the last fruit machine session supports the view that rather more replies were given in terms of sessions than of times the machine was actually operated. Half the regular players spent *over* ten minutes at the machine, and this is hardly compatible with only 18 per cent of the men and 30 per

TABLE 10.4 *Time spent on fruit machines*

	Men	Women
Less than 5 mins	20	20
5–10 mins	14	13
11 or more	30	22
Not known	36	45
	100%	100%
	(n = 231)	(n = 204)

TABLE 10.5   *Most spent on a fruit machine (%)*

	Men	Women
1s.–5s.	66	76
6s.–19s. 9d.	22	11
£1 or more	3	1
Not known	9	2

cent of the women playing six times or more. However, fruit machines do vary in the times taken per game: while some cannot be influenced by the player at all once the spools are in motion, in others a spool can be restarted, a 'free' game can be won, etc., thus varying somewhat the amounts of time spent per game.

The 'ceiling' for spending per session on fruit machines was, for the vast majority, £1, and for two-thirds of the men and three-quarters of the women 5s. or so: only 3 per cent of the men and 1 per cent of the women had ever spent over £1 on a fruit machine at any *one* time. The men who showed a greater propensity than average to have exceeded the 5s. 'ceiling' were the young; the regular as distinct from the irregular players; the most affluent and (exceeding the £1 mark) those playing in pubs, golf clubs and social clubs (men) and gaming clubs (women). For men, higher proportions than average had staked over 5s. at some time in gaming clubs and working-men's clubs. By contrast, a third of the men and 80 per cent of the women claimed to have won on a single occasion sums of over £1, a quarter of the men and 3 per cent of the women in the past twelve months. Of the regular players, 60 per cent of the men and 26 per cent of the women made this claim. For the regular players, therefore, the pattern of rarely spending over 5s. per session but occasionally winning over £1 on jackpots, etc., interspersed with frequent winnings, could well blur completely any possibility of calculating even within limits of several games on a fruit machine just how much had been won and how much lost. This may explain why, for such an ephemeral and casual-seeming activity as playing a fruit machine, as many as 28 per cent of the men playing regularly and 17 per cent of the women 'set aside' money for the game: a trend mainly concentrated among the poorer and working class. At a guess, the money for fruit machine play is 'set aside' not in the sense of 'budgeting ahead' for a leisure activity but in the sense of taking note of the amount one is going to spend on the game at the outset and stopping when that amount is spent: knowing how much you 'start out with' rather than planning ahead, in order that *some* check is kept on

TABLE 10.6   *Use of winnings by size (%)*

Use	Not known	*Size of win* 1s.–5s.	1s.–19s. 9d.	£1 or more
Pocket	76	28	45	49
Rebet	15	49	25	4
Spree/gift	9	19	27	18
Save/home	0	4	3	29
	(n = 16)	(n = 60)	(n = 27)	(n = 14)

expenditure. If this is the case, then the vast majority of fruit machine players probably have little idea as to the amounts they have in fact spent on the game. This view is at least corroborated by the data on use of winnings. Overall, taking the largest single win over the past twelve months, only about 10 per cent of the winners, men or women, saved or spent their winnings on the home, 40 per cent of the men and a third of the women simply pocketed their winnings. A quarter of the men and almost half of the women rebet their winnings, and a fifth of the men and just over a tenth of the women spent them on 'sprees' or 'gifts'. In view of the extent to which pubs instal gaming machines which take only tokens that can be spent on drink alone, the 'spree/gift' choice was, for players in some pubs and gaming clubs, the only alternative to rebetting the money. The greatest determinant of the use of winnings again appears to be the amount won: by far the highest rate of winnings which were saved or spent on the home, etc., for wins of £1 or more, and by far the highest proportion of winnings *under 5s.* were rebet. The extent to which this trend determines the greater propensity of the poorest men to rebet their winnings, as is also the case for the occasional as distinct from the regular betters, is not known. The significant feature of playing fruit machines, especially as far as the poor are concerned, is the temptation to fritter away small amounts of money over a period of time which can almost by definition never produce a win of the size or in a setting commensurate with doing anything except rebetting or buying a few drinks.

Predicting the use of gaming machines

(i) *What factors predict how often people use gaming machines?*

The analysis of frequency revealed three groupings of people

191

associated with gaming machines, two tentatively linked to frequent, and one with infrequent, play. The first split to occur was not on a variable that had predominated in previous frequency analyses. It was 'women in work' differentiating these to whom it did not apply from the rest (Diagram 11) the former being unmarried men or a small number of those whose marriages were over.[2] The significance of this split is that it did not occur between the youngest and the rest but between men not involved in marital relationships and the rest. The non-married men played seven times as often as the rest and split next into those watching football sporadically and the rest. Those who watched sporadically were characterized by being young, upper working-class status, upward mobility, recent job change, an individualistic approach to increasing income and dissatisfaction with their free time. These may point to a pattern of individualism in work as a career and its intrinsic interest which cuts across traditional lines of class association. This is congruent with a sense of restlessness which is acted out in leisure.

That the split occurred between those watching football sporadically and the rest may indicate that where attachment to traditional class leisure forms is weakened, but not eliminated, the pull to restlessness in leisure is greatest, since class attachments have been shaken but not broken. This possibility is strengthened by the fact that the football predictor achieves two splits, the first described above, the second between those watching football occasionally and the rest (11:4). While nothing is beyond coincidence, it is at least *unusual* for this predictor to prove so powerful twice running for the non-married men. This time, however, the group singled out as relatively frequent players are middle-aged or elderly stable working-class men (who do not record either parent as gambling) who had never had a job they preferred to their current job, who assert that they have *enough* free time and who don't know how to increase their income. A high belief in luck was the next most powerful predictor for this split.

The second grouping emerged out of the married men, whose mean frequency of play was much lower (11:2). Their first predictor was pub-going with irregularity associated with non-use of gaming machines, a circular argument if pubs are seen as the main locale. In fact, we established in the previous section that they are not the sole context. The regular pub-goers then split over job autonomy with low autonomy, and a positive evaluation of one's job, associated with frequent gaming (11:7). At first this is linked to being working class, but on subsequent splits it emerges that some upper middle class also rate on low job autonomy. Apparently, frequent play may be linked to the conflicts peculiar to high job expectations and low autonomy.

192

The third grouping consists of infrequent players made up of all married men *and* all women who go to pubs infrequently. In this, as in other forms of gaming, pub-going seems a crucial indicator of social processes germane to gambling.

(ii) *What factors predict whether people play gaming machines?*

Separate runs were made for men and women. The two most effective predictors for men were *age* and then *parental gambling*. This confirms the latter variable's predominance as a predictor of gambling.

The inverse relationship with age affords the best clue to the attractions of this form of gambling, though the link with parental gambling again suggests the importance of a prior orientation to gambling flowing from family background (Diagram 12). Of all the forms of gambling, gaming machines offer least scope for substantial or steady reward for the investment of skill or effort, and little scope for *interpersonal* character contests. The limited autonomy allowed the player rests almost wholly on physical dexterity, and on quick reflexes, and then only in the more complex machines. (Observation, not the survey data, suggests, though, that players frequently attempt to 'read' a machine, passing from one to another until they settle on one that 'feels' right – or 'getting to know' a machine in a place they frequent.) But the decline in gaming-machine play with age may simply reflect the learning process at work, in that the 'fun' content is quickly exhausted and the reward content is negligible. The younger the player, the less likely the novelty will have worn off.

For the youngest men, parental gambling (of both parents) is the best predictor of high proportions participating (50 per cent). Other strong predictors are affiliation to the Church of England, medium to high risk-taking, and an individualistic approach to increasing income. The other combination of traits which stands out most clearly with high proportions who use gaming machines are the experience of social mobility, and high rather than low conventionalism and risk-taking. It is just possible to discern some link here between an individualistic world-view and concentration on this form of gambling. In slightly different sequence, these results of age and parental gambling are comparable with those for women.

11 All gambling

Total gambling: distribution and description

The proportions participating at least occasionally and, separately, regularly in each type of gambling surveyed are shown again in Table 11.1, as a summary of Chapters 6–10. How are these figures related to each other? Do the same people participate in each type of gambling or is each a very distinctive activity? Clearly there are differences between each type of gambling in the extent to which it combines with other forms. In Tables 11.2, we summarize the findings on how far gambling is a composite activity. Doing the pools is obviously an activity that does not link closely with other gambling – almost 50 per cent of both men and women who do the pools engage in no other form of gambling at all regularly. It is associated most nearly with general betting or use of betting shops, especially for men, where almost a quarter do both. About a sixth of women who do the pools also play bingo.

Use of betting shops is at the opposite extreme. Few of those who use betting shops do *nothing else*: only 6 per cent of both men and women, but a quarter of the women. Over half of the regular betters also do the pools regularly, and almost half bet in other ways occasionally. Over a quarter play games in pubs regularly or regularly play bingo. Women also combine this with other gambling – 70 per cent also do the pools and over half play bingo. So betting in shops is not a unique activity.

Gaming in pubs and on fruit machines are also not clearly isolated activities – only 12 per cent regularly just use fruit machines and 16 per cent just game in pubs. For men, these activities overlap with pools most closely – over 50 per cent of both groups do the pools regularly. For women who use fruit machines this is also

194

true but for women who game in pubs half do no other form of gambling.

Finally, playing bingo is a fairly separate activity – over half the women and almost a quarter of the men do nothing else. For a third of the women bingo playing is combined with regular pools; this is true for 45 per cent of the men. For the men, almost 40 per cent also use betting shops.

It seems possible then to examine the characteristics of those who gamble on one or more forms as a composite rather than a discrete activity. In an attempt to construct a more comprehensive set of gambling indicators than those simply covering involvement in a specific type of gambling, we grouped together those taking part regularly in any of the nine forms and constructed a typology (see Chapter 3). We then tabulated the two gambling indicators – Type I and Type II – against the major socio-economic and attitude variables. The main effect of using the more exhaustive Type II indicator is to reduce the proportions of 'non' gamblers to as low as 8 per cent for men and 15 per cent for women, compared with 21 per cent for men and 50 per cent for women on the more restricted Type I indicator (see Table 11.3). If we had been completely exhaustive in our coverage and had included premium bonds, betting by proxy, and speculative investment on the Stock Exchange, we would arguably have approached *zero* for no gambling at all. However, it is debatable whether an indicator which includes the majority of the population who buy raffle tickets

TABLE 11.1   *Forms of gambling: proportions participating*

	At least occasionally		Regularly	
	Men	*Women*	*Men*	*Women*
Pools	52·5	26·2	47·4	22·1
Betting shops	27	7	17	2
Bet by agent/runner	8	5	4	1
Bet on-course horses	9	3·5	0	*
Bet on-course dogs	4	1	2	1
Bet on Ascot Gold Cup	20	10		
Bet on Derby	44	27		
Bet on Grand National	46	28		
Private bets	15·7	0·7	2·3	0·1
Bingo	17	16	11	10
Pub gaming	19·7	1·9	16·5	1·1
Casino gaming	3·5	1·5	0·1	0·3
Private gaming (with stakes)	15	9	7	4
Gaming machines	29	17	9	2

H*

TABLE 11.2.1   *Proportions of those who do the pools regularly who gamble in other ways (percentages)*

	Men	Women	Both
None	43·9	56·9	47·9
Regular bet shop	20·5	5·3	15·1
Regular pub games	18·2	0·9	12·0
Regular bingo	10·4	16·0	12·4
Regular gaming machines	10·1	4·2	8·0
Occasional general bets	23·5	22·3	23·1
Occasional casinos	4·0	1·3	3·1
Private bets	13·4	0·8	8·9

TABLE 11.2.2   *Proportions of those who use betting shops regularly who gamble in other ways (percentages)*

	Men	Women	Both
None	3·9	24·7	6·1
Regular pools	56·6	69·7	57·9
Regular pub games	29·2	8·4	27·0
Regular bingo	25·3	53·3	28·3
Regular gaming machines	18·8	3·9	17·2
Occasional general bets	47·0	10·4	43·2
Occasional casinos	4·6	—	4·1
Occasional private bets	31·9	—	28·6

TABLE 11.2.3   *Proportions of those who game in pubs regularly who gamble in other ways (percentages)*

	Men	Women	Both
None	12·7	50·4	15·5
Regular pools	52·2	18·5	50·0
Regular bet shop	30·3	12·6	29·0
Regular bingo	19·8	25·2	20·2
Regular gaming machines	20·2	—	18·7
Occasional general betting	36·5	24·4	35·6
Occasional casinos	10·8	—	10·0
Occasional private bets	35·3	5·9	33·1

TABLE 11.2.4 *Proportions of those who play bingo regularly who gamble in other ways*

	Men	Women	Both
None	21·1	51·3	36·9
Regular pools	44·5	34·8	39·4
Regular bet shop	39·3	8·8	23·4
Regular pub games	29·6	2·8	15·6
Regular gaming machines	33·8	11·5	22·1
Occasional general betting	15·3	7·2	11·1
Occasional casinos	5·7	1·0	3·2
Occasional private bets	29·7	0·9	14·7

TABLE 11.2.5 *Proportions of those who use gaming machines regularly who gamble in other ways*

	Men	Women	Both
None	11·2	15·3	12·0
Regular pools	54·8	49·5	53·7
Regular bet shop	36·9	3·5	30·1
Regular bingo	42·7	62·3	46·7
Regular pub games	38·3	—	30·5
Occasional general bets	10·7	24·4	13·5
Occasional casinos	12·1	6·0	10·9
Occasional private bets	25·0	1·1	20·2

TABLE 11.3 *Indicators of gambling*

Gambling	Type I		Type II	
	Men	Women	Men	Women
High	22	7	27	11
Medium	43	26	45	38
Low	13	17	20	36
Nil	21	50	8	15
	100%	100%	100%	100%

annually as 'low' gamblers, is of great utility. At any rate, we need to take *both* into account in our assessment of the social distribution of gambling; and distributions obtained by the two typologies are broadly similar.

Our main focus is on the distribution of those rated as 'high'

197

TABLE 11.4   *Area (men only) (%)*

Gambling		Type I			Type II		
		Sheffield	Swansea	W & W	Sheffield	Swansea	W & W
High	(n = 119)	18	25	10	24	30	13
Medium	(n = 336)	47	42	41	48	45	44
Low	(n = 138)	12	13	22	24	16	33
Nil	(n = 223)	23	20	27	4	9	10

TABLE 11.5   *Area (women only) (%)*

Gambling		Type I			Type II		
		Sheffield	Swansea	W & W	Sheffield	Swansea	W & W
High	(n = 53)	6	8	3	9	12	5
Medium	(n = 241)	24	27	21	37	39	27
Low	(n = 222)	18	16	23	43	32	51
Nil	(n = 621)	52	49	53	10	17	17

and rated jointly 'high' or 'medium' gamblers. Taking Type I first, the obvious contrast is that by *sex*: men are three times as likely as women to be rated 'high' gamblers, twice as likely to be rated 'high' or 'medium'. The variable which stood out as a relatively powerful discriminant for specific gambling especially among men – *age* – shows surprising uniformity; except that the elderly, are markedly less likely to be rated 'high' than the others (8 as opposed to over 20 per cent). However, the youngest men *are no more gambling-prone* than older (except the elderly) for *both* high and medium and on both indicators. One explanation for this is that the older are more specialized than younger gamblers, who take part in more forms of gambling regularly but who do not take part in any one activity with the same intensity of involvement as the older.

Social class, another powerful discriminator of specific gambling, especially bingo and use of betting shops, also presents far more uniformity than might have been assumed. Ratings for men of 'high' and 'medium' involvement are much the same, about 20 and 40 per cent for both lower middle class and working class groups. Only the proportion of upper middle-class men as highly involved is lower (11 per cent). The stable middle class is only one-third as involved (with only 7 per cent) in 'high' gambling as those rated 'neither' class or stable 'working class'. The stable middle class again stand out as relatively uninvolved in gambling (40 per cent nil and 22 per cent low for men and 69 per cent nil for women) but there is little difference either for men or women between the downwardly mobile, the upwardly mobile and the stable working class. Education shows slightly greater variation in the expected direction in that men whose school was elementary or secondary modern were over twice as likely to be rated 'high' gamblers as those whose school was grammar, comprehensive, private or other (over 20 per cent versus 10 per cent). This was not the case for women. Part-time did not differ from those with no further education: but those with any full-time further education were distinctly less likely to be rated 'high' or 'medium' gamblers. Men and women did not differ. Only those men with qualifications or who left school two years after minimum leaving age were markedly less prone to gamble; for women, the trend was from 'high' to 'low' gambling with increasing formal educational attainment and involvement.

Religious affiliation and church attendance show trends in the direction we have been led to expect. Roman Catholics do indeed turn out to have the highest proportion (36 per cent) of 'high' gamblers, twice that for Nonconformists (17 per cent) and higher than Anglicans (21 per cent). But those disclaiming *any* religious affiliation also have a rate of 23 per cent and the outstandingly low rate for 'high' gambling involvement is that of 'other' religious affiliations – mainly Jews. Also, even the Roman Catholic rate for 'medium' gambling involvement (27 per cent) is much lower than that for Anglicans or those disclaiming affiliation to a church (both about 48 per cent). The trend for women on affiliation but not attendance is quite out of line with theories predicting that Protestants would in general tend more to gambling than non-Protestants. A higher percentage of men who go to church regularly than sporadically are rated 'high' gamblers (18 per cent to 10 per cent).

Income shows little variation, save that the poorest (10 per cent compared to over 30 per cent as high and 38 per cent versus about 45 per cent as medium) are rather *less* involved in gambling than the rest; but this is bound to be explained to some extent by the preponderance of the elderly. Among women, it is, if anything, the *most affluent* who display the least propensity to gamble. Marital status makes surprisingly little difference to gambling participation. Finally, in terms of *area*, the differences between Swansea and Sheffield are very slight, and the lower figures in the 'high' category for Wanstead and Woodford are almost certainly a reflection of the greater proportion of middle class in that area (see Table 11.4).

To summarize, we are left with a surprisingly uniform pattern of the distribution of gambling. Given that men are twice to three times as likely to be regular gamblers (in the weak sense of weekly involvement or the stronger sense of involvement two to three times per week) then we are left with a rather invariant pattern of rates of involvement in gambling *as a whole* by the rest of the population, save that the elderly are far less frequent gamblers than the rest; that the established and upper middle class are less prone to gambling, as are the very poor; and that the advantages of an élite education do seem to predispose against gambling on a regular basis. It is possible that our indicators were so constructed as to blur, rather than sharpen, the contours of involvement in gambling activity by different frequencies.[1] But it seems more likely that gambling taken as a whole transcends these socio-economic cleavages, which to some extent determine the type of gambling pursued and the type of institutional context within which that pursuit takes place, rather than the overall pattern of rates of involvement in gambling in general,

This conclusion is reinforced in terms of the attitudinal variables, whose yield is far lower than might have been assumed *a priori*. There is a slight and non-linear association between a generalized preference for *risk-taking* in everyday life and propensity to gamble (about 50 per cent have high ratings on risks for almost each indicator of gambling) with a difference in involvement of only 8 per cent for men and 9 per cent for women as between 'high' gamblers and 'non' gamblers. 'Conventionalism' – which might be defined as indicating a preference for a settled and hierarchical society – at least yields a weak relationship for men between preference for 'conventionalism' and propensity to gamble, 63 per cent of 'high' gamblers as compared with 50 per cent of 'low' gamblers falling in the two higher 'conventionalism' categories. A 'belief in luck' seems only randomly associated with gambling on these tabulations.

It may be of course that these indicators, extracted from factor analysis, were *too* diffuse to discriminate at all. But this was not borne out by charting their distribution by four key socio-economic variables – age, social class, mobility and income. 'Risk-taking' preferences were monotonically associated with age for both men and women and for men this relationship was linear, even if only weakly (though this factor was a-symmetrical when tabulated against the other variables). Likewise, 'conventionalism' was strongly associated – inversely – with age: among men, 34 per cent of the youngest, 45 per cent of the younger, 66 per cent of the older and 76 per cent of the elderly rated 'high' in terms of 'conventionalism'. In terms of income, the poorer and poorest were more 'conventionalism'-oriented than the more affluent. The propensity to 'conventionalism' also grew the lower the socio-economic group status – a trend far more marked for men than for women. Finally, the established middle class were far less 'conventionalism'-prone than other groups, especially the downwardly mobile and the stable working class. This paradox, that those better placed in the social hierarchy than others are less constrained by respect for 'authority' and stability, is a familiar one – we will not enter into its ramifications here, being mainly concerned to note the amount of variation produced by the socio-economic factors when tabulated against the attitudinal indicators compared with those produced by the gambling indicators. 'Belief in luck' behaved similarly, and strengthens our view that while the attitudinal factors may not have accounted for more than a slight fraction of the variation in gambling, this is *not* due to their being too diffuse to operate as factors at all. (The reverse, of course, also applies – that involvement in gambling was expected to make some impact on the attitudinal variables, but – in the event – did not.)

Predicting variations in gambling

The one-stage analyses of both frequency and expenditure, taking as the dependent variable the sum of the five forms of gambling – pools, betting, gaming, club bingo and gaming machines – did not reveal any significant predictors of gambling.[2] The only important finding was that men participate almost four times as often as women; men having 123 gambling sessions a year compared to women's 35 sessions per year. Some predictors of note were job factors, pub-going, watching football and parental gambling. The expenditure analysis was rendered difficult by the lack of comparability of categories of spending between types of gambling.

The two-stage analyses of whether or not people gamble, and of what factors best predicted gambling with the non-gambers excluded, were more productive. Data for men and women were run separately and both produce interesting results. The most effective predictor of *men's* gambling is church attendance (excluding that for baptisms, weddings and funerals) a result in line with Devereux's theory and seemingly at odds with the previous class-based or job-specific theories generated. The only other close variable was again parental gambling (Diagram 13). Since the overall proportion participating was 75·9 per cent, at least *some* participation in *some* form of gambling is clearly normative. Hence it is better to view relatively frequent church attendance as a predictor of non-gambling rather than infrequency as a predictor of gambling. Church attendance appears as the clearest indicator of commitment to a system of beliefs at odds with gambling.

TABLE 11.6   *Men: frequent church-goers – gambling participation*

Religious affiliation*	per cent p.a.	n	s. d.
'Other' affiliation	12·1	17	32·7
Nonconformists	27·5	38	44·6
Church of England	36·3	29	48·1
Roman Catholic	66·9	27	47·0

* Two cases of *no* religious affiliation were included as 'frequent' church-goers – by no means an impossibility, but we have excluded them.

That men can cheerfully embrace theoretically quite antithetical belief systems is revealed by the selection of 'belief in luck', when frequent church-going is held constant, as the most effective predictor, 67 per cent of those with a medium to high, compared with only 25 per cent of those with a low belief in luck, participating in gambling.

Controlling for frequent church attendance also produced another result in line with Devereux's theory: the higher propensity to gamble of Roman Catholics as compared with Protestants (Table 11.6). It is worth noting yet another example of a result which has cropped up systematically throughout: the very low means for gambling for those categorized as affiliated to religions other than the major institutional churches. *Sectarianism* is perhaps the strongest alternative to gambling that has emerged in this survey.

Given frequent church-going, other categories with low means for gambling proportions are: lower and upper middle class; the upwardly mobile and the stable middle class; those educated at grammar school and privately; the married; those who rated their job effort (in terms of physical or mental wear and tear) low or very low; those involved most frequently in political and/or community activity; and those watching TV less than daily. This constellation of attributes characterizes the Protestant middle-class core as *least* prone to gambling, a result emphatically in line with Devereux's theorization. The only qualification is whether it is appropriate to control for church attendance in assessing his theoretical framework, which posited Protestant as distinct from non-Protestant in broader terms. It could be argued, though, that 'C. of E.' is so clichéd a reply to questions on religious affiliation that control for some firmer criterion of commitment is called for. However, whilst church-going is a crucial intervening variable in the relation between Protestantism and gambling, this is not the case for Roman Catholics, whose participation in gambling is much

TABLE 11.7   *Men: infrequent church-goers or non-attenders –*
gambling participation

Religious affiliation	Mean per cent p.a.	n	s. d.
Roman Catholic	59·9	29	49·0
'Other' affiliation	74·0	11	43·8
Church of England	79·1	352	40·7
Nonconformist	81·8	84	38·6
No formal affiliation	84·2	227	36·5

the same irrespective of the extent of their church attendance
(Table 11.7). There is no doubt, however, that the best predictors
of men not gambling are marriage, frequent church attendance
and a disbelief in luck, the *combination* of which produces a mean
proportion of only 12·2 per cent. This would be even lower if we
had been able to control for social class or social mobility.

Turning to the sequence which flowed from infrequent church
attendance (13:3) the most powerful predictor is *parental gambling,*
the lower of the two gambling proportions being 70·4 per cent
for those with neither parent having gambled. This is also in line
with our findings for specific forms of gambling. The best predictor
in this grouping was *involvement in hobbies.* If we ignore the tiny
numbers who were exceptionally heavily involved in hobbies,
to the extent of pursuing them more than two hours daily, the
relationship between hobbies and gambling, for this group, is an
inverse one, suggesting that pursuit of a hobby involves a set of
satisfactions in some respects alternative to those involved in
gambling. (This relationship broadly holds for the whole sample,
but less strongly.) Controlling for this variable, the best predictor
is job autonomy, those with high job autonomy having a low

TABLE 11.8   *Men: infrequent attenders at church, neither*
parent having gambled – gambling participation

Involvement in hobbies	Mean per cent p.a.	n	s. d.
0–2 hrs daily	46·6	30	49·9
Weekly but not daily	53·6	51	49·9
Less than weekly	95·3	265	43·2
At least 2 hrs daily	100·0	3	0·0

gambling mean of 26·8 per cent (13:8). This combination does suggest that, even when non-attachment to belief systems which seek to preclude gambling opens up the probability of high gambling participation, the lack of stimulus from parental gambling, and a high degree of scope for character and personality expression in both work *and* leisure do preclude gambling to a very great extent. Those lacking such scope in either *work* (13:19) *or* leisure (13:7) produce far higher means – 75·8 per cent and 66·8 per cent. Those pursuing hobbies but lacking high job-autonomy split on another leisure indicator, 'fun' leisure, between those only rarely or never enjoying these forms of entertainment and those doing so at least sporadically.

Despite pursuit of hobbies, two clear alternative responses to, or correlates of, the lack of real autonomy at work seem to emerge, distinguishing those who actively seek enjoyable entertainment, of which gambling appears to be part, from those who do not.

The grouping, predominantly comprising those who did not pursue hobbies at all or only infrequently, divided over the amount of time they had spent in the same job, those spending over twenty years producing the lower gambling mean. Low mean correlates were social stability and a collectivist perception of increasing income. This grouping (13:8) was predominantly over forty-five years old and split next on social mobility. This suggests being thoroughly settled in a job and *not* experiencing social mobility in middle-age makes for exceptionally low participation in gambling.

High risk-taking also went with low means of gambling for this group, which emphasizes yet again that there is no simple relationship between gambling and risk-taking. It may well be that the experience of spending most of one's working life in the same job and staying socially in the same status operates to reduce the attractiveness of gambling, whether that attraction stems from the need to place one's character at risk or potentially to change one's life situation.

Those spending less time in the same job are best differentiated by the *luck* factor, again with those *disbelieving* producing the lower mean. The residual groupings which close this sequence suggest that home-centredness, indicated by the frequency of certain household tasks, is *not* at odds with high participation in gambling; and that excessive job-effort does not produce 'compensatory' gambling even within a relatively high-scoring group.

The mean gambling proportions for the group (13:5) whose members did not attend church or attended infrequently, and at least one of whose parents gambled, is 89·0 per cent. The best predictor is then, *income,* with the poorest being hived off as *less* inclined to participate in gambling at all. The most interesting correlate was low conjugal role-sharing. But this grouping (13:11) proved residual, with a mean of 92·7 per cent and merely confirms that the very poor participate in gambling less than the norm even when church-going and parental gambling are accounted for. Within this grouping, the higher gambling means went with being non-married and either very young or elderly: the poorest middle-aged produced the lower means for gambling.

There appear to be three main groupings of men, only one of which is heavily involved in gambling. One grouping, which rarely participates, is characterized by frequent church attendance and being Protestant middle class, a result in line with Devereux's theory. The other grouping which does not get heavily involved, being too poor, is associated with infrequent church attendance and some parental gambling. The grouping which *is* involved is predicted by regular parental gambling, involvement in hobbies and some job-specific factors.

The analysis of *only the men who gamble* found job-specific factors to be the most effective predictors (Diagram 15). Job dissatisfaction, therefore, seems a fairly clear-cut generator of high gambling frequency – though, again, the reverse is equally plausible. It is not so likely, however, that high gambling frequency would lead to an expression of a preference for a past job, unless that change had been brought about by excessive gambling. Among those who saw their jobs as lacking interest, however, the best predictor of variance was *marital status*, with the non-married

TABLE 11.9   *Gambling population only: men*

Job interest	Mean times per year	n	s. d.
Medium	125·5	214	158·6
High	127·4	199	169·9
Not known	148·2	41	210·7
Low	201·9	44	142·1
Nil	271·3	13	196·3
Neutral	282·1	52	340·3
Preferred past job			
Not known	114·8	27	153·9
No	126·2	402	153·8
Yes	229·9	134	262·7

having by far the highest mean. It seems to be the case, then, that low job interest is an efficient predictor of high gambling frequency mainly for those men who, presumably, lack family responsibilities. Where there is no compensation for dull jobs in a family relationship, we can suggest some such compensation may be found in gambling.

Among the married (15:6) lower means go with education other than elementary only; wives having either a full-time or part-time paid job; and either extremely low or the more affluent income-groups. The inference here is that the very poor simply cannot afford to gamble too frequently, and the well-off do not need to do so, despite job dissatisfaction.

The analysis of *whether women gamble* did not show anything like the same dependence on church attendance as that for men (Diagram 14). The most efficient predictor was again *parental gambling*, the division between those whose parents did not gamble and the rest. *Age* and involvement in *paid work* were the next most efficient, the age variable separated the elderly from the rest, and housewives were substantially less likely to participate in gambling than those in paid work, whether part-time or full-time.

Those whose parents gambled regularly split next on current social class, differentiating the working class and the self-employed from the middle class. The working class and self-employed grouping split unproductively over job interest. The next best predictor, *marital status* and involvement in *paid work* strengthen the trend outlined above. Since *age* is not a predictor of any account for this group, the very high means for those who are single are in all probability bound up with that for those in full-time jobs, so that married or single women in paid jobs of either kind, of working-class status, seem to produce the highest rates of participation in gambling, confirming the conclusion that the rate of gambling between women and men converge the more women approach full-time involvement in specifically working-class job-situations. The same trend is evident for those whose parents did *not* gamble (14:2), which first divides the women in paid jobs from the full-time housewives, and splits the former on social class – though with the transposition of upper working- and lower middle-class statuses, in this case.

The lowest means stem particularly from the parental non-gambling grouping, among whom housewives produce the lower mean of 25·8 per cent. The best predictor then was religious affiliation. Lower means were also associated with middle-class status and frequent church attendance. This was intended as an indicator of 'home-centredness', and comprises such activities as 'do-it-yourself', repairing and decorating the home, gardening, and

TABLE 11.10   *Middle-class women whose parents gambled*

'Active home leisure'	Mean times per year	n	s. d.
Alternate days	31·5	54	46·5
Less than alternate days	38·7	112	48·7
0–3 hours daily	61·6	65	48·6
3+ hours daily	80·4	12	39·7

car maintenance, etc. That the group that does these least is least prone to participation of any kind in gambling perhaps suggests another link betwen male-oriented work and gambling.

In the analysis of women's gambling the factors that had emerged in the specific forms of gambling were the most effective – class and job specific factors – and not the one that has emerged for men's composite gambling, that of church attendance.

12 Conclusion

The final analysis of the data for men ironically presents a position that would have been inferred from a combination of the theorizations of Devereux and Herman. It is also compatible with simple anomie theory, and aligns with some of the preconceptions about the relationship between gambling and uses of leisure. (Newman has also suggested that 'hobbies' as a pursuit cut across that of gambling.) There appears to be something for everyone here, whereas in our initial theory-testing there was nothing for anybody. How did this transformation of the relationship between theories and data come about?

From a sheerly technical point of view, three variables changed the shape of the patterns between the dependent variable (total gambling) and the independent variables most relevant for the theories under consideration:

(1) Church attendance, in the analysis of whether people gamble, was controlled for by its emergence as the single most efficient predictor: held constant, it altered the relationship between gambling and religious affiliation to produce a result more in line with Devereux's theorization.

(2) Job interest, in the analysis of gambling frequency only for those participating, was measured by statements by respondents about the job, rather than by factor-analysed scores on the job-autonomy scale: the results are compatible with the compensatory theory of Herman, but less so for married than for non-married men.

(3) The dependent variable was continuous and not categorized.

If reminder were needed that the difficulty in sociology of contributing useful theory is matched only by the ease with which it is possible to 'falsify' such theory by over-hasty or incomplete conceptual or empirical tests, this example might so remind us. There is also the problem that, having spent so much time combing data spread relatively thinly over several areas of inquiry, we have little left to expend on theory modification, let alone theory generation. It is possible, though, to make one or two points, and draw certain themes together.

First of all, a feature of virtually all the theories on gambling, whether pitched at macro- or micro-sociological levels, either implicitly or explicitly, is that they entail functional analysis for their major insights. If we look again at Devereux's theory, and strip it of the holistic notion that in some fashion American society 'needs' to retain its double standard with regard to gambling to the point of illegalizing it on the one hand and tolerating its existence on the other, then what remains is an exhaustive functional analysis of the way in which social groups differentially located in the hierarchies of power and status in America adopt or adapt different versions of the complex symbolic order which legitimizes the social structure. The pursuit, non-pursuit or attack on different forms and intensities of gambling attain functionality by providing a behavioural and symbolic repertoire which enables people to accommodate themselves better in, and make more sense of, their position in this social order. A historical dimension is added by the long drawn-out war of attrition between puritanism and counteracting or alternative ideologies, onto which we can graft Goffman's proposition that 'action' of an aleatory kind has come to supplant older, more production-oriented images of achievement (one thinks of Samuel Smiles's *Self-Help* in particular) as representative of 'character'. To this, Caillois contributes the view that industrial societies – or indeed societies that evolve *any* kind of administrative infrastructure – cannot survive unless the elements of 'play' most central to other civilizations – mimesis and vertigo – are sharply curtailed: though the growth of 'fringe' religions, the pursuit of *ecstasis* through drug-taking, and the unabated search for salvation in other ways, shows the resistance to such curtailment once the austerities of early industrialization are surmounted.

Second, while it should not be imagined that this primacy accorded to the indicator of church attendance in our results automatically entails an acceptance of Devereux's theory as a whole, taken together with other findings it does suggest that a modified version of that theory makes most sense of the problem in both its sociological and its social formulations. Certain variations in gambling – assuming its ornate normative character – do occur on the indicators of religious involvement, educational attainment, orientation to politics, pursuit of hobbies, social class, conjugal role-sharing and job interest. These suggest that competing and conflicting definitions of 'character' are differentially reinforced or attenuated by people's experience of life within formidable structural constraints. Some of these definitions are more favourable to gambling than others. The functionality and rationality of gambling may loom larger when other solutions to problems are blocked, as – for example – when people are caught in the 'poverty trap', or when political solutions or collective action appear remote possibilities for betterment. Economic gain in a purely acquisitive sense, however, does not seem to be a prime determinant of gambling: our data on the expenditure of large wins does not suggest they are rebet by more than a tiny minority. Yet these are the very sums that *should* be rebet if the proverbial 'big score' is to materialize. The pleasure to be derived from gambling, the fascination it exerts, seems more likely in a context which stresses a particular kind of masculine role in both work and leisure. A systematic finding was that even women tended to gamble more the more they come to share the work experience of men.

Third, while these themes provide the elements for a framework within which the social distribution of gambling can in modern Western industrial societies be accounted for, they cannot provide anything like an adequate inventory for the task of explaining the enormous variability of different forms of gambling in smaller-scale contexts. (The counter criticism, by Newman for example, that they cannot encompass an explanation of gambling as a *universal* phenomenon – in societies ranging from ancient China to English lake villages – hardly affects their utility as theories which seek to account for the nature of gambling in a *particular* social structure.) While our areas were too broadly defined to capture that kind of variability which stems from gambling sub-cultures, the survey did in part provide the social mapping of different kinds of gambling from which future inquiries might develop, and for which they would need to account. For example, the strong links between class and intergenerational gambling in bingo; the strong class and job-interest association with betting; the age gradient in gaming-machine play; and the pervasive influence throughout of parental gambling as a key predictor, point to fruitful directions for far more research: but it is only with the use of quite different methodologies, more sensitive to the meanings which inhere in particular kinds of gambling in particular groups, that these relationships might become intelligible and causal inferences be attempted.

Fourth, the notion that legalization of many forms of gambling in 1960 and 1963 precipitated a sharp increase in gambling, followed by a slackening of that increase and a more careful monitoring and assessment of its extent (Newman has carried out an important piece of demythologizing here), have meant that the 1960s as a decade saw the rise and fall of gambling as a dramatic 'social problem'. It appears from our data that pools attract almost exactly the same proportion of the population as in 1950; that betting has increased slightly, though the need to interpret that increase in the context of inflation and a rise in prosperity is paramount; gaming post-Act cannot be compared with gaming pre-Act, but seems more readily to find an outlet in informal contexts – the pub and private contexts – than in formal casinos or nightclubs; only with bingo and gaming machines has there been a real increase, since these forms of gambling were simply not commercially available before 1960 on any other than a very minor scale. The social regulation of *demand* for gambling (as distinct from its legal expression) seems to have operated effectively to limit the potential increase in its *supply* stemming from legalization. The persistence of patterns of variation across generations – indicated both by our early finding that the best correlate of betting shop profitability was the area incidence of unemployment in 1931 and by the pervasive impact of parental gambling as a predictor – makes sharp increases (or decreases) in the year-by-year magnitude of gambling distinctly unlikely. However, as the 1931 example suggests, radical changes in people's 'life chances' may produce radical changes in their adaptive responses. The inflation of the 1970s may prove an equivalent watershed. One of the ironies of our project was that our questioning of respondents about their almost invariably modest expenditure on betting and bingo was carried out against the backcloth of devaluation, the panic over sterling, rising unemployment and a sequence of economic shifts which underlined the precariousness of our relative prosperity. In the face of these events, the 'rationality' of capitalism comes under increasing strain : in the face of processes which can contrive or eliminate huge capital formations almost overnight, as was the case with IOS,[1] the expenditure of a few pounds per head on gambling per year seems very small beer indeed.

Fifth, while these considerations may lead one to dismiss gambling as of no account in macro-economic terms, the uneven distribution of gambling means that for some the implications, both socially and personally, are far heavier. The gambling boom of the early 1960s may have been over-reported, but it did imply abuses and excesses which escaped social regulation and which were of great consequence for the individuals caught up in them. Evidence given to the Home Office during the brief heyday of unregulated casino-type night-clubs in 1965 pointed to the influx of inexperienced and amateurish beginners who quickly found themselves committed to far higher outlays of money than they could afford. The subtle inducements to overspend in contexts of packaged action and 'fancy milling', the resort to coercion in debt-collection, and the vulnerability of clubs to criminal entrepreneurship, made legal change imperative. The 1968 Act seems broadly adequate in its regulatory powers to offset some of these unanticipated side effects of legalization. Social policy on gambling, however, is subject to a clash of objectives. Social objectives – the goal of minimizing criminal entrepreneurship – clashes with fiscal ends – the goal of drawing in some revenue for the State from gambling profits: the larger the revenue drawn from gambling, the greater the inducement to make illegal books. The overall trend, however, is towards gambling as a key component in large-scale, interlocking 'leisure' industries. Perhaps the American parallel will not seem too outlandish when these industries get into their stride, for it will mean that for millions the equation of 'character' and the aleatory form of 'action' will be complete.

Appendix 1 Construction and definition of social indicators

Indicator	*Diagram abbreviation*	*Basic source question(s)*	*Categories*
1 Area	Area		0 Swansea 1 Sheffield 2 Wanstead/ Woodford
2 Sex	Sex		0 Male 1 Female
3 Age	Age	Household composition table	0 18–25 1 26–45 2 46–65 3 66 +
4 Marital status	Mar. St.	Household composition table Plus 'You said you were single-married-divorced?'	0 Single 1 Married 2 Marriage over (includes separated, divorced, widowed)
5 Religious affiliation	Rel. Aff.	'Do you belong to a religion now?'	0 None 1 Church of England 2 Roman Catholic 3 Nonconformist 4 Other
6 Religiosity	Rgy	'How important would you say religion is in your life?'	0 Great 1 Moderate 2 Slight 3 None
7 Church attendance	Ch. Att.	'Apart from weddings, christenings and funerals, how often do you go to a service?'	*0 Often 1 Infrequently 2 Never

* In the cross-tabulations, these categories were: 0 = weekly; 1 = monthly; 2 = yearly; 3 = never.

Indicator	Diagram abbreviation	Basic source question(s)	Categories
8 Conventionalism	Conv.	Factor analysis (See Chapter 3, pp. 57–60)	0 Low 1 2 3 High 4 Not known
9 'Risk-taking'	Risk	Factor analysis (See Chapter 3, pp. 57–60)	0 Low 1 2 3 High 4 Not known
10 'Belief in luck'	Luck	Factor analysis (See Chapter 3, pp. 57–60)	0 Low 1 2 3 High 4 Not known
11 Net household income (per year) (1968)	Inc.	After filters to ascertain whether their replies were in terms of weekly, monthly or yearly earnings, respondents filled in a card which they then sealed in an envelope. We asked if they would put on the card 'the total of the household earnings after tax and incomes have been deducted. Include anything your husband/wife earns, and parents or children if they live with you. Also pensions, dividends and family allowances on same basis. . . .' Those not wishing to disclose the exact sum, or not knowing it, were asked to tick the nearest category on an incomes checklist. This process applied to both personal and household earnings	0 Under £612 1 £613–999 2 £1,000–£1,432 3 £1,433+ 4 Not known
12 Education	Educ.	'What was the last school you went to full-time? What kind was it?'	0 Elementary only 1 Secondary modern/ comprehensive 2 Grammar/ technical 3 Private/other 4 Not known
13 Current socioeconomic grouping	S.E.G.	'What is your job?' *Based on Registrar-General's 17 Category Scale as follows:* Upper middle = 1, 2, 3, 4 and 13 Lower middle = 5 and 6 Upper working = 8 and 9 Lower working = 7, 10, 11 and 15 Self-employed = 12 and 14 (Full-time students were counted	0 Upper middle 1 Lower middle 2 Upper working 3 Lower working 4 Self-employed 5 Not known

Indicator	*Diagram abbreviation*	*Basic source question(s)*	*Categories*
		as upper middle. No cases of the 16 and 17 categories – agricultural and armed forces – came into the survey.)	
14 Social mobility (intergenerational)	Soc. Mob.	As for 13, plus 'What job has your father had for most of his life?'	0 Downwardly mobile 1 Upwardly mobile 2 Stable middle 3 Stable working 4 Not known
15 Dependent children	Dep. Ch.	Household composition table	0 None (includes non-married) 1 1 2 2–3 3 4+
16 No. of adults in household	F. size	Household composition table	0 One 1 Two 2 Three 3 Four 4 Five+
17 Interview situation	Int. Sit.	Interviewer checklist	0 Respondent only 1 Spouse present 2 Others present (not spouse) 3 Interruptions
18 Parental gambling	Par. G.	'How often did your father do any of the following whilst you were growing up?' (a) Bingo (b) Bet on horses (c) Bet on dogs (d) Go to horse-races (e) Go to dog-tracks (f) Make bets with friends (g) Football pools (h) Play cards or dice for money The question was repeated for the respondent's mother. In constructing the parental gambling indicator, the highest frequency was taken, not the sum of the frequencies. The cutting point being *weekly* or more often on any *one* of the eight items for each parent in turn	0 Neither 1 Either 2 Both
19 Job autonomy	Job Aut.	Factor analysis (See Chapter 3, pp. 72–3)	0 High (See Note, Chapter 4, p. 88) 1

Indicator	*Diagram abbreviation*	*Basic source question(s)*	*Categories*
			2
			3 Low
			4 Not known
20 Job effort	Job Eff.	Factor analysis (See Chapter 3, pp. 72–3)	0 Low
			1
			2
			3 High
			4 Not known
21 Job interest	Job Int.	'Which of the statements comes closest to describing how you feel about your present job?' (1) My job is interesting *nearly* all the time. (2) While my job is interesting most of the time, there are some dull patches. (3) My job is neither interesting nor dull. (4) There are a few times when my job is interesting, but most of it is pretty dull and monotonous. (5) My job is completely dull and monotonous, there is nothing interesting about it.	0 Not known/not applicable 1 High 2 3 4 5 Low
22 Promotion prospect	Prom. Prosp.	'What sort of prospects for promotion would you say your job has?'	0 Not known/ or not applicable 1 A good deal 2 Some 3 Hardly any 4 None
23 No. years in same job	Yrs in job	'How long have you had this job?'	1 Under 2 (includes 'not applicable') 2 2–9 3 10–19 4 20+ 5 Not known
24 Past job preferences	Job. Pref.	'Have you ever had a job you liked better than this one?'	0 Not applicable/ not known 1 Yes 2 No
25 Job change reasons	Job Ch.	'Why did you change to this one?'	0 Not applicable/ not known 1 Forced 2 Voluntary
26 Increasing income	Inc. Inc.	'Do you think the easiest way of increasing your income is: (1) By yourself (2) Along with other people in your kind of job?'	0 Not applicable/ not known 1 By self 2 With others

Indicator	Diagram abbreviation	Basic source question(s)	Categories
27 Women's (wives') work	W. in W.	'Have you got a full-time job?' and 'Do you have any other work?' 'Are you paid for this?'	0 Not applicable/ not known 1 Full-time paid work (15+ hours) 2 Part-time paid work (1–14 hours) 3 Full-time house-wife
28 Free time	F. T.	'Do you have all the spare time that you want?'	0 Not known 1 Enough 2 Not enough 3 Too much
29 Conjugal role-sharing	Conj.	'How often do you (does your husband) help with the following types of housework?' (Highest frequency taken) (a) Shopping (b) Cooking/preparing meals (c) Washing up (d) Cleaning (e) Washing and ironing (f) Other	0 High (includes non-married) 1 Medium 2 Low
30 Political/ community activity	Pol/Com	'How often do you take part in any political group or activities?' (a) Go to local political party meetings (b) Go to union meetings (c) Canvass or help local political party (d) Give talks or organize local feeling on political issues, e.g. proposed road schemes (e) Be active in an unofficial way (f) Member of tenant/resident Association (g) Attend parents' meetings at school (h) Member of local societies (i) Local church/chapel membership (j) Other (k) Choir/operatic group (l) Drama group (m) local/music/pop group	0 Twice weekly+ 1 Fortnightly+ 2 Yearly+ 3 Nil

Indicator	Diagram abbreviation	Basic source question(s)	Categories
31 Study	Study	'How often do you study at home or at evening classes?' (a) Study connected with work (b) Study leading to qualifications (c) Study by radio or correspondence (d) Evening classes for a special course (e) Evening classes for pleasure	0 Twice weekly+ 1 Fortnightly+ 2 Yearly+ 3 Nil
32 'Active home leisure'	A.H.L.	'Apart from housework, how often do you do things for your home and family?' (a) decorating (b) repairing (c) do-it-yourself, e.g. furniture mending (d) gardening (e) working on vehicle (f) knitting (g) sewing/dressmaking (h) other	0 3 hours daily 1 0–3 hours daily 2 Alternate days 3 Less than alternate days
33 'Active child leisure'	A.C.L.	'How often do you (does your husband) help with the children in the following ways?' (a) Bathing/putting to bed (b) Taking to and from school (c) Playing with/reading to (d) Taking on outings (e) Looking after in general on own (f) Other	0 Not applicable 1 Daily 2 Alternate days 3 Weekly+ 4 Less than weekly (where children under 11)
34 Hobbies	Hobbies	'How often do you do your own hobbies?'	0 2+hours daily 1 0–2 hours daily 2 Weekly 3 Less than weekly
35 Football match attendance	F/Ball	'How often do you go to watch football as a spectator?'	0 Weekly 1 Monthly+ 2 Yearly+ 3 Nil
36 Pub-going	Pubs	'Go for a drink to a pub or hotel in the evenings?'	0 Weekly+ 1 Monthly+ 2 Yearly+ 3 Nil
37 Entertainment	Ent.	'How often do you go out to the following?' (a) Go to a cafe or restaurant in the evening or at the weekend? (b) Go to a film? (c) Go out to a party? (d) Go out to a dance?	0 Weekly+ 1 Monthly+ 2 Yearly+ 3 Never

218

Indicator	Diagram abbreviation	Basic source question(s)	Categories
38 TV-watching	TV	'How often do you watch TV?'	0 2+ hours daily 1 0–2 hours daily 2 Alternate days 3 Less than alternate days

Appendix 2   Diagrams 1-15

Notes to the Diagrams

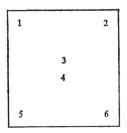

* Each box contains the following information: 1 = name of candidate group; 2 = selected categories for that group; 3 = weighted group mean; 4 = weighted standard deviation; 5 = group population size (unweighted); 6 = group number for each sequence. ◁⊦ = residual grouping achieved. Where absent, the sequence is incomplete or unproductive. Particular groupings a·e referred to in the text by diagram number and group number. For example, (14:7) refers to Diagram 14, group 7. Frequency = times per year.

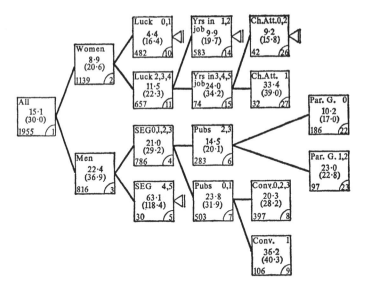

Diagram 1 POOLS FREQUENCY: whole population: 38 predictors

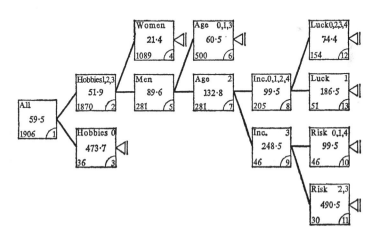

Diagram 2 POOLS EXPENDITURE: whole population: 38 predictors
(turnover in shillings p.a.)

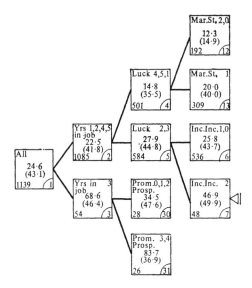

Diagram 3   POOLS: PROPORTIONS TAKING PART: women:
33 predictors

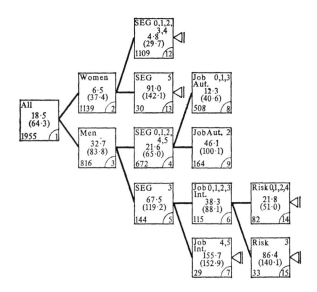

Diagram 4   BETTING FREQUENCY: whole population: 38 predictors

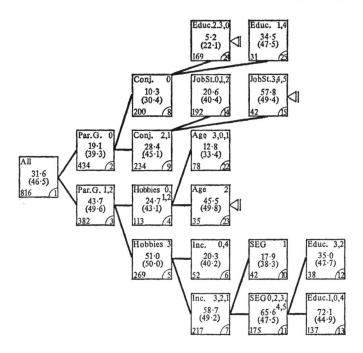

Diagram 5 BETTING: PROPORTIONS TAKING PART: men:
33 predictors

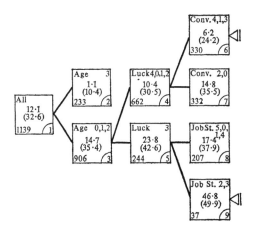

Diagram 6 BETTING: PROPORTIONS TAKING PART: women:
33 predictors

223

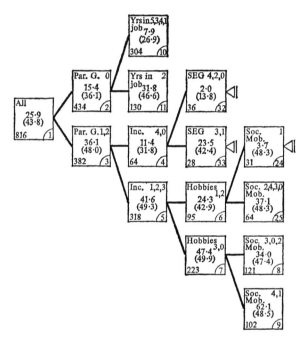

Diagram 7 GAMING: PROPORTIONS TAKING PART: men.
33 predictors

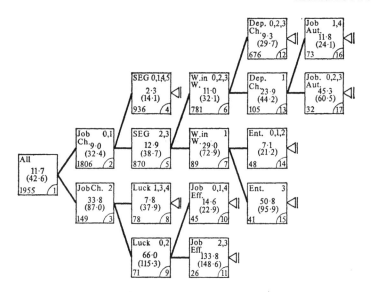

Diagram 8 CLUB BINGO FREQUENCY: whole population:
34 predictors

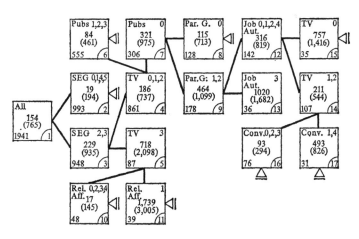

Diagram 9 CLUB BINGO EXPENDITURE: whole population:
33 predictors (in shillings p.a.)

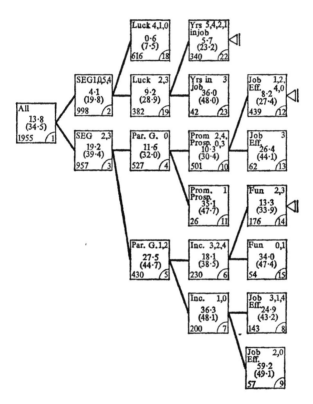

Diagram 10 CLUB BINGO: PROPORTIONS TAKING PART: whole population: 33 predictors

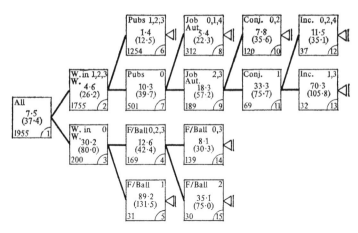

Diagram 11   GAMING MACHINES FREQUENCY: whole
population: 33 predictors

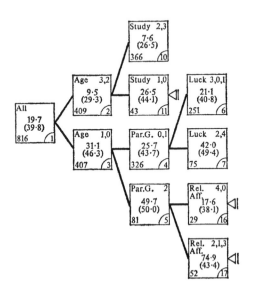

Diagram 12   GAMING MACHINES: PROPORTIONS TAKING
PART: men: 33 predictors

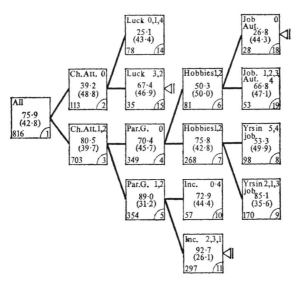

Diagram 13 TOTAL GAMBLING: PROPORTIONS TAKING
PART: men: 33 predictors

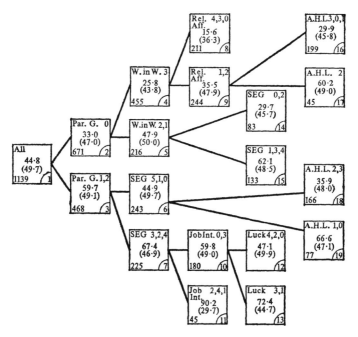

Diagram 14 TOTAL GAMBLING: PROPORTIONS TAKING
PART: women: 33 predictors

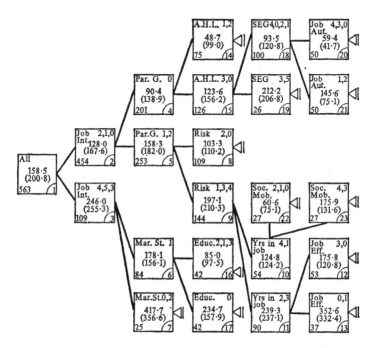

Diagram 15 TOTAL GAMBLING FREQUENCY: men: 33 predictors
(excluding non-gamblers)

Appendix 3 The betting office industry in Glamorgan, 1961-7

by Jeffery Dessant,
*Department of Business Studies,
Glamorgan Polytechnic, Pontypridd*

In 1961 a new industry of the betting office, born of the 1960 Betting, Gaming and Lotteries Act, came into being. The Act's chief purpose was to minimize the amount of gambling taking place in public places – to eliminate the street bookmaker. But once the industry was legalized it became very large and important. But it was not until 1967, when the first returns of the new betting tax became public, that it became apparent just how large, in terms of turnover, the industry was. The figures for turnover during the first eleven months operation of the betting tax are shown in Table 1. To put the figures in perspective, the total turnover was about one thirtieth the size of the national income of the economy, with betting office turnover as a large proportion.

TABLE 1 *Betting tax levied and turnover, October 1966–September 1967 (£ million)*

	Turnover	Tax
Off-course bookmakers	900	22·5
On-course bookmakers	124	3·1
Totalizators*	96	2·4
	1,120	28·0

* Includes greyhound racing.

There has not however been a factual study of the structure, organization and general economics of the bettting office industry. The result has been a plethora of rather sweeping, and sometimes inaccurate generalizations, since the industry is essentially different from other commercial enterprises.

This study attempts to fill the empirical vacuum. The third section examines the structure and organization of the industry in Glamorgan between the years 1961 and 1967. The second section considers the nature of the business that takes place in a betting office. It provides a background to the policy issues discussed in the final section of the appendix.

The nature of betting office trade

This section addresses two questions: first, what is the source of the bookmaker's gross profit margin and second, how large is that margin likely to be?

The term 'betting shop' has become a commonplace, implying that the owners have something to sell. Since no goods change hands the commodity for sale must be a service that satisfies a need of the consumer. This need is the desire to gamble and the transaction that takes place in a betting office is between two individuals, bookmaker and customer, as to the outcome of a race between two or more horses. The reasons why people gamble are many and varied yet hope of financial gain is *an* important motive.

The customer wants to win, but betting office owners also have to win to cover their running costs. The fact that the majority of betting offices continue to remain in business should constitute sufficient evidence that the betting office owners, in aggregate, have won on their transactions. By the same argument the customers, as a group, have lost. This means either that the customers are less proficient gamblers than the owners, or that whatever they are betting on is biased in favour of the owners. Alternatively, of course, both these possibilities may have some validity.

There is little doubt that some betting office customers are not particularly rational in their approach to gambling so that some of the bookmaker's margin of profit may derive from here. But basically the owner relies for his profit margin on the fact that the odds offered in each race are biased in his favour.[1] Consider this hypothetical example.

Table 2 considers six races at an actual meeting. If the bet is a fair one it should be possible to back every horse in a race to return a fixed sum if it wins, and break even. For the purposes of the example a return of £20 is aimed for. So that at the end of the day the bookmaker's accounts would look as shown in Table 3. Clearly the bet is not a fair one. The odds are framed to favour the owner

TABLE 2

	1st race				2nd race	
Horse	*Starting price*	*Stake required for return of £20*		*Horse*	*Starting price*	*Stake required*
		£	p			£ p
1	5–4	8	90	1	11–10	9 50
2	5–1	3	35	2	2–1	6 66½
3	15–2	2	35	3	13–2	2 66
4	8–1	2	22½	4	100–8	1 48
5	10–1	1	81½	5	100–7	1 32½
6	100–9	1	65	6	25–1	77
7	100–7	1	32½	7	33–1	59
8	20–1		95	8	33–1	59
9	20–1		95	9	33–1	59
10	20–1		95	10	33–1	59
11	20–1		95	11	33–1	59
12	20–1		95			
	Total stake	26	36½		Total stake	25 35
	Loss on race 1	26	36½		*Loss on race 2*	25 35
		−20	0			−20 0
		= 6	36½			5 35

	3rd race				4th race	
Horse	*Starting price*	*Stake required*		*Horse*	*Starting price*	*Stake required*
		£	p			£ p
1	2–5	14	28½	1	8–11	11 56
2	7–2	4	44½	2	7–2	4 44½
3	6–1	2	86	3	9–1	2 0
				4	10–1	1 81½
	Total stake	21	59	5	100–7	1 32½
				6	25–1	77
				7	25–1	77
					Total stake	22 18½
	Loss on race 3	21	59		*Loss on race 4*	22 18½
		−20	0			−20 0
		1	59			2 18½

Horse	5th race Starting price	Stake required		Horse	6th race Starting price	Stake required	
		£	p			£	p
1	6–4	8	0	1	13–8	7	60½
2	11–2	3	7½	2	5–1	3	33½
3	6–1	2	86	3	11–2	2	86
4	8–1	2	22½	4	6–1	3	7½
5	10–1	1	81½	5	10–1	1	81½
6	10–1	1	81½	6	110–8	1	48
7	100–8	1	48	7	100–6	1	20
8	100–6	1	20	8	20–1		95
9	20–1		95	9	20–1		95
10	20–1		95	10	20–1		95
11	20–1		95				
12	20–1		95		Total stake	24	22
	Total stake	26	27				
	Loss on race 5	26	27		*Loss on race 6*	24	22
		−20	0			−20	0
		6	27			4	22

TABLE 3

		Turnover £ p		Profit £ p	
1st race		26	36½	6	36½
2nd race		25	35	5	35
3rd race		21	59	1	59
4th race		22	18½	2	18½
5th race		26	27	6	27
6th race		24	22	4	22
	Total	145	98	25	98

and in the examples quoted the bias gives an 18 per cent gross profit margin on turnover. It is tempting to suggest that this rate of profit indicates the sort of margins to which betting offices typically work. However, for a number of reasons, such a suggestion would be misleading.

In the first place, the example implicitly assumes that the odds

233

offered approximately indicate the true chance of winning. But the odds in horse-racing are man-made, such that the odds offered against a horse may in no way reflect its true chance of winning. This fact allows certain informed people effectively to implement 'betting *coups*', to the detriment of the betting office owner's profit margin. On the other hand of course, if the betting market is misleading, the fact that inside information is not available to the majority of customers should work in the betting office's favour.

Second, the example assumes 'win only' betting whereas a large proportion of betting office trade is of the 'each-way' variety, which can be less profitable for the betting offices. Whether it is or not depends on the fraction of the win odds offered for a place. Thus it is in the hands of the betting office owner to increase the profitability of each-way betting by adjusting the odds offered for a place appropriately. It is noticeable that, during the period studied, the odds offered for a place in betting offices in Glamorgan, generally became less attractive.

Third, it must be pointed out that many owners, particularly the smaller ones, very rarely have all the horses backed in a race, as is suggested in the example. The single office owner will frequently have a very 'unbalanced book' on a particular race which means that if a certain horse wins he stands to lose heavily. However, in the long run, this should not materially influence the rate of profit, provided that the odds offered against the heavily backed horses accurately reflect their chances of winning. If the odds underrate the true chances, as would be the case in a genuine betting *coup*, the profit margin would be reduced.

In any form of gambling enterprise, the money wagered circulates back and forth between the parties involved. For this reason, other things being equal, the turnover tends to be high relative to other types of business. A gross rate of profit on turnover in the vicinity of 18 per cent would then imply the betting office industry to be highly lucrative. However the actual gross profit margin depends on a number of factors, such as the type of trade attracted, the odds given for place betting, the limits imposed on winning bets, and the efficiency of management in 'laying-off' large wagers. In particular one would expect the larger firms, handling substantial 'informed' wagers to be operating on a relatively small gross margin, but compensated by a large turnover; the reverse being true of the smaller firm handling the trade of the ordinary man in the street.

Whatever the gross margin may be, nearly all the betting offices in Glamorgan during the period studied boosted that margin by the imposition of limits on winning bets. Two broad types of limit were observable. First, some offices put a limit on the amount that any one customer could win on a single day's racing. It could be argued that this is justifiable because it informs the public exactly where they stand in relation to the betting office's ability to pay out, but probably it was imposed to lessen the firm's liabilities on a bad day.

The second type of limit imposed is that on specialized types of bet, such as doubles, trebles and accumulators, since odds offered are determined largely by win and each-way betting. If the betting office customer wishes to indulge in special varieties of wagers, the betting office owner is entitled to state the terms on which he is prepared to accept them, particularly if these types of wager tend to be less profitable than straightforward win and each-way betting. There is no particular reason to suppose that the specialized types of bet are less profitable. This is confirmed by Table 4, which gives the rate of return for various types of bet in three betting offices for a single day.

Probably a more important reason for this second imposition is to restrict the ability of the customer to win large amounts of money for a small stake. Provided the customer receives his winnings in small amounts over time, the owner has a good chance of regaining a significant proportion of this money through increased gambling. But if a customer who wagers in shillings has a windfall of one hundred pounds, the owner is less likely to get much of this back. Such a sum is more likely to be spent on the purchase of a consumer durable good (see Table 7.18).

Limits may be regarded as serving three functions. They afford protection against very large losses for the owner. They guard against large sums of money being won for small stakes and thus prevent those sums disappearing from the stock of money available for gambling. Finally, they increase the betting office owner's profit margin.

TABLE 4 *Percentage return on stake for various types of commission, in three betting offices*

	Office A	Office B	Office C
Win	$2\frac{1}{2}$	7	−25·2*
Each way	49	19·8	47
Win doubles and trebles	2·7	68·3	36·6
Each way doubles and trebles	71·2	50·3	72
Forecasts	77·3	67·3	1·8
Cross bets	84·6	72·7	40·2

* Loss.

Structure and organization of the industry

This section gives a factual account of the structure of the industry during the period studied and attempts to explain that structure in terms of its competitiveness and locational trends.

When betting offices became legalized in 1961 the proprietors came from two main sources. First, the large credit betting concerns had, of necessity, to enter the market to sustain their trade. The five largest firms in Glamorgan, in terms of offices owned, were all established postal and/or credit betting concerns before 1961. Between them they owned 47 per cent of all offices in Glamorgan at the beginning of 1967. In addition there were eleven medium-size firms owning over twelve offices of which several operated in the postal/credit betting market before 1961. The percentage of offices owned by these 'large' firms rises to 60 per cent.

The second source of ownership are the small one-man concerns whose trade, before 1961, was partly or wholly illegal, the street bookmaker. At the end of 1966 there were eighty-one single office owners, representing 10·4 per cent of the total. Another seventy-two offices were under the control of bookmakers who owned two or three offices, bringing the percentage up to 19·6 per cent. The true proportion of offices owned by the smaller firm was somewhat less than this because some owners, although operating under their own names, were in fact agents for the larger concerns. In terms of turnover, the proportion of trade handled by the small firms was undoubtedly smaller still, since the more expensive and attractive sites were generally obtained by the large firms. Table 5 gives a fuller picture of the size structure of the industry.

There were approximately[2] 640 betting offices in Glamorgan at the end of 1961 compared to 770 at the end of 1966. Table 6 shows that of this net increase of 130, 89 went to the five largest firms and 41 to the other firms: an increased concentration of ownership. During the period studied 107 betting offices closed down, although in a few cases licences for new premises were immediately granted in lieu of closure. This high rate of closure partly reflects the frenzied rush that took place in 1961 to make sure of obtaining a licence. Some applicants had undoubtedly failed to give sufficient consideration to the commercial viability of their chosen site.

There were seventy-five takeovers of betting offices during the period, mostly by the large firms of the small single offices. The few instances of reverse takeovers were perhaps due to the larger firms divesting themselves of marginally profitable premises. One large firm used the takeover as a major form of growth, obtaining eleven out of its twenty-four betting offices; a second firm obtained five of its sixteen offices by this means. Two of the largest firms,

TABLE 5 *Size distribution of firms in Glamorgan by number of offices owned, December 1966*

Number of offices	Number of firms	TOTAL OFFICES OWNED
50 and over	5	366
25–49	0	0
12–24	11	188
7–11	0	0
4–6	13	66
1–3	112	150
	141	770

Source: Calculated from information provided by Magistrate's Clerks Offices.

TABLE 6 *Betting office licences held by the five largest firms, Glamorgan, 1961 and 1967*

Area	Licences granted to five largest firms 1961	TOTAL granted 1961	%	Licences held by five largest firms December 1966	TOTAL Licences December 1966	%
Cardiff	77	138	55·8	113	163	69·3
Glamorgan Merthyr Tydfil Swansea	221	502	44·0	264	607	43·5
Total	298	640	46·6	377	770	49·0

Source: Calculated from data provided by Magistrate's Clerks Offices.

each owning over fifty offices obtained a fifth of their premises in the same way.

One final point is that during 1966 twenty-seven offices opened and twenty-five closed, giving a net increase of only two. It is tempting to argue that this slow rate of growth is evidence of market saturation in the region. However, in practice, it is difficult to know what influence the refusal of the authorities to grant planning permission and licences had in determining this slow growth rate. Certainly the region had and still has a high density of betting offices per head of population, shown in Table 7, which tends to

TABLE 7   *Number of betting offices per head of population: England and Wales, June 1966*

Area	Licences in force	1000 population served by each
England and Wales	14,123	3·38
Glamorgan	484	1·57
Cardiff	163	1·60
Merthyr Tydfil	57	1·02
Swansea	58	2·94

Source: Betting, Gaming and Lotteries Act, 1963 (Permits and Licences).

TABLE 8   *Areas of England and Wales with high density of betting offices, June 1966*

Area	1000 population served by each office	Area	1000 population served by each office
Merthyr Tydfil	1·02	St Helens	1·58
Wigan	1·41	Cardiff	1·60
Warrington	1·44	County of Monmouth	1·64
Gateshead	1·49	Blackpool	1·71
Newport	1·50	Barnsley	1·76
Liverpool	1·50	County of Durham	1·78
Great Yarmouth	1·55	County of Glamorgan	1·57
Newcastle-upon-Tyne	1·56	South Shields	1·57

Note: Table excludes the City of London.
Source: Betting, Gaming and Lotteries Act, 1963 (Permits and Licences).

confirm the impression of market saturation and an excessively large number of betting offices. Specifically all the old industrial areas of England and Wales exhibit the same high density (see Table 8) and the small valley communities of Glamorgan similarly encourage the observed high incidence of betting offices. How do we account for the unbalanced size-structure of the industry, the profusion of small firms and the enormous gap that exists between the size of the five largest firms and the rest.

Small firms may be explained by the backgrounds and origins of the owners; the pool of pre-1961 street bookmakers, who perhaps are not primarily businessmen. Their expertise is in the intricacies of gambling rather than building up and running a large business.

Further, the average age of these owners confirms their origins: of a sample of forty betting office owners in Glamorgan it was in the low fifties. The small single-office firms might be deterred from even limited expansion by the fact that the additional profit gained from running two or three similar offices might not appear to be worth the effort of having to delegate management.

The five largest firms in the county during the period studied owned over fifty betting offices each but there was no other firm of even half this size. The chief explanation of this could be that, in a saturated market, the medium-sized firms simply were not able to find profitable opportunities to expand. Alternatively, it is possible that there exists what might be called a 'size threshold'; once it is passed, expansion is easy and attractive.

As a firm grows in size it is possible that certain operational difficulties arise. Specifically it is true that each race involves the owner in making decisions as to what bet to accept and whether to 'lay off' any money. The owner also has to take care that accumulator bets do not mount up and involve him in heavy liabilities. But the large firms would tend to benefit from the law of large numbers. A small firm might be concerned to find that it had bets totalling say £1,000 going onto one horse. It would therefore have to keep a careful check on all bets struck in its various offices, communicate relevant information from the offices to the central organization and delegate staff to decide whether some money should be laid off, and if so how much. It may also on occasions prove difficult and sometimes impossible to lay money off in the trade.

The larger firm is less likely to be beset by such problems because the stake would be a much smaller proportion of its total stake on the race and would be better able to balance its books. Consider Table 9 as an example, which shows the win money staked on each horse for the same race in three actual betting offices. The maximum betting office X can lose is £20, if horse D wins. For betting office Y it is £12 if horse B wins and for Z it is £16 if horse C wins. Now consider what happens if all three betting offices are owned by the same firm. The stakes then appear in the total column and it can be seen that the most the firm can lose is £6 if horse C wins, significantly less than any of the offices taken individually. The greater the number of offices the more pronounced the effect is likely to be.

Moreover, the greater financial reserves of the larger firm should tend to make it relatively oblivious to the possibility of quite heavy short-term losses and thus to avoid the complications that arise from attempts to avoid such losses.

Having reached a size where 'laying off' and associated problems

TABLE 9 *Distribution of stake money in three betting offices (shillings)*

	Starting price	Betting office X	Betting office Y	Betting office Z	Total
Horse A	2–1	66	46	100	212
Horse B	7–2	12	89	26	127
Horse C	4–1	28	11	118	157
Horse D	5–1	106	10	16	132
Horse E	10–1	26	4	6	36

Note: For the purposes of the example only the first five horses in the betting are included.

are manageable, it is now attractive to expand the business to utilize the central facilities, since the staff, building and equipment, constitute a fixed cost.

Can there be competitiveness in an industry in which all the firms offer the same product at an identical price? There are ways in which the firm can vary the terms on which it provides its service. Although the firms take the prices they offer from the market formed on the race-course, the amount customers *can win* is influenced by the imposition of limits, by the odds offered for place betting and by the rate of betting tax imposed, which are all under the control of the individual firm. The effect of the forces of competition can bring benefit to the customer.

Concentration of ownership can reduce or eliminate competition. For Glamorgan during the period studied, the general level of concentration of ownership is shown in Table 6. Five-firm concentration figures were chosen because of the substantial difference in size between the five largest firms and the rest. There is no necessary suggestion in these figures of undue market dominance, but in the context of the betting office industry the important question to ask is whether particular towns and individual districts within large towns and cities are dominated by one or two firms. Table 10 shows that for a number of towns this is true. Further many smaller communities, districts and towns have only one or two betting offices, giving the public little or no choice.

It is rare, except in the centre of the larger towns and cities to find betting offices sited close together, no doubt partly due to the policy of the licensing authorities. Each office tends to build up a regular clientèle drawn from its immediate vicinity. If a certain office tries to increase its trade through raising limits or lowering the betting tax levied, it would have to offer the improved facilities

TABLE 10   *Percentage of offices owned by two largest firms in each area, December 1967*

Penarth	100
Treharris	100
Merthyr Vale	100
Glynneath	80
Treorchy	80
Maesteg	75
Mountain Ash	75
Bargoed	67
Aberavon	62

Source: Calculated from data supplied by Magistrate's Clerks Offices.

to its existing customers. It may be doubted whether the marginal increase in trade that follows would do anything to improve the overall profitability of the firm. There is little incentive to take competitive action. This is aggravated by the pattern of concentration; especially if all the betting offices in particular towns are owned by one or two firms.

Finally, in Glamorgan during the period studied, competition was restrained by the existence of a strong bookmaker's federation, to which the majority of betting office owners belonged. The initial effect which has since declined was to impose a rigorous uniformity on the terms offered throughout the industry, with few firms deviating from recommended terms.

Two pieces of evidence can be put forward to support the conclusion that there is very little competitiveness. First, the surprising uniformity of imposed limits and place odds offered and second, the levying of the full rate of betting tax at one shilling in the pound, by the majority of firms in Glamorgan. Although the tax is on gambling and not on betting offices, this is not the result one would expect from a competitive industry, where economic theory predicts that the incidence of the tax will fall partly on the consumer and partly on the producer. Further, at that time, there was a national recommendation that the customer should be asked to pay eightpence in the pound towards the cost of the betting tax. In Glamorgan the majority of firms felt able to ignore this recommendation and charge the full rate.

As regards the location of betting offices, the single outstanding feature is the general close proximity of betting offices to public houses and clubs. For example, a survey of Cardiff completed in December 1966 showed that over 50 per cent of all betting offices were either part premises of, adjacent to or directly opposite a public house or club. Considerably more were just a few seconds walk away. If one accepts the value judgment that it is undesirable to encourage drinking and gambling, then this close juxtaposition of buildings could be objected to.

It has to be remembered however that the locations described are usually the logical sites for betting offices, since before 1961 the illegal part of the trade was generally centred on public houses. Further, any conscious policy to separate the two institutions might well lead to a sharp increase in illegal gambling and thus defeat a major aim of the 1961 legislation.

Policy considerations

(i) *The betting tax*

On pages 232–3 it was shown that the odds offered in each race contain a bias in favour of the bookmaker which, in principle, gives him his margin of profit. If a betting tax of the type currently in operation is imposed, its effect must either be to increase the effective bias against the customer or to reduce the gross profit rate of the betting office, or some combination of the two. If the industry lacks competitiveness the tax is less likely to be financed out of the bookmaker's gross margin and in any case there is a very sharp limit to the extent to which the tax can satisfy its appetite from this source. But equally, the degree to which the tax can be financed through increasing the bias against the customer, is limited.

For example, assume a horse-race in which the odds constitute a fair bet. The odds offered against a certain horse winning are four to one, a true reflection of the animal's chance. Now admit the bookmaker's margin of profit, which biases the odds against the customer. Thus the odds obtainable fall say to three to one. The government now imposes a betting tax which is levied on the customer so that the effective odds fall perhaps to two to one. Thus the odds offered represent half the horses' true chance of winning. Clearly there is a limit to this process. At some level of the tax, many customers will find betting in this way unattractive. Turnover will fall and diminishing returns to the tax be encountered. What is more important, it is likely that this result will be achieved at quite low rates of the tax. For example consider Table 11, which shows the actual starting price and the true starting price after tax for a particular wager, assuming that the tax is paid out of winnings. Remember that the actual starting price is itself biased against the customer since it allows for the bookmaker's margin.

TABLE 11   *Effect of betting tax on rate of return*

Stake	Starting price	Gross return if horse wins	Rate of tax (%)	Return after tax	True starting price after tax
£5	1–1	£10	40	£6	1–5 on
£5	1–1	£10	30	£7	2–5 on
£5	1–1	£10	25	£7·10	1–2 on
£5	1–1	£10	15	£8·10	4–6 on (app)

Note: The example assumes that the tax is levied on winning bets.

Although the effect is less dramatic if the tax is levied on stake money, it is still true that betting must become unattractive to many people at fairly low rates of tax. So that it is arguable that even marginal increases in the tax from its present level increases the danger of two things occurring. The first is a sharp fall in betting office turnover giving rise to a fall in the total yield of the tax. Second, a higher betting tax is likely to encourage the growth of illegal gambling. In Glamorgan during the period studied there was already evidence of increased illegal betting. The book-maker operating from a public house has few overheads and pays no betting tax and should therefore be able to give the public better value for money. He is more happily placed to cater for those who wish to bet on evening racing, since betting offices are for the most part closed when this racing takes place. Any further biasing of the odds against the customer, caused by a higher betting tax, would undoubtedly encourage the betting public to try to avoid the tax by making use of the illegal market.

The existence of the illegal market does, of course, reinforce the first point that it constitutes an alternative for the customer to the betting office, so that as the tax rises the betting office trade is more likely to fall and with it the tax yield. In the field of gambling the government have on a previous occasion indulged in a policy of killing off the goose that lays the golden egg. It effectively caused the demise of fixed-odd betting on football matches through imposing a high rate of tax.

(ii) *Tote monopoly*

Could a tote monopoly produce a more efficient industry, in terms of cost of production, than presently exists and offer an acceptable service to the public at large?

There are some 'cost' savings that should certainly follow from the creation of a tote monopoly. Most obviously the bookmaker's profit margin would be removed and to the extent that the margin is swelled by monopoly elements, further savings would accrue. Second, if, as suggested by this study, there exists excess capacity in the industry then gains in efficiency could be obtained through rationalization. Finally, it would seem likely that the cost of a central organization to run a tote monopoly would be considerably less than the cost of all the individual central organizations required to run the industry as presently constituted. It might be contended that the bureaucratic inefficiency that arguably characterizes state-run enterprises would dissipate the advantages listed. This is unlikely in the case of a tote monopoly since it would not appear to be an industry where the administrative and executive staff have to make frequent and important decisions. In fact the decision-making process would seem to be largely automatic.

The benefits, such as they are, could be distributed in various directions. They could be used to increase the revenue of the government. It has been shown that it is presently difficult to increase the taxation of the industry. Under a tote monopoly such an increase could obviously be more easily effected. Alternatively the benefits could be used to improve the racing industry in this country. Leaving aside the thorny question of to what extent gambling on racing should support the sport of racing, few would deny that the racing industry needs financial help. The best British bloodstock is increasingly being bought to be exported abroad. In France, which has a tote monopoly, track facilities are better and prize money is generally considerably higher than in this country. In fact the discrepancy is so marked that many of the more able British race-horses spend most of their time racing in France. Finally the benefits described could go to the betting public in the form of improved odds.

Whether these benefits can in fact be reaped depends very much on the answer to whether a tote monopoly could provide an acceptable service. It is argued that even if it could be shown unequivocally that a tote monopoly is desirable in principle, practical difficulties would destroy its viability. A large illegal market would once again grow up, fed by the pool of unemployed bookmakers that a tote monopoly would create. Thus the viability of such an organization would be destroyed.

There is no doubt that the service provided by the bookmaker and that provided by a tote monopoly, as conventionally conceived, are not the same. Whereas with a bookmaker one can know with some accuracy the odds being offered, such information is not available on the tote. Whether this difference is sufficient to cause the rebirth of substantial illegal gambling, as is so often predicted, is something that would only be discovered in the event. An obstacle to the growth of substantial illegal bookmaking is that since there would be no market on the race-course, some other way of forming a market would have to be devised.

But is this conventional conception of the tote the only one that it is possible to envisage? Is it not possible that in an age of computers and rapid communication, some system could be devised that would keep the customers of a tote monopoly fairly accurately informed as to the current state of the betting market? If such a system could be made operational then the major distinction between the service of the tote and of the bookmaker disappears. There is no reason why the tote should not offer the public a very similar variety of bets as the bookmaker, and indeed increase its attractiveness by instituting a selection of 'jackpot-type' bets.

Further useful discussion of the question of tote monopoly is precluded by the dearth of empirical study. As suggested it would be particularly useful to have some estimate of the extent to which such a nationalized concern could bring about increases in efficiency and to know whether an organization could be devised for the tote that would produce a service attractive to the betting public.

Notes

Chapter 1 Gambling as a sociological problem

1 Johan Huizinga, *Homo Ludens: A Study of the Play Element in Culture*, Routledge & Kegan Paul, 1949; Paladin, 1970.

2 Roger Caillois, *Man, Play and Games*, Thames & Hudson, 1962.

3 Caillois refers to the situation in Brazil in 1958.

4 Erving Goffman, 'Where the action is', in *Interaction Ritual*, Allen Lane, 1972. First published 1967.

5 E. Goffman, 'Fun in games', in *Encounters*, Bobbs-Merrill, 1961.

6 For this and other crucial connections I am grateful to Richard Daventry.

7 Marvin Scott, *The Racing Game*, Aldine, 1968.

8 See D. Matza and G. Sykes, 'Delinquency and subterranean values', *American Sociological Review*, September 1962.

9 W. B. Miller, 'Lower class culture as a generating milieu of gang delinquency', *Journal of Social Issues*, 14 (3), 1958, pp. 5–19.

10 Edward C. Devereux, Jr, 'Gambling and the social structure: a sociological study of lotteries and horse racing in contemporary America', 2 vols, unpublished Ph.D. thesis, Harvard University, 1949.

11 George Homans, 'Bringing men back in', *American Sociological Review*, 1962.

12 Ernest Gellner, 'Concepts and society', in *Transactions of the Fifth World Congress of Sociology*, Washington, 1962, vol. I, pp. 153–84.

13 See, for example, R. M. Titmuss, 'Authoritarianism and the family', in *Essays on the Welfare State*, Allen & Unwin, 1958.

14 Robert K. Herman, 'Gambling as work: a sociological study of the race track', in *Gambling*, Harper & Row, 1967.

15 But see Jon Halliday and Peter Fuller (eds), *The Psychology of Gambling*, Allen Lane, 1974, for Fuller's introductory analysis of the different reactions to gambling of the Roman Catholic as distinct from the Protestant Church.

Chapter 2 Gambling as a social problem

1 William J. Chambliss, 'The laws on vagrancy', *Social Problems*, 1964.

2 A. Rubner, *The Economics of Gambling*, Macmillan, 1966.
3 Hansard, vol. 82, cols 793–6.
4 2nd Report from the Select Committee on Lotteries (1808).
5 Minutes of Evidence, 1844, Select Committee on Gaming, pp. v, vi.
6 Ibid., pp. 193–202.
7 Ibid., p. 16.
8 See James Mott, 'Popular gambling from the decline of the lotteries to the rise of the pools' in Raphael Samuel (ed.), History Workshop Series (forthcoming).
9 See in particular, Kai T. Eriksen, *Wayward Puritans*, Wiley, 1966.
10 The following letter from Professor A. L. Goodhart illustrates this well (*The Times*, 28 March 1972):

> Sir, In the spring of 1941, Maynard Keynes, Sir Wilfrid Greene and I were in Estoril on the outskirts of Lisbon, waiting for a sea-plane to fly us to New York. One evening we went to the local casino where Keynes and Greene, who were following a carefully planned system, seemed to be inexorably unsuccessful while I, a novice, recouped our depleted [sic] finances.
>
> When we left, Keynes explained that a player's success depended more on intuition than on intelligence. He gave as an illustration his own reputation as an astute business man because he had made staggering profits both for King's College (Cambridge) and for himself by investing in the shares of a Chicago traction company.
>
> For no particular reason he had sold these holdings two weeks before the stock market collapsed in the autumn panic of 1929. If he had not done so the College would have been in serious financial difficulties and he would have been wiped out. It was not reason but chance that had made him choose the crucial date. The fact that he was an economist, he said, was irrelevant.

11 A time-bargain was in the nature of a stock option today with the difference that failure to pay in the event of a loss could not then be enforced. In 1773, the City had petitioned the Commons to suppress the illegal lotteries, perhaps with the aim of reinforcing the distinction between Gambling and Commercial investment (Rat. 1933 Royal Commission). (Not, however, mentioned in C. L. Ewen, *Lotteries and Sweepstakes*, Heath, Cranton, 1932.)
12 Charles Lamb, *Essays of Elia*, Dent, Everyman, 1964.
13 Brian Harrison, contribution to discussion on 'Work and leisure in pre-industrial society' by Keith Thomas, presented at 7th *Past and Present* Conference, 1964: *Past and Present*, no. 29, December 1964, pp. 63–6.
14 This was also the intention of the 1960 Act.
15 Graham, 1845 Games and Wagers Act Amendment, second reading.
16 Para. 3098, 1844 Minutes of Evidence.
17 Hansard, 3rd series, vol, 8718, col. 129.
18 Harrison, op. cit.
19 See Dennis Craig, *Horse Racing*, Penguin, 1944.
20 T. Burns, 'Leisure, work and the social structure', B.S.A. Conference Paper (unpublished), 1967.
21 Guy Chapman, *Culture and Survival*, Cape, 1940, p. 80.

22 Burns, op. cit., p. 8.

23 Wages were subsistence only, but their provision gave employers a total power which differed from the previous relationship between journeymen and craftsmen and the market.

24 *Past and Present* Conference, loc. cit.

25 Guy Chapman, op. cit., p. 115: his chapters on the 'Delimitation' and the 'Exploitation' of leisure could not have been quoted here but for Burns's demonstration of their value in his 1967 paper.

26 Henry James, *English Hours*, Heinemann, 1905, p. 173.

27 See his evidence to the Select Committee on Gaming, 1844.

28 As by Clough, in the Committee stage: Hansard, 1906, vol. 167, col. 1162.

29 Ibid., col. 1164.

30 See P. Quennell (ed.), *Mayhew's London*, Spring Books, pp. 46–51.

31 Lady Bell, *At the Works*, 1906 (1911 edn, Nelson, p. 359).

32 Select Committee on Lotteries, 1808, Minutes of Evidence.

33 Royal Commission on Lotteries, 1933, Minutes of Evidence, 15 December 1932, 20th day.

34 The Commission did not take too kindly to the suggestion. For example: *Sir David Owen:* 'I do not quite know myself what an economist is. What is his function? Is it to add to the cheerfulness and frivolity of life?' – 'My object, I think, in this was to promote clear thinking on these matters.' – 'I should say you are a humourist.' 'All the expenses to be paid by the Sunday papers.' 'Everyone in the country waking up on Sunday morning stretching out for the Sunday paper.' What economic factor underlies that suggestion? – 'You would have to have some means of publication, and this would be a means whereby the profits of the State would be intact, without the subtraction of the expenses.' (7879–82).

35 Donald Cressey, *Organised Crime and Criminal Organisations*, Heffers, 1971; *Criminal Organisation*, Heinemann Educational, 1972.

36 Quoted in Burns, op. cit., p. 12.

37 Ibid.

Chapter 3 The research strategy

1 W. F. F. Kemsley and D. Ginsburg, *Betting in Britain*, Social Survey Reports: New Series, 710/4, HMSO, 1951.

2 O. Newman, *Gambling: Hazard and Reward*, Athlone Press, 1972.

3 E. C. Devereux, Jr, 'Gambling and the social structure: a sociological study of lotteries and horse racing in contemporary America', 2 vols, unpublished Ph.D. thesis, Harvard University, 1949.

4 See C. Rosser and C. Harris, *The Family and Social Change*, Routledge & Kegan Paul, 1965; P. Willmott and M. Young, *Family and Class in a London Suburb*, Routledge & Kegan Paul, 1960.

5 C. A. Moser and G. Kalton, *Survey Methods in Social Investigation*, Heinemann, 1958, pp. 83–4.

6 F. Yates, *Sampling Methods for Censuses and Surveys*, Griffin, 1953.

7 H. Blalock, *Causal Inference in Non-Experimental Research*, Chapel Hill, 1965.

8 All the analyses would be weighted by the reciprocal of the sampling fractions to give us true estimates of the population proportions. The unweighted data would no longer be a true reflection of the class structure of each area.

9 See L. Kish, *Survey Research*, 1965, p. 400 f.

10 Hyman distinguished between surveys whose aims are principally descriptive and those whose aims are mainly explanatory (see H. H. Hyman, *Survey Design and Analysis*, (Free Press, Chicago, 1954)). Our aim was both to describe and explain variations in gambling. Far fewer variables were needed for adequate descriptive tabulations.

11 H. O. Selvin and A. Stuart, 'A critique of tests of significance in survey research', *American Sociological Review*, 1957, 22, 519–27.

12 The only weakness perhaps lies in taking as 'high' those gambling twice a week on only one form of gambling. A 'high' rating would then go to a respondent who plays a fruit machine twice a week and nothing else, whereas a respondent who played only once a week but also spent a fortune at a dog-track weekly would be counted as 'medium'. There is no foolproof way of avoiding these possibilities. The overwhelming likelihood is that the dog-track better gambles in other ways, one of which is more than once a week.

We developed another indicator of Multiple Gambling, Type II, which is exactly the same as Type I, but incorporates betting at big races, fixed odds betting, newspaper competitions, raffles, lotteries and non-club bingo as elements needed for a truly comprehensive gambling indicator. Type I seems a better indicator, since the categories become too diffuse when loaded with very occasional punters or raffle-ticket buyers.

13 E. C. Devereux, Jr, op. cit.

14 T. Adorno et al, *The Authoritarian Personality*, Norton, New York, 1969.

15 Adorno's F-scale covered the following domains of importance and the attitude configuration:
   (a) conventionalism, mainly rigid adherence to group values
   (b) power and toughness – exaggerated assertions of strength and toughness, over-emphasis on conventionality of the individual, preoccupation with dominance-submission
   (c) authoritarian submission, namely submissive, uncritical attitude towards idealized moral authority of the ingroup
   (d) anti-intraception, namely opposition to the subjective, the imaginative, the tender-minded
   (e) superstition and stereotypy, namely the belief in mystical determinants of an individual's fate, the disposition to think in rigid categories
   (f) projectivity, namely disposition to believe that wild and dangerous things go on in the world.

16 Most of the statements were selected from those found to be of value in personality inventories and studies of superstition.

17 The items not expected to be correlated with conventionalism were items 2 and 5. However there is a reasonable explanation for this seeming failure to obtain desired dimensions. The five 'risk' items were

not all stated in the same way. Yet the two items which were related to 'authoritarianism' empirically were negatively related to 'risk-taking' – that is, if one agreed with the statements one did *not* take risks – whereas the other three items were positively related to 'risk-taking'. Thus although a bi-polar continuum was expected, it does not appear to exist. The absence of a bi-polar continuum on the risk-taking variable can be shown by looking at the correlations between the items (see appended tables). There are virtually zero correlations between item 2 and items 8, 11, 14 and item 5 and items 8, 11, 14 in all the area analyses and in the total sample analysis. The two risk items that have significant loadings on Factor I seem to reflect 'projectivity' which is one of the dimensions of the 'authoritarian' construct. (Projectivity is a fear that the world is getting too violent.) Thus there is little doubt Factor I, which accounts for the most of the variance in the analysis, is a factor relating to opinions about life styles and may be said to relate to rigid adherence to conventional values. We can properly identify the variable as 'conventionalism'.

18 Additional evidence showing how little the pattern differed between the three factors is the proportion of the variance accounted by each factor in each area, shown above.

19 The programme is described in John A. Sonquist and James N. Morgan, *The Detection of Interaction Effects*, Survey Research Center, Institute for Social Research, University of Michigan, 1964.

20 The whole sample is first split into two in the way that makes the largest reduction in the variance. In doing so, it considers all the binary splits between classes of each independent variable. It does so subject to the constraint that classes that are not contiguous (in the sample group considered) are not grouped together. The procedure is then repeated for that sample group that has the largest total sum of squares. In this way an AID 'tree' is formed, out of a series of binary splits. The procedure is stopped either if the ratio of the between group sum of squares to total sum of squares to reduce the unexplained sum of squares is smaller than a predetermined constant, or if the total sums of squares is less than a second predetermined constant. See Selvin and Stuart, op. cit.

21 This judgment is aided by other information printed on the AID output. One form of information is the details of optimal splits on all variables for each group at each stage.

22 See H. M. Blalock, 'Theory building and the concepts of interaction', *American Sociological Review*, 1965, pp. 374–80. Atkinson's theory was stated in 'Motivational determinants of risk-taking behaviour', *Psychological Bulletin*, 1954, pp. 63–4.

23 The distinction between the two forms of interaction effect must not be exaggerated. In a technique based on binary splits, the one is the obverse of the other.

24 In principle, of course, it can explain all the variation if the constraints are set liberally enough.

25 Unlike multiple regression analysis, however, the program used did not allow the combination of continuous and classified predictors.

26 'Interviewing effects on a survey of drinking practices', *Sociological Quarterly*, 13, 2, 1972.

NOTES

Chapter 4   Tests of hypotheses about patterns of gambling

1 This reference should not be taken to include the more specifically psychological theories of gambling, which deal with gambling, subjective probability and risk-taking: these fell outside our range. See, for example, J. Cohen, *Behaviour in Uncertainty*, Allen & Unwin, 1964.

2 Edward C. Devereux, Jr, 'Gambling and the social structure: a sociological study of lotteries and horse racing in contemporary America', 2 vols, unpublished Ph.D. thesis, Harvard University, 1949.

3 The most ambitious attempt to argue this case, with somewhat different data in mind, is to be found in Barney Glaser and Anselm Strauss, *The Discovery of Grounded Theory: Strategies for Qualitative Research*, Aldine, 1968.

4 R. K. Merton, *Social Theory and Social Structure*, 2nd rev. edn, Free Press, 1957, chs 4 and 5.

5 T. Hirschi and H. Selvin, *Delinquency Research: An Appraisal of Analytic Method*, Free Press, 1967.

6 W. G. Runciman, *Relative Deprivation and Social Justice*, Routledge & Kegan Paul, 1966.

7 D. M. Downes, *The Delinquent Solution: A Study in Subcultural Theory*, Routledge & Kegan Paul, 1966.

8 J. Horton, 'The dehumanisation of alienation and anomie: a problem in the ideology of sociology', *British Journal of Sociology*, 15, December 1964, pp. 283–300. Horton argues that survey work has emptied these concepts of their original moral content. To a large extent one can only agree, but remain reluctant to abandon these concepts to the realm of metaphysics.

9 Robert Blauner, *Alienation and Freedom*, University of Chicago Press, 1964.

10 See, for example, N. Dennis, F. Henrique and F. Slaughter, *Coal is our Life*, 1956, and I. K. Zola, 'Observations on gambling in a lower-class setting', *Social Problems*, Spring 1963.

11 R. K. Herman, 'Gambling as work: a sociological study of the race track' in Herman (ed.) *Gambling*, 1967, pp. 87–104.

12 E. Goffman, op. cit.

Chapter 5   The social distribution of gambling

1 Clearly there are problems of equivalence involved; and the indicator excludes forms of gambling which arguably should have been included – such as newspaper competitions, raffles, premium bonds, etc. Elsewhere, in Chapter 11, we show the close parallelism in the distribution of gambling as measured by an indicator which excluded, and one that included, these forms of gambling. On balance, however, we excluded them because their inclusion tended to dilute the variation achieved, and because they represent forms of gambling whose status as such is more problematic. For example, betting on premium bonds takes the form of prizes allotted from the interest which accrues from the stakes, which are recoverable: this is certainly gambling, but raises the issue of whether or not we should regard betting and gaming in general as *double* gambling, since not only the stake, but the interest which would accrue had the stake been invested, are subject to loss.

The gambling industry has yet to announce a scheme whereby punters could ultimately recover their stakes, and winnings are paid for out of the investment the stakes originally provided. Another limitation of the results is that adjustment for the other factors could be obtained three ways but not four, since a four-way split would involve too small cell numbers. Hence, the results take the form sex × age × income; sex × age × class; and sex × income × class rather than sex × age × income × class. Even as things are, the results increase in tentativeness the smaller the base cell size for each grouping.

Introduction
1 The presence of predictors with 'don't know' or 'not applicable' categories into which many respondents fall inevitably produces some unproductive splits. To eliminate this possibility means eliminating either all respondents falling into such categories or eliminating all predictors where large numbers of respondents fall into such categories, and either choice limits the utility of the method more than the obstacle it is designed to overcome. Also a split, once made, rules out other, possibly more fruitful splits, on predictors of marginally lesser efficiency.

Chapter 6   Football pools
1 W. F. F. Kemsley and D. Ginsberg, *Betting in Britain*, Social Survey Reports, New Series 710/4 HMSO, 1951.
2 The bivariate tables do not control for variations due to other factors.
3 N. Tec, *Gambling in Sweden*, Bedminster Press, New Jersey, 1965.
4 E. Goffman, 'Where the action is', in *Interaction Ritual*, Allen Lane, 1972 (first published 1967).
5 On the unweighted data, however, the last proposition *is* borne out, the proportions of saving or spending winnings on the home, etc., *rising* with the amounts won, from 21 per cent for those winning £2 or less to 62 per cent for those winning over £100.
6 See Marvin B. Scott, *The Racing Game*, Aldine, 1968.
7 Edward C. Devereux, Jr, 'Gambling and the social structure; a sociological study of lotteries and horse racing in contemporary America', 2 vols, unpublished Ph.D. thesis, Harvard University, 1949.
8 Two groupings (1:5 and 2:3) looked interesting, but on closer examination they derived from very high scores for sub-groups too small to make further analysis worth while.

Chapter 7   Betting
1 It should be stressed, however, that Hill had declared himself an opponent of the Act, and the actual years used in any comparison can be manipulated to some extent to heighten the conclusion desired.
2 Otto Newman, *Gambling; Hazard and Reward*, Athlone Press, 1972.
3 As estimated by S. Roman and H. D. Paley in their 1962 'Report to the New York State Legislature', on off-course betting in Britain.
4 No allowance is made for laying off betting in any of these figures; though Newman makes such allowances in his calculations for 1962

and 1967, he does not do so for the 1947 data, hence we have left them in for the later periods.

5 Ibid., Tables III, IV, VI and VII.

6 Private communication from the Secretary, the Churches' Council on Gambling, 1971. See also 'The Rise of the "Money Factories"', Churches' Council on Gambling, 1972.

7 Hence, in all types of gambling except pools and bingo, we rely for our knowledge of outlay on frequency and stake data taken separately.

8 *Daily Mail*, 25 March 1971.

9 *Minutes of Evidence taken before the Select Committee on Betting Duty, 1923* HMSO, 1924, p. 506, para. 8875.

10 Particularly on the unweighted data: where 80 per cent of weekly, 60 per cent of monthly and 33 per cent of yearly betters claim a skill element.

11 The unweighted data show exactly the reverse, with those using 'singles' displaying a 'no win' rate over twice as high as the long-odds 'treble' (36:15). The explanation may be that those less experienced back at shorter odds, so that they unduly inflate the figure for 'singles', while those betting at longer odds win at least once in the year because of the greater frequency of their betting. On the other hand, the trend for winning larger amounts, of over £10 and over £100, *does* accord with expectations, the longer odds broadly correlating with the larger 'peak' winnings.

12 Ginsberg and Kemsley, op. cit.

13 Ibid.

14 Broadly speaking, the 1950 income-groups should be doubled in terms of £'s to compare with the 1968 money values – thus £500+ in 1950 terms is equivalent to £1,000+ in 1968 terms.

15 In the case of horse-track betters, a base population of thirty rather than fifty-three occurs. This loss is due to the overlap which occurred when respondents took part in more than one form of the betting styles covered in the section: rather than asking them to answer in relation to two, three, four or possibly five ways of betting, we asked them to select that which they took part in most frequently. As horse-track betting is a relatively infrequent activity, those who also took part in betting through an agent – or betting at dog-tracks – would have answered in relation to these. Data on horse-track betting is based, in what follows, on respondents who did not, except very infrequently, bet via agents or on dog-tracks. Hence they cannot be generalized to *all* horse-track betters, whereas *in principle*, for the areas covered at least, data on *frequency* of horse-track betting can be so generalized. The data on on-track horse-race betters may, as a result, err on the side of underestimation.

16 There are contextual and methodological difficulties involved in comparison: basically the questions asked differed and the samples were not of the same order. The 1950 survey was based on a national sample of some 3,000 respondents, stratified by area and including rural areas; the 1968 survey took place in three urban areas only. The 1950 survey gives no breakdown of the prevalence of gambling by different urban/rural indicators, so we have no way of knowing how far

a concentration on urban areas either inflates or reduces the overall prevalence figures obtained. The sheer availability of *outlets* in an urban as distinct from rural areas would suggest that an urban sample would *inflate* rather than *reduce* prevalence figures compared with a truly national sample. There are other differences between the samples, e.g. the 1950 data are drawn from sixteen-year-olds and above, the 1968 data on eighteen-year-olds and above: but the difference flowing from these factors is arguably negligible. Grounds for comparability also stem from the finding that area variation in most forms of gambling activity were negligible, once the main social and economic variables had been controlled for; this gives a better basis for comparison with the national sample than if area variation net of these variables had been marked.

17 Ginsberg and Kemsley, op. cit., p. 23.

18 The questions asked in the 1950 and 1968 surveys differed in form: the 1950 question related to whether respondents had bet on a stated major race in 1949; the 1968 questions related to whether respondents bet on a stated major race every year, every two to three years, less often or never.

19 Ginsberg and Kemsley, op. cit., p. 22.

20 Credit and cash postal betting were excluded for technical reasons though the very slight incidence is unlikely to have influenced the predictive outcome if they had been included.

21 Categorization of conjugal role-sharing leaves something to be desired: the non-married should have been separately categorized but were merged with the lowest conjugal role-sharing group instead. Effective comparisons are therefore limited to those categorized as 0 (high conjugal role-sharing) and 1 (low conjugal role-sharing).

Chapter 8   Gaming

1 *Mass-Observation: The Pub and the People: a worktown study*, 1943, Gollancz, pp. 307 and 309; the fieldwork for the study took place in 1938. The study documents a host of pub amusements now sadly extinct, and remains unique for its evocation of the pub as a key social institution in urban working-class communities. One of its chief merits was to demolish the myth that people went to pubs solely to get drunk.

2 Which is why the profit/loss figure for women exceeds their turnover in this calculation.

3 George and Weedon Grossmith, *The Diary of a Nobody*, 1892; Penguin edition, p. 176.

4 At the data-processing stage, considerations of time ruled out the production of separate sets of tabulations for pub gaming, club gaming and private gaming.

5 See below, p. 172; see also W. I. Thomas, 'The gambling instinct', *American Journal of Sociology*, 1901, pp. 750–63.

6 See Chapter 11 for the relevant matrix.

7 Not reproduced here. The expenditure indicator is even more unreliable for gaming than for other forms of gambling, since the circulation of money in most forms of gaming (except casino gaming in particular) involves a very high turnover relative to profit and loss.

NOTES

Chapter 10   Gaming machines
1 Roger Caillois, *Man, Play and Games*, Thames & Hudson, 1962.
2 The inclusion of women in this run prevented the split occurring on 'marital status'.

Chapter 11   All gambling
1 This limitation does not apply to the next section.
2 The units measured were *sessions*, not individual turns, goes or plays that make up a session.

Chapter 12   Conclusion
1 See C. Raw, B. Page and G. Hodgson, *Do You Sincerely Want to be Rich? Bernard Cornfeld and IOS: An International Swindle*, Penguin Books, 1972.

Appendix 3   The betting office industry in Glamorgan, 1961–7
1 The odds are determined on the race-course by the on-course bookmakers.
2 Approximately, because it is difficult to know in some cases exactly when the offices opened and closed.

Index